Southern Living®

Cooking for Christmas

Favorite Holiday Recipes to Share with Family and Friends

Oxmoor House®

ISBN-13: 978-0-8487-3448-0
ISBN-10: 0-8487-3448-3
Library of Congress Control Number: 2010936023

Printed in the United States of America
First Printing 2011

Oxmoor House

VP, Publishing Director: Jim Childs
Editorial Director: Susan Payne Dobbs
Brand Manager: Daniel Fagan
Senior Editor: Rebecca Brennan
Managing Editor: Laurie S. Herr

Southern Living Cooking for Christmas

Editor: Susan Hernandez Ray
Project Editor: Georgia Dodge
Designer: Allison L. Sperando
Director, Test Kitchens: Elizabeth Tyler Austin
Assistant Directors, Test Kitchens: Julie Christopher, Julie Gunter
Test Kitchens Professionals: Wendy Ball, Allison E. Cox, Victoria E. Cox, Margaret Monroe Dickey, Alyson Moreland Haynes, Stefanie Maloney, Callie Nash, Catherine Crowell Steele, Leah Van Deren
Photography Director: Jim Bathie
Senior Photo Stylist: Kay E. Clarke
Associate Photo Stylist: Katherine Eckert Coyne
Assistant Photo Stylist: Mary Louise Menendez
Production Manager: Greg A. Amason

Contributors

Copy Editor: Stacey B. Loyless
Proofreader: Julie Gillis
Indexer: Nanette Cardon
Interns: Sarah H. Doss, Alison Loughman, Caitlin Watzke
Test Kitchen Professionals: Kathleen Royal Phillips, Lindsay A. Rozier
Photographer: Mary Britton Senseney
Photo Stylist: Mindi Shapiro Levine

Southern Living

Editor: Lindsay Bierman
Executive Editor: Rachel Hardage
Food Director: Shannon Sliter Satterwhite
Test Kitchen Director: Rebecca Kracke Gordon
Senior Writer: Donna Florio
Senior Food Editors: Shirley Harrington, Mary Allen Perry
Recipe Editor: JoAnn Weatherly
Assistant Recipe Editor: Ashley Arthur
Test Kitchen Specialists/Food Styling: Marian Cooper Cairns, Vanessa McNeil Rocchio
Test Kitchen Professionals: Norman King, Pam Lolley, Angela Sellers
Copy Editor: Ashley Leath
Senior Photographers: Ralph Anderson, Gary Clark, Jennifer Davick, Art Meripol
Photographer: Robbie Caponetto
Photo Research Coordinator: Ginny P. Allen
Senior Photo Stylist: Buffy Hargett
Assistant Photo Stylist: Amy Burke
Production Coordinator: Paula Dennis
Editorial Assistant: Pat York

To order additional publications, call
1-800-765-6400 or 1-800-491-0551.

For more books to enrich your life,
visit **oxmoorhouse.com**

To search, savor, and share thousands of recipes,
visit **myrecipes.com**

Cover: Roasted Dry-Rub Turkey with Gravy (page 152); Cornbread Dressing (page 172); Grandma Erma's Spirited Cranberry Sauce (page 173); Roasted Haricots Verts with Creole Mustard Sauce (page 183); Sweet Potato Biscuits (page 206); Bacon-Arugula-Apple Bites (page 65); Crunchy–PecanPie Bites (page 268); Raspberry–Red Velvet Petits Fours (page 228)
Back Cover: Lemon-Garlic Green Beans (page 50); Fennel-Crusted Rib Roast (page 55); Mocha Java Cakes (page 239)

Red Velvet Brownies, page 226

Potato Gratin with Rosemary
Crust, page 186

CONTENTS

Elizabeth

GET SET
for celebrating

stylish SETTINGS

Set the mood for merriment with a dining room dressed for the holidays. Here are a few ways to get started.

dining room details

1 Centerpiece
Keep the centerpiece low so that guests can see each other across the table. Magnolia blossoms in a brass pedestal bowl make for an easy, elegant arrangement.

2 Linens
Use casual linens, such as machine-washable cotton napkins, to temper the formal feel of a set table and to avoid a dry-cleaning bill.

3 Color scheme
Pull colors from throughout the room onto the table. The fabric on these dining chairs served as inspiration for the place setting's soft blue-green and deep red color palette.

4 Stemware
Mix amber glass stemware with clear glass water goblets to coordinate with the gold accents.

5 Flatware
Opt for brass flatware instead of sterling silver for an updated look; no polishing required.

6 Place cards
Add a seasonal touch with unique place card holders, such as these golden pinecones. Use handwritten cards to direct guests to their seats.

7 China patterns
Layer patterns for unexpected flair. Don't be afraid to mix colors and styles, but be sure to pull the look together with a consistent accent color.

inspiring ideas

- Add red and green for a simple way to create a holiday look. Mix in color with linens, stemware, flatware, and flowers.

- For a twist on traditional, try dashes of hot pink, lime, or orange. Add gerbera daisies, strings of brightly colored beads, and some coordinating candles for a fun and funky look.

- Use burlap for an inexpensive, rustic fabric to wrap potted rosemary topiaries and cut greenery for a natural look.

- Scatter ornaments down the middle of your table for an easy accent. Choose colors that complement your china.

- Create vases for flowers and greenery with serving pieces from your collection—such as bowls, teacups and saucers, coffee mugs, and pitchers. Place them on a cake stand for added height.

- Make decorative place cards by covering a florist foam ball with flowers, as shown on page 8, top right. Place the flowered ball on a festive plate, and insert the place card into the ball.

Christmas charm

Just when you were beginning to think your red-and-green china should be a thing of Christmas past, it's time to bring it out and let it shine. Vintage or antique patterns and designs, including those with holly, nutcrackers, and the standard tree, are elegant and classic when paired with bright red accents and a little gold and silver sparkle.

Stylemaker and flea-market-shopper–extraordinaire Eddie Ross put together this table, which combines a cheerful holly design with secondhand pieces such as mismatched vintage silverware and a ceramic compote-turned-centerpiece. Here are his four essential elements.

1 Napkin rings: Tie fresh sprigs of holly from your yard onto linen napkins with red ribbon.

2 Place setting: Mix various white china patterns, antique or new, for a layered look.

3 Salt and pepper: Add some character to the table with unique vintage salt cellars or shakers.

4 Centerpiece: Combine red roses and poinsettias with fresh greenery and berries for a classic arrangement.

fresh CENTERPIECES

Show off your creative side with fun and easy-to-make arrangements. Use seasonal fruits, florals, and greenery for eye-catching decorations that are guaranteed to be the center of attention at your holiday table.

fruits of the season

In no time you can put together a centerpiece for your table that will earn a big "wow" from your guests. Fill basic glass cylinder vases with glass beads and jewel-like berries, and settle an African violet into each one. Relax the look with pomegranates that you've cut in half and placed in the center of square silver trays. (Insert a chef's knife just into the top of the pomegranate, and rock the knife until the fruit spills open.) Fill in the trays with vivid clusters of kumquats, limes, and lemons, and then scatter votive candles throughout the centerpiece for added glow.

Another option for a fruitful centerpiece includes fresh oranges with whole cloves tied with ribbon and placed in a footed bowl. Or try stacking cake stands of graduated sizes and accenting them with seasonal fruit and sprigs of holly.

a lasting impression

If you are looking for a long-lasting centerpiece, try using some simple naturals and florals, such as the mix of roses, hydrangeas, and evergreen branches seen here. Place them in a solid container so that you can water and nurture your centerpiece throughout the holiday season.

hanging around

Accent your light fixture by hanging ornaments from it. These transparent glass ornaments are hung with pieces of narrow ribbon. Other tricks to try: Suspend little glass vases filled with flowers from gold cording; or wrap tiny party favors, and hang them from the chandelier. After the event, cut the ribbons, and present a favor to each guest.

what's old is new again

The best place to start for a holiday centerpiece is to use what you already have. Collection pieces, such as heirloom silver trays and mint julep cups, can be mixed with votives, baskets, and ornaments. Add in some greenery, berries, and flowers for a fresh touch.

create a beautiful
BUFFET

You don't need an enormous table to entertain in style. Just follow these tips for setting up a fetching sideboard for serving.

mix old and new

1 Buffet beauty
Create a welcoming buffet by using what you have. Put your hand-me-downs on display. This mahogany buffet fits perfectly into a niche that's the right size.

2 Mix and match
Update old-fashioned pieces with modern accessories, such as a pair of mod white lamps.

3 Heirloom pieces
Don't forsake your sentimental heirlooms; decorate with them and use them for entertaining.

4 A touch of glass
Mix in additional modern pieces, such as glass bowls, with your heirloom serving pieces for a richer look.

highs and lows

5 Arrange it right
Create a cascade of varying heights with serving pieces and decorations. On this sideboard, the candles and hydrangeas are set higher than the food serving dishes.

6 Candle charm
Check the position of the votive candles by pretending to serve yourself—the last thing you would want is for a guest to be burned.

7 Serve with style
Don't forget to set out serving pieces—placing them on napkins makes sure that these pretty utensils will stand out.

19

location, location

That's the key when setting up your serving spots for entertaining—think about where you want guests to gather. Don't just keep the party in the formal dining room. A spot in the kitchen, such as this island, can make a great serving place.

finishing touches

These must-have serving pieces are not only beautiful, but they also make serving a holiday dinner effortless.

Carving set
Anyone faced with the task of carving a bird or roast knows how important it is to have a good knife and fork. Be sure to maintain the blade with regular honing and sharpening.

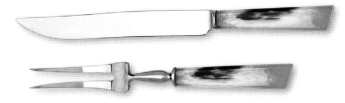

Slotted spoon
This is a must for the buffet table when vegetables render a lot of liquid. This spoon's gold finish adds an elegant touch.

Soup ladle
Skip your full formal collection, and introduce pieces with interesting patterns and handles. This ladle can handle gravies and sauces, as well as soups.

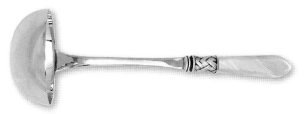

Cake server
For cake, pie, quiche, and even sliced pizza, a cake server is as versatile as a spatula—only prettier.

Salad servers
These sturdy servers only look dainty—use them to serve up a salad or vegetables, such as green beans or asparagus.

Tongs
A good pair of tongs comes in handy for a variety of tasks: cooking, serving, even turning linens when soaking them to remove post-party stains.

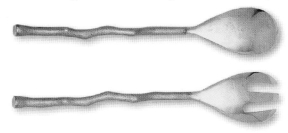

Tray
Large platters are workhorses when it comes to entertaining. Try lining them with hearty leaves of kale, cabbage, or chard for a pretty presentation. Mix it up with shapes other than the standard oval.

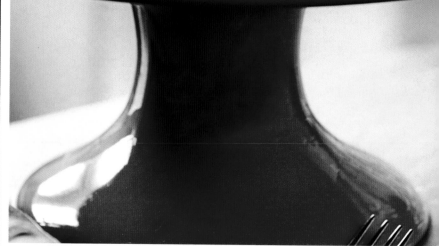

Christmas MENUS

Roast Pork with
Garlic-Onion Gravy

NEW ORLEANS
style menu

menu for 8

Roast Pork with Garlic-Onion Gravy
Oyster Dressing
Creamed Collards
Stuffed Mirlitons
Coconut-Almond Cream Cake

up to one week ahead:
• Prepare Oyster Dressing recipe as directed through cooking the oysters; cover and freeze.

2 days ahead:
• Prepare Coconut Almond Filling; cover and chill.

1 day ahead:
• Place oyster dressing mixture in refrigerator to thaw.
• Prepare Coconut-Almond Cream Cake and frosting.
• Complete cake preparation; cover cake, and keep at room temperature.
• Prepare Sizzlin' Skillet Cornbread.
• Make cuts in roast, and stuff with garlic. Tie roast with kitchen string, and cover and chill.
• Prepare Béchamel Sauce; cover and chill.

morning of:
• Chop onion, celery, bell pepper, green onions, and garlic for the Stuffed Mirlitons; cover and chill.
• Trim and chop collards for Creamed Collards; cover and chill.

6 hours ahead:
• Cook Roast with Garlic-Onion Gravy; keep warm.
• Cook Mirlitons; let cool and set aside.

2 hours ahead:
• Complete preparation of Stuffed Mirlitons; keep warm.
• Complete preparation of Creamed Collards; keep warm.

1½ hour ahead:
• Complete preparation of Oyster Dressing; keep warm.

Roast Pork with Garlic-Onion Gravy

Makes 8 servings
Hands-on Time: 48 min.   **Total Time:** 5 hr., 8 min.

1	(5- to 6-lb.) bone-in pork shoulder roast
10	garlic cloves, halved
	Kitchen string
5	tsp. Cajun seasoning
2	Tbsp. vegetable oil
3	medium onions, halved and sliced
3	celery ribs, chopped
1	(14½-oz.) can low-sodium chicken broth
3	Tbsp. all-purpose flour
5	Tbsp. cold water

Garnishes: red grapes, sliced pears, collard green leaves, persimmons

1. Preheat oven to 325°. Make 20 small, deep cuts in roast, and insert garlic pieces. Tie roast with kitchen string, securing at 2-inch intervals. Rub Cajun seasoning onto roast.
2. Cook roast in hot oil in a large heavy skillet over high heat 2 minutes on all sides or until browned. Remove roast from skillet. Reduce heat to medium. Add sliced onions and celery to skillet; cook, stirring frequently, 5 to 8 minutes or until tender. Place onion mixture in a roasting pan; top with roast. Add broth. Cover loosely with heavy-duty aluminum foil.
3. Bake at 325° for 3½ to 4 hours or until a meat thermometer inserted into thickest portion registers 180° to 185°. Remove roast from pan; cover with foil, and let stand 20 minutes before slicing.
4. Pour pan drippings through a wire-mesh strainer into a measuring cup to equal 2 cups, adding additional broth or water, if necessary. Discard solids.
5. Whisk together 3 Tbsp. flour and 5 Tbsp. cold water in a medium saucepan. Whisk in pan drippings. Cook, whisking often, over medium-high heat 6 to 7 minutes or until thickened. Serve with pork. Garnish, if desired.

Oyster Dressing

Oyster Dressing

Makes 8 servings
Hands-on Time: 54 min. **Total Time:** 2 hr., 49 min., including cornbread

- 2   medium onions, diced
- 4   celery ribs, diced
- 2   red bell peppers, diced
- 2   green bell peppers, diced
- 4   garlic cloves, minced
- ¼   cup olive oil
- 2   (8-oz.) containers fresh oysters, drained and coarsely chopped
- ⅔   cup dry white wine
- ½   cup chicken broth
- ¼   cup butter
- 3   bay leaves
- 2   Tbsp. fresh thyme leaves
- 2   tsp. black pepper
- 1   tsp. salt
- 1   tsp. crushed dried red pepper
- 1   tsp. hot pepper sauce
- 2   large eggs
- ½   cup grated Parmesan cheese
-     Sizzlin' Skillet Cornbread, crumbled
-     Garnishes: fresh parsley sprig, grated Parmesan cheese

1. Preheat oven to 375°. Sauté first 5 ingredients in hot oil in a large skillet over medium heat 15 to 20 minutes or until tender and lightly browned. Stir in oysters and next 9 ingredients; cook 3 to 4 minutes or until edges of oysters begin to curl. Remove from heat; let stand 10 minutes. Remove bay leaves.
2. Place mixture in a large bowl; stir in eggs and cheese. Fold in cornbread. Place mixture in a lightly greased 3-qt. or 13- x 9-inch baking dish.
3. Bake at 375° for 40 to 45 minutes or until lightly browned. Garnish, if desired.

make-ahead tip

To make ahead, prepare recipe as directed through cooking the oysters. Cover tightly, and freeze up to 1 month. Thaw in refrigerator 24 hours. Let stand at room temperature 30 minutes. Proceed with recipe as directed.

Sizzlin' Skillet Cornbread

Makes 6 servings
Hands-on Time: 15 min. **Total Time:** 1 hr.

- 2   Tbsp. bacon drippings
- 2   cups buttermilk
- 1   large egg
- 1¾ cups self-rising cornmeal mix

1. Preheat oven to 450°. Coat bottom and sides of a 10-inch cast-iron skillet with 2 Tbsp. bacon drippings; heat in oven 10 minutes.
2. Whisk together remaining ingredients; pour batter into hot skillet.
3. Bake at 450° for 15 minutes or until lightly browned. Invert cornbread onto a wire rack. Cool completely (about 30 minutes).

Enliven your table and offer a nod to the enduring strength of this unique city and its food.

editor's favorite

Creamed Collards

Makes 8 to 10 servings
Hands-on Time: 20 min. **Total Time:** 1 hr., 19 min., including sauce

- 4½   lb. fresh collard greens*
- 1   lb. bacon, chopped
- ¼   cup butter
- 2   large onions, diced
- 3   cups chicken broth
- ½   cup apple cider vinegar
- 1   tsp. salt
- ½   tsp. pepper
- Béchamel Sauce

1. Rinse collard greens. Trim and discard thick stems from bottom of collard green leaves (about 2 inches); coarsely chop collard greens.
2. Cook bacon, in batches, in an 8-qt. stock pot over medium heat 10 to 12 minutes or until crisp. Remove bacon with a slotted spoon, and drain on paper towels, reserving drippings in stock pot. Reserve ¼ cup bacon.
3. Add butter and onions to hot drippings in skillet. Sauté onion 8 minutes or until tender. Add collards, in batches, and cook, stirring occasionally, 5 minutes or until wilted. Stir in chicken broth, next 3 ingredients, and remaining bacon.
4. Bring to a boil. Reduce heat to low, and cook, stirring occasionally, 15 minutes or to desired degree of tenderness. Drain collards, reserving 1 cup liquid.
5. Stir in Béchamel Sauce. Stir in reserved cooking liquid, ¼ cup at a time, to desired consistency. Transfer to a serving dish, and sprinkle with reserved ¼ cup bacon.

*2 (1-lb.) packages fresh collard greens, thoroughly washed, trimmed, and chopped, may be substituted.

test-kitchen secret

Try this easy method for cutting up the bacon: Remove wrapping from bacon. Place the entire pound of cold bacon on a cutting board, and slice into ½-inch cubes.

Béchamel Sauce

Béchamel (bay-shah-MEHL) is the French term for white sauce. This sauce can be made ahead.

Makes about 4½ cups
Hands-on Time: 10 min. **Total Time:** 19 min.

- ½   cup butter
- 2   medium shallots, minced
- 2   garlic cloves, pressed
- ¾   cup all-purpose flour
- 4   cups milk
- ½   tsp. salt
- ½   tsp. pepper
- ¼   tsp. ground nutmeg

1. Melt butter in a heavy saucepan over low heat; add shallots and garlic, and sauté 1 minute. Whisk in flour until smooth. Cook 1 minute, whisking constantly.
2. Increase heat to medium. Gradually whisk in milk; cook over medium heat, whisking constantly, 5 to 7 minutes or until mixture is thickened and bubbly. Stir in salt, pepper, and nutmeg.

make-ahead tip

You can make the sauce ahead and store it in an airtight container in the refrigerator up to 2 days. Warm sauce over low heat before using.

Creamed Collards

Stuffed Mirlitons

Stuffed Mirlitons

Makes 8 servings
Hands-on Time: 30 min. **Total Time:** 1 hr., 12 min.

4	medium mirlitons (chayote squash) (about ¾ lb. each)
1¼	lb. peeled, medium-size raw shrimp (31 to 35 count)
½	cup butter
1	medium onion, finely chopped
½	medium-size green bell pepper, chopped
2	celery ribs, finely chopped
3	green onions, chopped
3	garlic cloves, minced
¼	cup chopped fresh parsley
1¼	cups fine, dry breadcrumbs, divided
¾	tsp. salt
½	tsp. black pepper
¼	tsp. ground red pepper
1	large egg, lightly beaten
2	Tbsp. butter

1. Place mirlitons in salted water to cover in a large Dutch oven; bring to a boil over medium-high heat. Cook 45 to 50 minutes or until very tender when pierced with a fork. Drain mirlitons, and cool 30 minutes.
2. Devein shrimp, if desired. Coarsely chop shrimp. Preheat oven to 350°. Cut mirlitons in half length-wise; remove and discard seeds. Carefully scoop out pulp into a bowl, leaving a ¼-inch-thick shell. Finely chop pulp.
3. Melt ½ cup butter in a large, deep skillet or Dutch oven over medium heat; add onion, and cook, stirring occasionally, 5 minutes or until tender. Reduce heat to low; add bell pepper and next 4 ingredients; sauté 12 minutes or until tender. Stir in mirliton pulp; cook, stirring often, 5 minutes. Stir in 1 cup breadcrumbs until combined. Remove from heat; stir in shrimp. Stir in salt and next 3 ingredients.
4. Microwave 2 Tbsp. butter at HIGH 10 to 15 seconds or until melted. Spoon mirliton mixture into shells, pressing down lightly. Sprinkle with remaining ¼ cup breadcrumbs. Place mirlitons in 2(11- x 7-inch) baking dishes. Drizzle with melted butter.
5. Bake at 350° for 30 minutes or until lightly browned.

Note: We tested this recipe with an 1,100-watt microwave.

Stuffed Squash: Omit steps 1 and 2. Substitute 7 medium zucchini or yellow squash for mirlitons. Microwave squash at HIGH 3 minutes. Cut each in half lengthwise. Carefully scoop out pulp into a bowl, leaving a ¼-inch-thick shell. Finely chop pulp. Devein shrimp, if desired; coarsely chop shrimp. Proceed with recipe as directed, beginning with melting ½ cup butter.

Coconut-Almond Cream Cake

If the tops of the layers are a little rounded, level them with a serrated knife. This is a tall cake, and it needs to be level if you want your friends to admire your work before they devour it—as they absolutely will.

Makes 12 servings
Hands-on Time: 30 min. **Total Time:** 10 hr., 42 min., including filling and frosting

  2   cups sweetened flaked coconut
  ½   cup sliced almonds
  Parchment paper
  3½   cups all-purpose flour
  1   Tbsp. baking powder
  ½   tsp. salt
  1½   cups unsalted butter, softened
  1¼   cups granulated sugar
  1   cup firmly packed light brown
       sugar
  5   large eggs
  1   cup whipping cream
  ⅓   cup coconut milk
  1   Tbsp. vanilla extract
  1   Tbsp. almond extract
  Coconut-Almond Filling
  Coconut–Cream Cheese Frosting
  Garnishes: kumquats, currants, fresh mint sprigs

1. Preheat oven to 325°. Bake coconut in a single layer in a shallow pan 6 minutes. Place almonds in a single layer in another shallow pan; bake, with coconut, 7 to 9 minutes or until almonds are fragrant and coconut is lightly browned, stirring occasionally.
2. Line 3 (9-inch) round cake pans with parchment paper. Grease and flour paper. Sift together flour, baking powder, and salt in a very large bowl.
3. Beat butter at medium speed with a heavy-duty electric stand mixer until creamy; gradually add sugars, beating until blended. Beat 8 minutes more or until very fluffy, scraping bottom and sides of bowl as needed. Add eggs, 1 at a time, beating well after each addition (about 30 seconds per egg). Stir in whipping cream and next 3 ingredients.
4. Gently fold butter mixture into flour mixture, in batches, just until combined. Pour batter into prepared pans.
5. Bake at 325° for 30 to 32 minutes or until a wooden pick inserted in center comes out clean. Cool in pans on wire racks 10 minutes; remove from pans to wire racks, and cool completely (about 1 hour).

6. Place 1 cake layer on a serving plate. Spread half of chilled Coconut-Almond Filling over cake layer. Top with 1 layer, pressing down gently. Repeat procedure with remaining half of Coconut-Almond Filling and remaining cake layer.
7. Gently spread Coconut–Cream Cheese Frosting on top and sides of cake. Press toasted coconut onto sides of cake; sprinkle toasted almonds on top. Garnish, if desired.

Coconut-Almond Filling

This filling acts as a glue to hold the layers together. It works best when chilled, so don't skip that step.

Makes 3 cups
Hands-on Time: 15 min. **Total Time:** 8 hr., 15 min.

  2   Tbsp. cornstarch
  1   tsp. almond extract
  1¼   cups whipping cream
  ½   cup firmly packed light brown sugar
  ½   cup unsalted butter
  2¼   cups loosely packed sweetened flaked coconut
  ¼   cup sour cream

1. Stir together cornstarch, almond extract, and 2 Tbsp. water in a small bowl.
2. Bring whipping cream, brown sugar, and butter to a boil in a saucepan over medium heat. Remove from heat, and immediately whisk in cornstarch mixture. Stir in coconut and sour cream. Cover and chill 8 hours.

Coconut–Cream Cheese Frosting

Makes about 3 cups
Hands-on Time: 10 min. **Total Time:** 10 min.

  2   (8-oz.) packages cream cheese, softened
  ½   cup unsalted butter, softened
  2   cups powdered sugar
  1   Tbsp. cream of coconut
  1   tsp. vanilla extract

1. Beat cream cheese and butter at medium speed with an electric mixer until creamy. Gradually add powdered sugar, beating at low speed until blended. Increase speed to medium, and beat in cream of coconut and vanilla extract until smooth.

Coconut-Almond Cream Cake

Roasted Pork with Dried Fruit and Port Sauce

traditional
FAMILY DINNER

menu for 8

Roasted Pork with Dried Fruit and Port Sauce
Brussels Sprouts with Pancetta
Mashed Potatoes en Croûte

2 days ahead:
• Place pork tenderloin in refrigerator to thaw, if frozen.

1 day ahead:
• Cook and crumble pancetta for Brussels sprouts.
• Trim and cut Brussels sprouts in half; cover and refrigerate.
• Prepare mash potato mixture; cover and chill.

4 to 5 hours ahead:
• Roast pork, and prepare dried fruit and port sauce; cover and chill.

2 hours ahead:
• Take potato mixture out of refrigerator, and bring to room temperature.

1 hour ahead:
• Complete preparation of Brussels sprouts.
• Assemble Mashed Potatoes en Croûte, and bake.

last minute:
• Warm pork and sauce.
• Carve pork.

party pointers

• Set the table, and pick out the serving dishes early in the day.
• Limit your table setting to no more than three colors. When in doubt, use simple white linens.
• Keep centerpiece arrangements low. Otherwise, guests won't be able to see each other.

Roasted Pork with Dried Fruit and Port Sauce

Prepare the meat and sauce separately, and then warm them together just before the guests arrive.

Makes 8 servings
Hands-on Time: 21 min. **Total Time:** 49 min.

- 3 lb. pork tenderloin
- 1 tsp. salt
- ½ tsp. pepper
- 7 tsp. olive oil, divided
- 1 cup dried apricots
- 1 cup dried pitted plums
- 1 cup dried peaches
- ½ cup dried tart cherries
- ¼ cup pine nuts
- 1 cup port wine
- 1 cup pomegranate juice
- 2 (2½-inch) cinnamon sticks
- ½ cup chicken broth

1. Preheat oven to 425°. Remove silver skin from tenderloin, leaving a thin layer of fat. Sprinkle pork with salt and pepper. Cook pork in 6 tsp. hot oil in a large skillet over medium-high heat 3 minutes on each side or until golden brown. Transfer pork to a lightly greased jelly-roll or roasting pan, reserving drippings in skillet.
2. Bake pork at 425° for 18 to 20 minutes or until a meat thermometer inserted into thickest portion registers 150°. Remove from oven; cover and let stand 10 minutes or until thermometer registers 155°.
3. Meanwhile, add remaining 1 tsp. oil to hot drippings in skillet. Add apricots and next 4 ingredients, and sauté over medium-high heat 3 minutes or until pine nuts are toasted and fragrant. Add port wine and next 2 ingredients. Bring to a boil; reduce heat to low, and simmer 5 minutes or until mixture slightly thickens. Stir in broth, and simmer 15 minutes or until fruit is tender. Serve with pork.

Brussels Sprouts with Pancetta

Makes 8 servings
Hands-on Time: 10 min. **Total Time:** 27 min.

- 2   lb. fresh Brussels sprouts, trimmed and halved
- 2   Tbsp. olive oil
- ¼   tsp. salt
- ¼   tsp. pepper
- 6   (⅛-inch-thick) pancetta slices
- 1   Tbsp. freshly grated Parmesan cheese

1. Preheat oven to 425°. Toss together Brussels sprouts and next 3 ingredients in a 15- x 10-inch jelly-roll pan. Bake 17 to 20 minutes or until sprouts are tender and edges are lightly browned, stirring occasionally.
2. Meanwhile, cook pancetta in a large skillet over medium heat 8 to 10 minutes or until crisp. Remove pancetta, and drain on paper towels. Crumble pancetta.
3. Remove sprouts from oven, and place in a large serving dish. Top with cheese and crumbled pancetta.

Brussels Sprouts with Pancetta

Mashed Potatoes en Croûte

Add a decorative touch to Mashed Potatoes en Croûte by topping it with pretty pastry leaves. Simply cut out leaves from another puff pastry sheet, using a small leaf-shaped cutter, and arrange on top of the crust before baking.

Makes 10 to 12 servings
Hands-on Time: 30 min. **Total Time:** 1 hr., 24 min.

- 4   lb. Yukon gold potatoes, peeled and cut into 1-inch cubes
- ½   cup milk
- 2   bay leaves
- ½   cup butter
- ½   cup heavy cream
- 1   tsp. salt
- ½   tsp. freshly ground pepper
- ¼   tsp. ground nutmeg
- 2   egg yolks
- ¼   cup freshly grated Parmesan cheese
- 1   (17.3-oz.) package frozen puff pastry sheets, thawed
- 1   large egg
- 1   Tbsp. half-and-half

1. Preheat oven to 425°. Bring 2 qt. salted water to a boil in a large Dutch oven over medium-high heat. Add potatoes and next 2 ingredients, and cook 25 minutes or until potatoes are tender. Drain potatoes, and discard bay leaves. Mash potatoes with a potato masher until soft and fluffy.
2. Microwave butter and cream in a small microwave-safe bowl at HIGH 1 minute. Stir until smooth; add salt, pepper, and nutmeg. Stir butter mixture into mashed potatoes. Stir in egg yolks and cheese until smooth.
3. Press 1 pastry sheet into a 9-inch deep-dish pie plate, allowing edges to hang over sides. Spoon mashed potatoes into pie plate, and top with remaining pastry sheet. Crimp and fold edges inward. Cut several slits in top of pastry for steam to escape. Whisk together egg and half-and-half; brush over pastry.
4. Bake at 425° for 24 minutes or until pastry is golden and has risen slightly.

test-kitchen secret

Mash the Yukon gold potatoes by hand. Don't even think about using a blender or food processor. Giving in to such temptation will result in a dense, inedible paste.

Mashed Potatoes en Croûte

Warm Lemon-Rosemary Olives

festive
GIRLS' LUNCH

menu for 8

Warm Lemon-Rosemary Olives
Leafy Green Salad with Pears
Latina Lasagna
Green Beans with Garlic
Mexican Chocolate Pound Cake

2 days ahead:
• Prepare Latina Lasagna, but do not bake; cover and chill.

1 day ahead:
• Prepare Mexican Chocolate Pound Cake; cover and keep at room temperature.
• Prepare Mexican Chocolate Sauce; cover and chill. Double recipe to give as gifts to your guests, if desired.

3 hours ahead:
• Bake Latina Lasagna; add an extra 20 to 30 minutes to baking time if made ahead.

1 hour ahead:
• Prepare Warm Lemon-Rosemary Olives; do not unfold foil until ready to serve.
• Prepare Green Beans with Garlic; cover and keep warm.

last minute:
• Assemble Leafy Green Salad with Pears.
• Plate and garnish all dishes, if desired.
• Warm Mexican Chocolate Sauce, and garnish pound cake, if desired.

quick and easy

Warm Lemon-Rosemary Olives

Makes 3 cups
Hands-on Time: 10 min. **Total Time:** 40 min.

3   cups mixed olives
2   fresh rosemary sprigs
1   tsp. dried crushed red pepper
1   tsp. lemon zest
1   tsp. olive oil
Garnishes: rosemary sprig, lemon rind strips

1. Preheat oven to 400°. Place first 4 ingredients on a large piece of aluminum foil; drizzle with oil. Fold foil over olive mixture, and pinch edges to seal.
2. Bake at 400° for 30 minutes. Serve warm. Garnish with rosemary and lemon, if desired.

test-kitchen secret

Mixed olives are available at most grocers.

Kick off the holiday season by getting some of your friends together for a marvelous midday meal.

Leafy Green Salad with Pears

Latina Lasagna

Leafy Green Salad with Pears

Makes 16 servings
Hands-on Time: 10 min. **Total Time:** 10 min.

  1   Tbsp. honey
  ½   cup bottled olive oil-and-vinegar dressing
  8   cups torn butter lettuce
  2   Anjou pears, sliced
  1   (3.5-oz.) package roasted glazed pecan pieces

1. Stir honey into olive oil-and-vinegar dressing. Place lettuce and pears in a bowl. Drizzle with dressing, and sprinkle with pecan pieces.

Note: We tested with Naturally Fresh Salad Toppings Roasted & Glazed Pecan Pieces.

make ahead • editor's favorite
Latina Lasagna

You can assemble and chill this up to 2 days ahead, and bake before serving. Simply add 20 to 30 minutes to the baking time.

Makes 8 servings
Hands-on Time: 28 min. **Total Time:** 1 hr., 48 min.

  1½   lb. fresh chorizo sausage, casings removed
   2   (24-oz.) jars tomato-and-basil pasta sauce
   1   cup chopped fresh cilantro
   1   (4.5-oz.) can chopped green chiles
   1   (15-oz.) container ricotta cheese
   1   cup whipping cream
   2   large eggs, lightly beaten
  12   no-boil lasagna noodles
   1   (16-oz.) package shredded Mexican four-cheese blend

Green Beans with Garlic

1. Preheat oven to 375°. Cook sausage in a Dutch oven over medium heat 8 to 10 minutes or until meat is no longer pink, breaking sausage into pieces while cooking. Drain; return sausage to Dutch oven. Reduce heat to medium-low. Stir in pasta sauce, cilantro, and chiles; cook, stirring often, 5 minutes.

2. Stir together ricotta cheese, whipping cream, and eggs until smooth.

3. Spoon 1 cup sauce mixture into a lightly greased 13- x 9-inch pan. Top with 4 lasagna noodles. Top with half of ricotta cheese mixture, one-third of shredded Mexican cheese blend, and one-third of remaining sauce mixture. Repeat layers once, beginning with noodles. Top with remaining 4 noodles, sauce mixture, and shredded cheese blend. Cover with aluminum foil.

4. Bake at 375° for 45 minutes. Uncover and bake 15 more minutes or until golden and bubbly. Let stand 20 minutes before serving.

editor's favorite

Green Beans with Garlic

Makes 12 to 16 servings
Hands-on Time: 23 min. **Total Time:** 23 min.

- 3 lb. green beans, trimmed
- 3 large garlic cloves, thinly sliced
- 2 Tbsp. olive oil
- 1 tsp. salt
- ½ tsp. freshly ground pepper

1. Cook beans in boiling salted water to cover 5 minutes or just until tender. Drain well.

2. Cook half of garlic in 1 Tbsp. hot oil in a Dutch oven over medium heat 1 minute or until golden. Add half of beans, and sprinkle with ½ tsp. salt and ¼ tsp. pepper. Cook, stirring constantly, 3 minutes. Transfer to a serving dish. Repeat procedure with remaining garlic, oil, beans, salt, and pepper.

Mexican Chocolate
Pound Cake

Mexican Chocolate Pound Cake

This moist cake is equally delicious without the sauce.

Makes 16 servings
Hands-on Time: 16 min. **Total Time:** 3 hr., 14 min., including sauce

- 1 (8-oz.) package semisweet chocolate baking squares, chopped*
- 1 cup butter, softened
- 1½ cups granulated sugar
- 4 large eggs
- ½ cup chocolate syrup
- 2 tsp. vanilla extract
- 2½ cups all-purpose flour
- 1 tsp. ground cinnamon
- ¼ tsp. baking soda
- ⅛ tsp. salt
- 1 cup buttermilk
- Powdered sugar (optional)
- Mexican Chocolate Sauce
- Garnish: toasted sliced almonds

1. Preheat oven to 325°. Microwave chocolate baking squares in a microwave-safe bowl at HIGH 1 minute and 15 seconds or until chocolate is melted and smooth, stirring at 15-second intervals. Beat butter at medium speed with a heavy-duty electric stand mixer 2 minutes or until creamy. Gradually add granulated sugar, beating 5 to 7 minutes or until light and fluffy. Add eggs, 1 at a time, beating just until yellow disappears after each addition. Stir in melted chocolate, chocolate syrup, and vanilla until smooth.
2. Combine flour and next 3 ingredients; add to butter mixture alternately with buttermilk, beginning and ending with flour mixture. Beat at low speed just until blended after each addition. Pour batter into a greased and floured 10-inch (14-cup) tube pan.
3. Bake at 325° for 1 hour and 10 minutes or until a long wooden pick inserted in center of cake comes out clean. Cool in pan on a wire rack 10 to 15 minutes; remove from pan to wire rack, and let cool completely (about 1 hour and 30 minutes). Sprinkle with powdered sugar, if desired. Serve with Mexican Chocolate Sauce. Garnish with almonds, if desired.

*2 (4.4-oz.) packages Mexican chocolate, chopped, may be substituted. Omit ground cinnamon.

great gift

Mexican Chocolate Sauce

Makes about 1½ cups
Hands-on Time: 8 min. **Total Time:** 8 min.

- 1 (8-oz.) package semisweet chocolate baking squares, chopped
- ¾ cup whipping cream
- 2 tsp. light brown sugar
- ¼ tsp. ground cinnamon
- ¼ tsp. almond extract
- Pinch of salt
- 1 Tbsp. butter

1. Cook first 6 ingredients in a small saucepan over low heat, whisking occasionally, 3 to 4 minutes or until mixture is smooth and chocolate is melted. Remove from heat. Whisk in butter until melted. Serve immediately.

test-kitchen secret

We replicated the flavor profile of Mexican chocolate using semisweet chocolate and cinnamon. If you prefer to use Mexican chocolate, look for it with the hot drink mixes or on the Hispanic food aisle.

STRESS-FREE *celebration*

(Pictured on page 42 at bottom right)

menu for 8

Wayne's French 75
Spiced Butternut-Pumpkin Soup
Caesar Salad Bites
Baked Goat-Cheese Dip
Bacon-Grits Fritters

up to 1 month ahead:
• Prepare Baked Goat-Cheese Dip; do not bake. Cover and freeze.

up to 1 week ahead:
• Prepare Bacon-Grits Fritters; do not fry. Put into freezer bag, and freeze.

1 day ahead:
• Cut assorted vegetables for Baked Goat-Cheese Dip.
• Chop English cucumber for Caesar Salad Bites.
• Prepare Spiced Butternut-Pumpkin Soup; cover soup and chill.
• Thaw Baked Goat-Cheese Dip in refrigerator for 24 hours.

5 to 6 hours ahead:
• Prep your bar; prepare drink station, and chill Champagne.
• Make lemon rind twist for Wayne's French 75; chill in cold water.

1 hour ahead:
• Bring cheese dip to room temperature, and bake as directed.
• Fry Bacon-Grits Fritters.
• Assemble Caesar Salad Bites.

last minute:
• Make guest a Wayne's French 75.
• Plate appetizers, and garnish, if desired.

Wayne's French 75

Makes 1 cocktail
Hands-on Time: 5 min. **Total Time:** 5 min.

3   Tbsp. brandy
1   Tbsp. orange liqueur
Crushed ice cubes
1   lemon wedge
1   lemon rind twist
½   cup Champagne or sparkling wine

1. Combine brandy, orange liqueur, and crushed ice cubes in a cocktail shaker. Cover with lid, and shake until thoroughly chilled. Strain into a glass. Squeeze juice from lemon wedge into glass. Add lemon rind twist and Champagne or sparkling wine.

Get your party started with a tart beverage and standout appetizers that are mostly make-ahead.

Spiced Butternut-Pumpkin Soup

This yields more than enough for appetizer-size servings. Divide up the leftovers, and freeze for a last-minute meal during the busy month of December.

Makes 15 cups
Hands-on Time: 30 min. **Total Time:** 1 hr., 35 min.

2	Tbsp. butter
1	large sweet onion, diced
1	large red bell pepper, chopped
3	garlic cloves, minced
2	Tbsp. finely grated fresh ginger
1	medium-size butternut squash, peeled and cubed (about 1¾ lb.)
1	small pumpkin, peeled and cubed (about 1¾ lb.)
1	large sweet potato, peeled and cubed
1	large Granny Smith apple, peeled and cubed
1	(32-oz.) container low-sodium chicken broth
2	bay leaves
1½	tsp. red curry paste*
½	tsp. ground pepper
¾	cup whipping cream
1	Tbsp. fresh lime juice
Salt and pepper to taste	

1. Melt butter in a large Dutch oven over medium-high heat; add onion and bell pepper, and sauté 8 minutes or until onion is golden. Stir in garlic and ginger, and cook 1 minute. Add squash, next 7 ingredients, and 4 cups water. Bring to a boil, reduce heat to medium-low, and simmer 20 minutes or until vegetables are tender. Remove from heat, and let stand 30 minutes, stirring occasionally. Remove and discard bay leaves.
2. Process soup, in batches, in a blender until smooth. Return to Dutch oven, and stir in cream. Bring to a simmer over medium heat; stir in lime juice, and season with salt and pepper to taste.

*1 tsp. curry powder may be substituted.

Note: 3 lb. butternut squash may be substituted for 1¾ lb. butternut squash and 1¾ lb. pumpkin.

Caesar Salad Bites

Turn these appetizers into a pretty salad by layering veggies and croutons in a clear ice bucket or trifle dish and topping with dressing and parsley.

Makes 8 servings
Hands-on Time: 20 min. **Total Time:** 20 min.

2	romaine lettuce hearts
⅔	cup bottled refrigerated creamy Caesar dressing
½	English cucumber, chopped
1¼	cups small seasoned croutons
1	cup halved grape tomatoes
¼	cup coarsely chopped fresh parsley
Freshly ground pepper to taste	

1. Separate romaine hearts into 24 medium leaves, and arrange on a large platter. Spoon dressing lightly down center of each leaf. Top with chopped cucumber and next 3 ingredients. Sprinkle with pepper to taste.

Note: We tested with Marie's Creamy Caesar Dressing.

Caesar Salad Bites

Baked Goat-Cheese Dip

Baked Goat-Cheese Dip

Makes 12 servings
Hands-on Time: 20 min. **Total Time:** 45 min.

- 1 small onion, diced
- 1 Tbsp. olive oil
- 2 garlic cloves, minced
- 2 Tbsp. tomato paste
- ¼ tsp. dried crushed red pepper
- Pinch of sugar
- 1 (14.5-oz.) can petite-diced tomatoes
- ¼ cup chopped sun-dried tomatoes in oil
- ¼ cup torn basil leaves
- Salt and pepper to taste
- 2 (4-oz.) goat cheese logs, softened
- 1 (8-oz.) package cream cheese, softened
- Assorted cut vegetables and bread cubes

1. Preheat oven to 350°. Sauté onion in hot oil in a 3-qt. saucepan over medium-high heat 5 minutes or until tender. Stir in garlic and next 3 ingredients, and cook, stirring constantly, 1 minute. Stir in diced and sun-dried tomatoes. Reduce heat to medium-low, and simmer, stirring occasionally, 10 minutes or until very thick. Remove from heat, and stir in basil and salt and pepper to taste.
2. Stir together goat cheese and cream cheese until well blended. Spread into a lightly greased 9-inch shallow ovenproof dish. Top with tomato mixture.
3. Bake at 350° for 15 to 18 minutes or until thoroughly heated. Serve with assorted vegetables and bread cubes.

make-ahead tip

Prepare recipe as directed through Step 2. Cover and freeze up to 1 month. Thaw in refrigerator overnight. Let stand at room temperature 30 minutes. Bake as directed.

Bacon-Grits Fritters

Makes about 32 fritters
Hands-on Time: 35 min. **Total Time:** 4 hr., 40 min.

- 1 cup uncooked quick-cooking grits
- 4 cups milk
- 1 tsp. salt
- 1½ cups (6 oz.) shredded extra-sharp white Cheddar cheese
- ½ cup cooked and finely crumbled bacon (about 8 slices)
- 2 green onions, minced
- ½ tsp. freshly ground pepper
- 2 large eggs
- 3 cups Japanese breadcrumbs (panko)
- Vegetable oil

1. Prepare grits according to package directions, using 4 cups milk and 1 tsp. salt. Remove from heat, and let stand 5 minutes. Stir in cheese and next 3 ingredients, stirring until cheese is melted. Spoon mixture into a lightly greased 8-inch square baking dish or pan, and chill 4 to 24 hours.
2. Roll grits into 1½-inch balls. Whisk together eggs and ¼ cup water. Dip balls in egg wash, and roll in breadcrumbs.
3. Pour oil to depth of 3 inches in a large, heavy skillet; heat over medium-high heat to 350°. Fry fritters, in batches, 3 to 4 minutes or until golden brown. Drain on paper towels. Keep fritters warm on a wire rack in a pan in a 225° oven up to 30 minutes. Serve warm.

make-ahead tip

Prepare recipe as directed through Step 2. Cover and chill in a single layer up to 4 hours. Fry as directed. You may also prepare through Step 2, and freeze on a baking sheet for 30 minutes or until firm. Transfer to a zip-top plastic freezer bag, and freeze. Cook frozen fritters as directed in Step 3, increasing cooking time to 5 to 6 minutes or until golden and centers are thoroughly heated.

Bacon-Grits Fritters

Cherry-Pecan Brie

an *ELEGANT* *holiday dinner*

menu for 8

Cherry-Pecan Brie
Tossed Greens-and-Grapes Salad
Easy Asiago-Olive Rolls
Pancetta-Wrapped Beef Tenderloin with Whipped
Horseradish Cream
Crispy Potatoes with Fennel
Lemon-Garlic Green Beans
Chocolate Truffle Cheesecake

2 weeks before:
• Toast pecans for the Brie; freeze in an airtight container.

2 days ahead:
• Thaw tenderloin in refrigerator if frozen.
• Gather a pretty bouquet of fresh herbs for garnishing. Refrigerate in a glass of water.
• Make vinaigrette. Cover and chill. Let stand at room temperature 30 minutes; whisk before serving.

1 day ahead:
• Stir together topping for the Brie the day before, and chill.
• Trim and slice fennel for potatoes. Wrap in a damp paper towel, seal in a zip-top plastic freezer bag.
• Bake cheesecake—the texture is better when the cheesecake is well chilled.

8 hours ahead:
• Prepare Whipped Horseradish Cream; cover and chill.

Cherry-Pecan Brie

Makes 8 servings
Hands-on Time: 10 min. **Total Time:** 10 min.

⅓ cup cherry preserves
1 Tbsp. balsamic vinegar
⅛ tsp. freshly ground pepper
⅛ tsp. salt
1 (16-oz.) warm Brie round with rind removed from top
Garnish: toasted pecans
Crackers

1. Stir together cherry preserves, balsamic vinegar, pepper, and salt in a bowl. Drizzle over Brie. Top with chopped toasted pecans. Serve with crackers.

Tossed Greens-and-Grapes Salad

Makes 8 servings
Hands-on Time: 15 min. **Total Time:** 15 min.

¾ cup olive oil
¼ cup red wine vinegar
1½ Tbsp. Dijon mustard
1½ tsp. honey
⅛ tsp. salt
⅛ tsp. pepper
1 (5-oz.) package spring greens mix or sweet baby greens
2 cups seedless red grapes, halved
1 cup salted, roasted cashews
2 oz. Manchego cheese, shaved

1. Stir together olive oil and next 5 ingredients in a large serving bowl. Add spring greens and next 3 ingredients, and toss. Serve immediately.

test-kitchen secret

Manchego cheese has a firm texture with a nutty, buttery, mildly sharp flavor that's easy to like. Use a vegetable peeler to shave cheese into big pieces.

Easy Asiago-Olive Rolls

Pancetta-Wrapped Beef Tenderloin with Whipped Horseradish Cream

Makes 8 servings
Hands-on Time: 20 min. **Total Time:** 1 hr., 25 min., including cream

- 1   (5- to 6-lb.) beef tenderloin, trimmed
- 2   tsp. kosher salt
- 1   tsp. coarsely ground pepper
- 3   Tbsp. olive oil, divided
- 14 very thin pancetta slices
-     Wax paper
- 3   garlic cloves, minced
- 2   Tbsp. chopped fresh rosemary
-     Kitchen string
-     Whipped Horseradish Cream

1. Preheat oven to 425°. Sprinkle tenderloin with salt and pepper. Cook in 2 Tbsp. hot oil in a skillet over medium-high heat 5 minutes on each side or until browned. Let cool 5 minutes.
2. Meanwhile, arrange pancetta slices in 2 rows on a large piece of wax paper, overlapping to form a rectangle. Sprinkle garlic and rosemary over tenderloin. Place tenderloin on edge of 1 long side of pancetta. Tightly roll up tenderloin with pancetta, using wax paper as a guide. Discard wax paper. Tie tenderloin with kitchen string, securing at 1-inch intervals. Transfer to an aluminum foil–lined baking sheet, and brush with remaining 1 Tbsp. oil.
3. Bake at 425° for 30 minutes or until pancetta is crispy and a meat thermometer inserted into center of tenderloin registers 120° (rare). Let stand 10 minutes. Discard kitchen string before slicing. Serve with Whipped Horseradish Cream.

Note: For medium-rare, cook tenderloin to 135°, or to 150° for medium.

Whipped Horseradish Cream

Makes 2¼ cups
Hands-on Time: 10 min. **Total Time:** 10 min.

- 1   cup whipping cream
- ¼   cup horseradish
- 2   Tbsp. chopped fresh parsley
- ¼   tsp. salt

1. Beat whipping cream at medium speed with a heavy-duty electric stand mixer 1 minute or until soft peaks form. Fold in remaining ingredients. Serve immediately, or cover and chill up to 8 hours.

Easy Asiago-Olive Rolls

Asiago [ah-SYAH-goh] has a sweeter flavor than Parmesan and Romano.

Makes 8 to 10 servings
Hands-on Time: 10 min. **Total Time:** 25 min.

- 1   (13.8-oz.) can refrigerated classic pizza crust dough
- ¼   cup refrigerated olive tapenade
- ½   cup grated Asiago cheese
- 1   tsp. chopped fresh rosemary
- 1   Tbsp. butter, melted

1. Preheat oven to 450°. Unroll pizza crust dough. Spread olive tapenade over dough, leaving a ¼-inch border. Sprinkle with cheese and rosemary. Gently roll up dough, starting at 1 long side. Cut into 10 (1¼-inch-thick) slices. Place slices in a lightly greased 9-inch round cake pan. Brush top of dough with melted butter. Bake 15 to 20 minutes or until golden. Serve immediately.

Pancetta-Wrapped Beef Tenderloin with
Whipped Horseradish Cream; Crispy Potatoes
with Fennel (recipe on page 50); Lemon-Garlic
Green Beans (recipe on page 50)

Crispy Potatoes with Fennel

Do not use a traditional cookware skillet unless the skillet and handle are labeled oven safe to at least 475°. (Pictured on page 49)

Makes 8 servings
Hands-on Time: 15 min. **Total Time:** 1 hr., 5 min.

1   fennel bulb
3   Tbsp. olive oil
2   lb. red potatoes, thinly sliced
2   tsp. chopped fresh thyme
1½ tsp. salt
½   tsp. pepper

1. Preheat oven to 475°. Rinse fennel thoroughly. Trim and discard root end of fennel bulb. Trim stalks from fennel bulb, reserving fronds for another use. Thinly slice bulb.
2. Add oil to a 9-inch cast-iron skillet. Arrange half of potato slices in skillet. Layer with fennel slices and remaining potatoes. Sprinkle with thyme, salt, and pepper. Cover with aluminum foil.
3. Bake at 475° for 35 minutes. Uncover and bake 15 more minutes or until vegetables are browned. Serve hot or at room temperature. Transfer to serving bowl, if desired.

Lemon-Garlic Green Beans

(Pictured on page 49)

Makes 8 servings
Hands-on Time: 15 min. **Total Time:** 21 min.

1½ lb. fresh haricots verts (tiny green beans), trimmed
2   tsp. salt, divided
3   garlic cloves, minced
3   shallots, sliced
2   Tbsp. olive oil
¼   cup chopped fresh basil
3   Tbsp. fresh lemon juice
¼   tsp. pepper
Garnishes: lemon zest, fresh basil leaves

1. Cook beans with 1 tsp. salt in boiling water to cover 4 to 5 minutes or until crisp-tender; drain. Plunge beans into ice water to stop the cooking process; drain.

2. Cook garlic and shallots in hot oil in a large nonstick skillet over medium heat 2 minutes or until just golden brown; remove from heat. Stir in basil, next 2 ingredients, and remaining 1 tsp. salt. Add green beans, and toss to coat. Garnish, if desired.

Chocolate Truffle Cheesecake

To make the snowflake garnish on this cheesecake, see page 281.

Makes 10 servings
Hands-on Time: 20 min. **Total Time:** 12 hr., 25 min., including ganache topping

1½ cups crushed dark chocolate-and-almond shortbread cookies (about 18 cookies)
2   Tbsp. melted butter
2   (4-oz.) semisweet chocolate baking bars, chopped
1   cup whipping cream
4   (8-oz.) packages cream cheese, softened
1   (14-oz.) can sweetened condensed milk
2   tsp. vanilla extract
4   large eggs
Ganache Topping
Garnish: fresh raspberries or White Chocolate Snowflake

1. Preheat oven to 300°. Combine crushed cookies and butter. Press mixture on bottom of a 9-inch springform pan.
2. Microwave chocolate and cream at HIGH 1½ minutes or until melted, stirring at 30-second intervals.
3. Beat cream cheese at medium speed with a heavy-duty electric stand mixer 2 minutes or until smooth. Add sweetened condensed milk and vanilla, beating just until combined. Add eggs, 1 at a time, beating at low speed just until blended after each addition. Add chocolate mixture, beating just until blended. Pour batter into prepared crust.
4. Bake at 300° for 1 hour and 5 minutes or just until center is set. Turn oven off. Let cheesecake stand in oven with door closed 30 minutes. Remove cheesecake from oven; gently run a knife around outer edge of cheesecake to loosen from sides of pan. Cool completely in pan on a wire rack (about 1 hour). Cover and chill 8 to 24 hours.
5. Remove sides of pan, and place cheesecake on a serving plate. Slowly pour warm Ganache Topping over cheesecake, spreading to edges. Chill 1 hour before serving. Garnish with rasbperries or White Chocolate Snowflake, if desired.

Ganache Topping

Makes 1¼ cups
Hands-on Time: 10 min. **Total Time:** 30 min.

1   cup whipping cream
1   (4-oz.) semisweet chocolate baking bar
1   (4-oz.) dark chocolate baking bar

1. Bring whipping cream to a light boil in a saucepan over medium heat.

2. Process chocolate bars in a food processor until coarsely chopped. With processor running, pour cream through food chute in a slow, steady stream, processing until smooth. Let mixture cool until slightly warm (about 20 minutes).

Chocolate Truffle Cheesecake

feast with FRIENDS

menu for 8

Quick Winter Pickled Veggies
Deviled Ham Terrine
Kumquat Martini
Fennel-Crusted Rib Roast
Roasted Asparagus
Warm Greens with Cornbread Croutons
Buttermilk Panna Cotta with Zinfandel-Poached Figs

up to 1 month ahead:
• Prepare Super-Simple Syrup; store in an airtight container in refrigerator up to 1 month.

up to 1 week ahead:
• Prepare Quick Winter Pickled Veggies; store in an airtight container up to 1 week. Make extra to put into mason jars and send home with your guests as party favors.
• Prepare cornbread croutons; store in an airtight container at room temperature.

2 days ahead:
• Prepare Deviled Ham Terrine; cover and chill.

1 day ahead:
• Prepare Molasses Vinaigrette; cover and chill.
• Prepare Buttermilk Panna Cotta, and divide mixture; cover and chill.
• Prepare Zinfandel-Poached Figs; cover and chill.

4 hours ahead:
• Prepare and roast Fennel-Crusted Rib Roast; let rest for 15 minutes to 1 hour before carving.

1 hour ahead:
• Prepare Warm Greens.
• Prepare Roasted Asparagus with remaining drippings from rib roast.
• Prepare bar with all the ingredients needed to make a Kumquat Martini.

last minute:
• Bring Deviled Ham Terrine to room temperature.
• Assemble Warm Greens with Cornbread Croutons.
• Bring Zinfandel-Poached Figs to room temperature.
• Have bar area completely ready for guests to make drinks; make a demo drink if desired.
• Carve rib roast, plate dish, and garnish, if desired.

Laughter is always on the menu when you get together with friends over a seasonal supper.

Quick Winter Pickled Veggies

Serve alongside Deviled Ham Terrine, or add to your favorite martini or Bloody Mary. Make extra as a takeaway for your guests. Pickles may seem summery, but you can enjoy them using seasonal fall and winter produce.

Makes about 8 cups
Hands-on Time: 35 min. **Total Time:** 2 hr., 5 min., plus 1 day for chilling

2	cups apple cider vinegar
⅔	cup sugar
¼	cup kosher salt
3	garlic cloves
1	tsp. mustard seeds
1	tsp. fennel seeds
1	tsp. black peppercorns
½	tsp. dried crushed red pepper
8	cups assorted cut vegetables

1. Bring first 8 ingredients and 2½ cups water to a boil in a large nonaluminum saucepan over medium-high heat, stirring until sugar is dissolved; boil 1 minute. Let stand 30 minutes.
2. Meanwhile, cook vegetables, in batches, in boiling water to cover 1 to 2 minutes or until crisp-tender; drain. Plunge into ice water to stop the cooking process; drain.
3. Transfer vegetables to a large bowl or 2½-qt. container. Pour vinegar mixture over vegetables. Let stand 1 hour. Cover and chill 1 day before serving. Store in an airtight container in refrigerator up to 1 week.

test-kitchen secret

These veggies are perfect for pickling: Cauliflower florets, Swiss chard stalks, carrot sticks, halved Brussels sprouts, sliced parsnips, radishes, sliced fennel, green beans, and bell pepper rings.

Quick Winter Pickled Veggies; Deviled Ham Terrine (recipe on page 54)

Deviled Ham Terrine

This recipe can be halved easily. (Pictured on page 53)

Makes 4¾ cups
Hands-on Time: 20 min. **Total Time:** 8 hr., 50 min.

1½	lb. smoked ham, coarsely chopped (about 4 cups)
½	cup finely chopped fresh parsley
½	cup mayonnaise
6	Tbsp. butter, softened
¼	cup whole-grain Dijon mustard
3	Tbsp. dry white wine
1	celery rib, finely chopped
2	green onions, finely chopped
1	tsp. lemon zest
¾	tsp. black pepper
¼	tsp. ground red pepper
	Crackers
	Quick Winter Pickled Veggies (recipe on page 53)
	Garnish: sliced pickled okra

1. Pulse ham, in batches, in a food processor 4 to 6 times or until shredded. (Do not over-process.)
2. Stir together parsley and next 9 ingredients. Stir in ham until well blended. Cover and chill 8 hours. Store in an airtight container in refrigerator up to 3 days. Let stand at room temperature 30 minutes before serving. Serve deviled ham with crackers and Quick Winter Pickled Veggies. Garnish, if desired.

party pointer

Use the best quality ham you can find. For a great serving idea, simply line a 5-cup serving piece or 2 (2½-cup) serving pieces with plastic wrap, spoon in deviled ham, cover, and chill. When you're ready to serve, unmold it onto a serving plate, discarding plastic wrap.

quick & easy

Kumquat Martini

Get in the cheer with this sipping cocktail. It's a cross between a mint julep and a classic martini. Take the pressure off the hostess: Prep the ingredients separately in small bowls, and let guests muddle and shake their drinks to order.

Makes 1 serving
Hands-on Time: 10 min. **Total Time:** 15 min., including syrup

2	kumquats, sliced
5	fresh mint leaves
1	to 2 Tbsp. Super-Simple Syrup
	Crushed ice
¼	cup vodka

1. Combine first 3 ingredients in a cocktail shaker. Press leaves and kumquat slices against bottom of shaker using a muddler or back of a wooden spoon to release flavors; add ice and vodka. Cover with lid, and shake vigorously until thoroughly chilled (about 30 seconds). Strain into a chilled martini glass. Serve immediately.

Super-Simple Syrup:

Makes about 2½ cups
Hands-on Time: 5 min. **Total Time:** 5 min.

1. Microwave 1 cup water in a microwave-safe 4-cup glass measuring cup at HIGH 1 minute and 30 seconds or until very hot. Add 2 cups sugar; stir 20 seconds. Microwave at HIGH 45 seconds; stir until sugar is dissolved and mixture is clear. Cover and chill until ready to use. Store in an airtight container in refrigerator up to 1 month.

Fennel-Crusted Rib Roast

Makes 8 servings
Hands-on Time: 20 min. **Total Time:** 3 hr., 5 min.

- 1 (7- to 9-lb.) 4-rib prime rib roast, trimmed
- 2 tsp. black peppercorns
- 2 tsp. fennel seeds
- 1½ tsp. coriander seeds
- 1 Tbsp. olive oil
- 4 tsp. kosher salt
- Garnishes: fresh cranberries, oranges, gray sea salt

1. Preheat oven to 400°. Let roast stand at room temperature 30 minutes.

2. Pulse peppercorns, fennel, and coriander in a spice grinder 5 times or until coarsely ground. (Or place spices in a zip-top plastic freezer bag, and crush using a rolling pin or skillet.) Rub roast with oil, and sprinkle with salt. Press spice mixture onto all sides of roast. Place on a rack in a roasting pan.

3. Bake roast at 400° for 2 hours or until a meat thermometer inserted into thickest portion registers 120° to 125° (medium-rare) or to desired degree of doneness. Let stand 15 minutes to 1 hour before slicing. If desired, reserve pan drippings to coat Roasted Asparagus. Garnish, if desired.

test-kitchen secrets

Follow our tips for standing rib roast first-timers.
- This recipe calls for a 4-rib roast (a full roast has 7 ribs). One rib provides 2 generous servings of beef.
- Ask the grocery store butcher to "french" or trim the meat around the bones.
- Roast to an internal temperature of 120°. The roast's temperature continues to rise, ensuring a perfect medium-rare in the center and ends that are more medium to medium-well.

Fennel-Crusted Rib Roast

Roasted Asparagus

Roasted Asparagus

Makes 8 servings
Hands-on Time: 15 min. **Total Time:** 20 min.

2   lb. fresh asparagus
2   Tbsp. pan drippings from Fennel-Crusted Rib Roast*
1   lemon, thinly sliced

1. Preheat broiler with oven rack 3 inches from heat. Snap off and discard tough ends of asparagus; toss asparagus with rib roast pan drippings and lemon slices. Arrange in a single layer in a 17- x 12-inch jelly-roll pan. Broil 4 to 9 minutes or until browned.

*2 Tbsp. olive oil and salt and pepper to taste may be substituted for pan drippings.

Warm Greens with Cornbread Croutons

Reserve and freeze a large wedge of cornbread when you make your Thanksgiving dressing. It will save time when you make the croutons. Warm salad not your speed? Try Baby Greens with Molasses Vinaigrette.

Makes 8 servings
Hands-on Time: 22 min. **Total Time:** 37 min.

4   cups (¾-inch) cornbread cubes
2   Tbsp. melted butter
1   tsp. kosher salt, divided
1   tsp. coarsely ground pepper, divided
1   medium-size red onion, halved and sliced
1   garlic clove, minced
¼   cup olive oil
⅓   cup apple cider vinegar
2   Tbsp. molasses
1   Tbsp. coarse-grained Dijon mustard
4   bunches frisée, torn*

1. Preheat oven to 400°. Gently toss 4 cups cornbread cubes with 2 Tbsp. melted butter, ¼ tsp. salt, and ½ tsp. pepper. Arrange in a single layer on a baking sheet.
2. Bake at 400° for 15 to 25 minutes or until toasted.
3. Sauté onion and garlic in hot oil in a Dutch oven over medium heat 5 minutes. Stir in vinegar, molasses, mustard, and remaining ¾ tsp. salt and ½ tsp. pepper; cook 1 minute.

Warm Greens with
Cornbread Croutons

Add frisée, and toss to coat. Cook, stirring constantly, 1 to 2 minutes or until frisée just begins to wilt.
4. Transfer onion mixture to a serving dish, and sprinkle with cornbread croutons; serve immediately.

*2 bunches curly endive may be substituted.

Baby Greens with Molasses Vinaigrette:
Whisk together ⅓ cup olive oil, ¼ cup apple cider vinegar, 2 Tbsp. molasses, 1 Tbsp. coarse-grained Dijon mustard, 1 minced garlic clove, ¾ tsp. kosher salt, and ½ tsp. pepper. Toss desired amount of dressing with 1 (5-oz.) package thoroughly washed spring greens mix. Top with ¼ red onion, thinly sliced, and cornbread croutons. Serve with remaining dressing. Hands-on Time: 15 min.; Total Time: 15 min.

Buttermilk Panna Cotta with Zinfandel-Poached Figs

make ahead

Buttermilk Panna Cotta with Zinfandel-Poached Figs

Panna cotta, an eggless custard, is generally served unmolded on a serving plate.

Makes 8 servings
Hands-on Time: 22 min. **Total Time:** 8 hr., including figs

- 2   cups heavy cream
- ½   vanilla bean, split
- 1   envelope unflavored gelatin
- ½   cup plus 2 Tbsp. sugar
- 2½ cups buttermilk
-     Zinfandel-Poached Figs
-     Garnish: freshly grated nutmeg

1. Combine cream and vanilla bean in a small saucepan; sprinkle gelatin over cream, and let stand 10 minutes.
2. Cook cream mixture over medium-low heat, stirring constantly, 5 minutes or until gelatin is dissolved. Increase heat to medium; add sugar, and stir until sugar is dissolved (about 2 to 3 minutes).
3. Remove from heat. Scrape seeds from vanilla bean into cream mixture with back of a knife; discard vanilla bean. Whisk in buttermilk.
4. Divide mixture among 8 (10-oz.) glasses. Cover and chill 6 hours to 2 days. Spoon 2 to 3 Tbsp. Zinfandel-Poached Figs into each glass just before serving. Garnish, if desired.

Zinfandel-Poached Figs

The remaining Zinfandel wine is the perfect companion for the succulent roast.

Makes about 1½ cups
Hands-on Time: 25 min. **Total Time:** 1 hr., 25 min.

- 1   cup halved dried Mission figlets
- 1   cup red Zinfandel wine*
- ½   cup chopped dried apricots
- ⅓   cup honey
- ½   vanilla bean, split**
- ⅛   tsp. ground cinnamon
-     Pinch of salt and pepper

1. Combine figlets, wine, apricots, and remaining ingredients in a small saucepan.
2. Bring fig mixture to a boil over medium-high heat; reduce heat to medium-low, and simmer, stirring occasionally, 10 to 12 minutes or until mixture is slightly thickened.
3. Scrape seeds from vanilla bean into fig mixture; discard vanilla bean. Cool 1 hour. Serve immediately, or cover and chill until ready to serve.

*1 cup cranberry-grape juice cocktail and 2 tsp. apple cider vinegar may be substituted.

**½ tsp. vanilla extract may be substituted. (Stir extract into figs after removing saucepan from heat.)

Note: Store in an airtight container in refrigerator up to 2 weeks. If chilled, let stand at room temperature 30 minutes before serving.

Winter Fruit Compote;
Gentleman's Casserole
(recipe on page 60)

Christmas Eve
BRUNCH

menu for 4

Winter Fruit Compote
Gentleman's Casserole (double recipe)
Cranberry-Orange Tea Bread Muffins
Kane's Peppery Bloody Mary (double recipe)

up to 2 months ahead:
• Bake Cranberry-Orange Tea Bread Muffins, but do not glaze. Freeze in a zip-top plastic freezer bag.

1 day before:
• Make Candied Kumquat Slices for muffins. Cover loosely with plastic wrap, and let stand at room temperature.
• Make Gruyère Cheese Sauce for Gentleman's Casserole. Cover and chill.
• Make Winter Fruit Compote, and chill.
• Bake puff pastry shells for Gentleman's Casserole. Store at room temperature in a zip-top plastic freezer bag.

day of:
• Make Kane's Peppery Bloody Mary.
• Make Orange–Cream Cheese Glaze.
• Thaw muffins at room temperature; top with glaze and kumquat slices.
• Reheat puff pastry shells on a baking sheet at 350° for 5 minutes.
• Microwave Gruyère Cheese Sauce.
• Scramble eggs, and fold in cheese sauce.

Winter Fruit Compote

To avoid having leftover Champagne, buy a split (187 milliliter) for this recipe.

Makes 4 servings
Hands-on Time: 40 min. **Total Time:** 3 hr., 15 min.

½ cup sugar
1 cup Champagne or sparkling wine
2 Ruby Red grapefruits, peeled and sectioned
2 oranges, peeled and sectioned
Garnish: maraschino cherries with stems

1. Cook sugar in a small saucepan over medium heat, tilting pan occasionally, 10 minutes or until caramel colored. Remove from heat, and gradually pour Champagne over sugar (mixture will bubble and seize). Let stand 5 minutes.
2. Cook Champagne mixture over medium-low heat, stirring occasionally, 15 minutes or until sugar is dissolved (mixture will be syrupy). Remove from heat, and let cool 30 minutes.
3. Combine grapefruit and orange sections in a bowl. Pour Champagne mixture over fruit. Cover and chill 2 to 24 hours. Garnish, if desired.

White Grape Winter Fruit Compote:
Substitute white grape juice for Champagne. Proceed with recipe as directed.

Enjoy this fireside brunch on Christmas Eve morning—it's mostly make-ahead, so you can relax and enjoy the beginning of the holiday.

Gentleman's Casserole

This recipe easily doubles to serve 4. You can bake puff pastry shells the day before. Remove tops, and reheat on a baking sheet at 350° for 5 minutes. (Pictured on page 58)

Makes 2 servings
Hands-on Time: 31 min. **Total Time:** 1 hr., 7 min., including Gruyère Cheese Sauce

- 1 (10-oz.) package frozen puff pastry shells
- 1 Tbsp. butter
- ⅓ cup chopped cooked ham
- 1 Tbsp. chopped green onions
- 4 large eggs, lightly beaten
- Gruyère Cheese Sauce
- ¼ cup grated Gruyère cheese
- Dash of paprika
- Garnish: chopped green onions

1. Bake 4 pastry shells according to package directions. Reserve remaining shells for another use.
2. Melt butter in a medium-size nonstick skillet over medium heat; add ham and green onions. Sauté 2 minutes or until green onions are tender. Add eggs, and cook, without stirring, 1 to 2 minutes or until eggs begin to set on bottom. Gently draw cooked edges away from sides of pan to form large pieces. Cook, stirring occasionally, 1 to 2 minutes or until eggs are thickened and moist. (Do not over stir.) Gently fold in Gruyère Cheese Sauce.
3. Spoon egg mixture into prepared pastry shells. Sprinkle with cheese and paprika. Garnish, if desired. Serve immediately.

Chicken-and-White Cheddar Casserole:
Substitute extra-sharp white Cheddar cheese for Gruyère, Cheddar Cheese Sauce for Gruyère Cheese Sauce, and chopped cooked chicken for ham. Proceed with recipe as directed.

Gruyère Cheese Sauce

You can make this up to 2 days ahead, and store in the refrigerator. Reheat in a microwave-safe bowl at HIGH 1½ minutes, stirring halfway through.

Makes about ¾ cup
Hands-on Time: 16 min. **Total Time:** 16 min.

- ¾ cup milk
- 1 Tbsp. butter
- 1 Tbsp. all-purpose flour
- ½ cup grated Gruyère cheese
- ¼ tsp. salt
- ⅛ tsp. pepper

1. Microwave milk in a 2-cup microwave-safe glass measuring cup at HIGH 1 minute.
2. Melt butter in a small heavy saucepan over medium heat; gradually whisk in flour. Cook 1 minute, whisking constantly. Gradually whisk in warm milk; cook over medium heat, whisking constantly, 3 to 5 minutes or until thickened and bubbly. Remove from heat; whisk in cheese, salt, and pepper.

Cheddar Cheese Sauce: Substitute extra-sharp white Cheddar cheese for Gruyère. Proceed with recipe as directed.

Cranberry-Orange Tea Bread Muffins

Makes 2 dozen
Hands-on Time: 25 min. **Total Time:** 25 hr., 35 min., including glaze and candied kumquats

- ½ cup chopped pecans
- 2 cups all-purpose flour
- 1½ tsp. baking powder
- 1 tsp. salt
- ½ (12-oz.) package fresh cranberries (about 2 cups)
- 1 cup sugar
- ¼ cup butter, softened
- 1 large egg, lightly beaten
- ¾ cup orange juice
- 24 aluminum foil miniature baking cups
- Vegetable cooking spray
- Orange–Cream Cheese Glaze
- Garnish: Candied Kumquat Slices

1. Preheat oven to 350°. Bake pecans in a single layer in a shallow pan 8 to 10 minutes or until toasted and fragrant, stirring occasionally.

2. Whisk together flour, baking powder, and salt.

3. Pulse cranberries and sugar in a food processor 3 to 4 times or just until chopped.

4. Beat butter at medium speed with an electric mixer until creamy. Add egg, beating until well blended. Gradually add flour mixture alternately with orange juice, beginning and ending with flour mixture. Beat at low speed until blended after each addition. Stir in cranberry mixture and pecans.

5. Place baking cups in miniature muffin pans; coat with cooking spray. Spoon batter into baking cups, filling completely.

6. Bake at 350° for 25 minutes or until a wooden pick inserted in center comes clean. Remove from pans to a wire rack; spoon Orange–Cream Cheese Glaze over warm muffins. Garnish with Candied Kumquat Slices, if desired.

Note: To make ahead, place unglazed muffins in a zip-top plastic freezer bag; freeze up to 2 months. Let thaw at room temperature before glazing.

Orange–Cream Cheese Glaze

Makes about 1 cup
Hands-on Time: 10 min. Total Time: 10 min.

  1   (3-oz.) package cream cheese, softened
  1   Tbsp. orange juice
  ¼   tsp. vanilla extract
  1½ cups sifted powdered sugar

1. Beat cream cheese at medium speed with an electric mixer until creamy. Add orange juice and vanilla extract; beat until smooth. Gradually add powdered sugar, beating until smooth.

Candied Kumquat Slices

You can strain the syrup left after making kumquat slices to flavor iced tea or lemonade.

Makes about 3½ dozen
Hands-on Time: 15 min. Total Time: 24 hr., 25 min.

  8   kumquats
  ¾   cup sugar, divided
  Wax paper

1. Cut kumquats into ⅛-inch-thick slices. Stir together ½ cup sugar and ½ cup water in a small heavy saucepan. Bring to a boil over medium heat. Reduce heat to medium-low, and stir in kumquat slices; simmer 10 minutes. Remove from heat; remove kumquat slices, 1 at a time, shaking off excess sugar-water mixture. Place kumquats in a bowl with ¼ cup sugar; toss to coat. Transfer kumquats to wax paper. Cover loosely with plastic wrap, and let stand 24 hours.

Cranberry-Orange Tea
Bread Muffins

Kane's Peppery Bloody Mary

This recipe received our Test Kitchens' highest rating.

Makes 2 servings
Hands-on Time: 10 min. **Total Time:** 10 min.

- 1 tsp. chopped fresh basil
- 1 tsp. chopped fresh cilantro
- 1 tsp. chopped fresh chives
- 1⅓ cups tomato juice
- ½ cup pepper vodka
- 6 Tbsp. fresh lemon juice
- 1½ to 3 tsp. green hot sauce
- 1 tsp. Worcestershire sauce
- Large pinch of celery salt
- Pinch of sea salt
- Freshly ground pepper to taste
- Garnishes: pickled okra, lemon wedges

1. Combine first 3 ingredients in a cocktail shaker. Press leaves against bottom of cup using a muddler or wooden spoon to release flavors; stir in tomato juice and next 7 ingredients. Transfer half of mixture to a 2-cup glass measuring cup.

2. Place ice in cocktail shaker, filling halfway full. Cover with lid, and shake vigorously until thoroughly chilled. Strain into a glass over ice. Repeat procedure with remaining tomato mixture. Garnish, if desired.

Kane's Bloody Mary: Substitute regular vodka for pepper vodka. Proceed with recipe as directed.

party pointer

Celebrate each addition to the family with personalized stockings. This is the perfect way to mark the birth of a child or to make a new daughter-in-law feel like a member of the family.

Kane's Peppery Bloody Mary

easy *SUPPER CLUB*

menu for 8

Uptown Figs or Bacon-Arugula-Apple Bites
Herbed Pork Roast
Roasted Fall Vegetables
Puffed Mashed Potatoes
Basil-and-Blue Cheese Salad
Brandy Alexander Cheesecake

1 month ahead:
• Prepare and bake Brandy Alexander Cheesecake; follow directions for proper freezing method.

2 days ahead:
• Prepare Puffed Mashed Potatoes through Step 2 in recipe; cover and chill.

1 day ahead:
• Cook bacon; cover and chill.
• Prepare dressing for salad; cover and chill.

2 hours ahead:
• Prepare and roast Herbed Pork Roast.
• Prepare and roast Fall Vegetables.
• Remove cheesecake from freezer, and thaw in refrigerator until ready to serve.

1 hour ahead:
• Prepare and assemble Uptown Figs or Bacon-Arugula-Apple Bites.
• Bring potato mixture to room temperature, and add remaining ingredients.

30 minutes:
• Bake mashed potatoes.

last minute:
• Plate and garnish appetizers, if desired.
• Assemble Basil-and-Blue Cheese Salad.
• Carve Pork Roast.

Uptown Figs: Cut a slit in large side of 24 dried figs, cutting to, but not through, stem end of figs. Stir together 1 (3-oz.) package softened cream cheese, 2 tsp. powdered sugar, and 2 tsp. orange liqueur. Fill each fig with cream cheese mixture and 1 roasted, salted almond. Press figs to secure fillings.

Bacon-Arugula-Apple Bites: Toss Red Delicious apple slices in lemon juice; pat dry. Spread each with about 2 tsp. garlic-and-herb spreadable cheese. Top with cooked and crumbled bacon, baby arugula sprigs, and freshly cracked pepper.

Note: We tested with Vermont Gourmet Garlic-and-Herb Spreadable Cheese.

Bacon-Arugula-Apple Bites

Herbed Pork Roast

We loved this roast with gravy. We used Knorr Classic Brown Gravy Mix prepared according to package directions.

Makes 8 servings
Hands-on Time: 26 min. **Total Time:** 1 hr., 6 min.

- 1 (4- to 5-lb.) untrimmed pork loin roast
- 1 tsp. kosher salt
- 1 tsp. coarsely ground pepper
- Kitchen string
- 5 Tbsp. olive oil, divided
- 2 Tbsp. chopped fresh sage
- 2 Tbsp. chopped fresh parsley
- 2 Tbsp. chopped fresh thyme
- 1 Tbsp. chopped fresh rosemary

1. Preheat oven to 425°. Sprinkle pork with kosher salt and gound pepper. Tie pork with kitchen string, securing at 2-inch intervals.
2. Cook pork, fat side down, in 3 Tbsp. hot oil in a stainless-steel skillet over medium-high heat 3 to 5 minutes on each side or until golden brown. Place, fat side up, on a wire rack in an aluminum foil–lined roasting pan. Remove kitchen string; make 5 (½-inch-deep) cuts in pork.
3. Stir together sage, next 3 ingredients, and remaining 2 Tbsp. oil. Stuff herb mixture into slits in pork.
4. Bake at 425° for 30 to 40 minutes or until a meat thermometer inserted into thickest portion registers 150°. Let stand 10 minutes before serving.

Roasted Fall Vegetables

Makes 8 servings
Hands-on Time: 20 min. **Total Time:** 50 min.

- 8 baby yellow beets
- 8 baby candy cane beets
- 10 small carrots with greenery
- 3 Tbsp. olive oil, divided
- 1 tsp. kosher salt, divided
- ½ tsp. pepper, divided

1. Preheat oven to 425°. Cut tops from yellow and candy cane beets, leaving ½-inch stems. Peel beets, and cut in half. Cut tops from carrots, leaving ½ inch of greenery on each.
2. Toss yellow beets and carrots with 2 Tbsp. olive oil in a large bowl; place in a single layer on 1 side of an aluminum foil–lined 15- x 10-inch jelly-roll pan. Sprinkle vegetables in pan with ½ tsp. salt and ¼ tsp. pepper.
3. Toss candy cane beets with remaining 1 Tbsp. olive oil; arrange beets in a single layer on remaining side of jelly-roll pan. Sprinkle with remaining ½ tsp. salt and ¼ tsp. pepper.
4. Bake at 425° for 15 minutes; stir once, and bake 15 more minutes or until tender.

test-kitchen secret

Candy cane beets are also known as Chioggia beets. We love this variety because they don't stain like traditional red beets.

This is one sit-down dinner that's dressy enough to impress yet doable enough to enjoy.

Puffed Mashed Potatoes

If you like Parmesan cheese, you'll like the Spanish cheese Manchego.

Makes 10 to 12 servings
Hands-on Time: 21 min. **Total Time:** 1 hr., 6 min.

 5   lb. Yukon gold potatoes, peeled and cut into 2-inch pieces
 1   Tbsp. salt, divided
 3   Tbsp. butter
 ¾   cup (3 oz.) shredded Manchego cheese*
 ¾   cup half-and-half
 2   large eggs, lightly beaten
 ½   tsp. pepper
 2   Tbsp. butter, melted

1. Bring potatoes, 2 tsp. salt, and water to cover to a boil in a large Dutch oven over medium-high heat. Boil 20 minutes or until tender; drain. Reduce heat to low.
2. Return potatoes to Dutch oven, and cook, stirring occasionally, 1 to 2 minutes or until potatoes are dry. Remove from heat; mash potatoes with a potato masher to desired consistency.

3. Preheat oven to 400°. Stir butter, next 4 ingredients, and remaining 1 tsp. salt into potatoes. Spread mixture into a lightly greased 2½- to 3-qt. baking dish. Brush mashed potatoes with melted butter.
4. Bake at 400° for 20 to 25 minutes or until thoroughly heated and puffed. Serve immediately.

*Shredded Parmesan cheese may be substituted.

Note: To make Puffed Mashed Potatoes ahead, prepare recipe as directed through Step 2. Cover and chill up to 2 days. Remove from refrigerator, and let stand at room temperature for at least 30 minutes. Proceed with recipe as directed.

party pointer

For a pretty presentation out of the oven, spread potato mixture in a baking dish, create swirls with the back of a spoon as you would frost a cake, and then brush with butter.

Herbed Pork Roast; Roasted Fall Vegetables; Puffed Mashed Potatoes

Basil-and-Blue Cheese Salad

It's ideal to slice pears and avocados at the last minute so they won't turn brown. You can do this 1 hour ahead and toss in a small amount of lemon juice. (Too much will alter the flavor of the vinaigrette.)

Makes 10 to 12 servings
Hands-on Time: 20 min. **Total Time:** 20 min.

⅓ cup olive oil
⅓ cup seasoned rice vinegar
1 tsp. country-style Dijon mustard
½ tsp. salt
¼ tsp. dried crushed red pepper
10 cups mixed salad greens
½ cup firmly packed fresh basil leaves, coarsely chopped
2 ripe pears, thinly sliced
2 fresh navel oranges, sectioned
2 avocados, sliced
1 (4-oz.) package blue cheese, crumbled

Basil-and-Blue Cheese Salad

1. Whisk together first 5 ingredients. Cover and chill until ready to use (up to 24 hours).
2. Toss together greens and basil. Top with pears, oranges, avocados, and blue cheese; toss. Drizzle with vinaigrette. Serve immediately.

make ahead • freezer friendly

Brandy Alexander Cheesecake

To freeze up to 1 month, wrap springform pan tightly with aluminum foil, and slide into a zip-top plastic freezer bag.

Makes 10 to 12 servings
Hands-on Time: 20 min. **Total Time:** 11 hr., 8 min.

1 (10-oz.) box chocolate-flavored bear-shaped graham crackers, crushed (about 2¼ cups)
6 Tbsp. butter, melted
2 Tbsp. sugar, divided
4 (8-oz.) packages cream cheese, softened
1¼ cups sugar
3 Tbsp. cornstarch
4 large eggs, at room temperature
4 Tbsp. brandy, divided
4 Tbsp. crème de cacao, divided*
1 (16-oz.) container sour cream
Garnishes: blackberries, currants, raspberries, strawberries

1. Preheat oven to 325°. Stir together crushed graham crackers, butter, and 1 Tbsp. sugar. Press mixture on bottom and halfway up sides of a 9-inch springform pan. Freeze 10 minutes.
2. Beat cream cheese, 1¼ cups sugar, and cornstarch at medium speed with an electric mixer 2 to 3 minutes or until smooth. Add eggs, 1 at a time, beating at low speed just until yellow disappears after each addition. Add 3 Tbsp. brandy and 3 Tbsp. crème de cacao, and beat mixture just until blended. Pour into prepared crust.
3. Bake at 325° for 1 hour or just until center is almost set.
4. During last 2 minutes of baking, stir together sour cream and remaining 1 Tbsp. sugar, 1 Tbsp. brandy, and 1 Tbsp. crème de cacao.
5. Spread sour cream mixture over cheesecake. Bake at 325° for 8 more minutes. Remove cheesecake from oven; gently run a knife along outer edge of cheesecake, and cool

Brandy Alexander Cheesecake

completely in pan on a wire rack (about 1½ hours). Cover
and chill 8 to 24 hours.

6. Remove sides of springform pan, and place cheesecake
on a serving plate. Garnish, if desired.

*Coffee liqueur may be substituted. We tested with Kahlúa.

test-kitchen secret

Allowing a cheesecake to chill is important for
developing its texture and flavor.

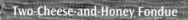
Two-Cheese-and-Honey Fondue

FONDUE *fun*

menu for 6

Two-Cheese-and-Honey Fondue
Tomato-and-Herb Fondue
mixed salad greens
Mississippi Mud Fondue

1 week ahead:
• Toast pecans; store in airtight container at room temperature or freezer.

1 day ahead:
• Prepare Two-Cheese-and-Honey Fondue; cover and chill.
• Prepare Tomato-and-Herb Fondue; cover and chill.
• Bake brownies, if not buying ready-made.

1 hour ahead:
• Warm up cheese fondue.
• Cut bread and fruit.
• Cook meats and pasta.
• Plate dessert accompaniments.

last minute:
• Transfer cheese to fondue pot.
• Heat Tomato-and-Herb Fondue.
• After your meal is over, allow guests to relax while you assemble Mississippi Mud Fondue for dessert.

test-kitchen secrets

• Allow 20 (1-inch) cubes of bread, 6 to 8 ounces of fruit or vegetables, or at least 4 cookies per person.
• Fill ceramic pots with cheese, chocolate, and dessert-based fondues.
• Use metal pots for oil, broth, or beer fondues.
• Keep portions bite-size.

Two-Cheese-and-Honey Fondue

Should there be leftovers of this dreamy delicacy, reheat it the next day and serve over pound cake or ice cream.

Makes 2¾ cups
Hands-on Time: 23 min. **Total Time:** 23 min.

Fondue:
- 1 cup heavy cream
- 1 cup chicken broth
- 1 Tbsp. honey
- 2 cups (8 oz.) freshly shredded Jarlsberg cheese
- ½ cup (2 oz.) freshly shredded Swiss cheese
- ¼ cup all-purpose flour
- ¼ tsp. dry mustard
- ¼ tsp. freshly cracked pepper

Serve with:
Cubed ciabatta bread, sliced pears, sliced apples

1. Bring heavy cream, chicken broth, and honey to a boil over medium-high heat; reduce heat to medium-low, and simmer. Meanwhile, combine cheeses, flour, mustard, and pepper in a large bowl. Slowly whisk cheese mixture into simmering broth until melted and smooth. Transfer to fondue pot; keep warm. Serve fondue with desired accompaniments.

Entertain the easy way—one pot, lots of flavor.

Tomato-and-Herb Fondue

Makes 3 cups
Hands-on Time: 21 min. **Total Time:** 21 min.

Fondue:
- 1 Tbsp. butter
- ¼ cup chopped sweet onion
- 2 garlic cloves, minced
- 2 (14.5-oz.) cans fire-roasted tomatoes
- 1 tsp. tomato paste
- ½ tsp. lemon zest
- ¼ cup chopped fresh basil

Serve with:
Cubed, lightly toasted French bread; cubed, toasted cheese bread; chopped, cooked chicken tenders; meatballs; tortellini

1. Melt butter in a large saucepan over medium heat; add onion and garlic, and sauté 3 minutes or until vegetables are tender. Add tomatoes, tomato paste, and lemon zest; cook, stirring occasionally, 8 to 10 minutes. Remove from heat, and stir in basil. Transfer to fondue pot; keep warm. Serve with desired accompaniments.

Mississippi Mud Fondue

Makes 4 cups
Hands-on Time: 18 min. **Total Time:** 18 min.

Fondue:
- 1 cup heavy cream
- 1 (12-oz.) package dark chocolate morsels
- 1 (7½-oz.) jar marshmallow crème
- ½ tsp. vanilla extract

Serve with:
Brownies, biscotti, graham crackers, marshmallows, chopped toasted pecans, chopped candied ginger

1. Bring cream to a boil in a large heavy-duty saucepan over medium-high heat; reduce heat to low, and simmer. Add chocolate morsels, and stir until melted and smooth. Stir in marshmallow crème and vanilla, stirring constantly until smooth. Transfer to fondue pot. Keep warm. Serve with desired accompaniments.

Tomato-and-Herb Fondue

test-kitchen secrets
- Cover a wooden table with a thick tablecloth to avoid damage to furniture and to catch spills.
- No double dipping.

Mississippi Mud Fondue

White Bean–and–Black Olive
Crostini; Sparkling Sippers
(recipe on page 76)

casual TEXAS holiday

menu for 8

White Bean–and–Black Olive Crostini
Sparkling Sippers
Citrus-Walnut Salad
Roasted Green Beans with Sun-dried Tomatoes
Chipotle Smashed Sweet Potatoes
Roasted Turkey Stuffed with Hazelnut Dressing
Upside-Down Apple Tart

1 month ahead:
• Prepare simple syrup for Sparkling Sippers; cover and chill.

1 week ahead:
• Prepare Cumin-Dijon Vinaigrette; cover and chill.

3 days ahead:
• Prepare brined turkey; cover and chill.

1 day ahead:
• Make White Bean–and–Black Olive mixture; cover and chill.
• Toast crostini and walnuts; store in an airtight container at room temperature.
• Prepare Upside-Down Apple Tart; store in an airtight container at room temperature.

7 hours ahead:
• Prepare turkey and dressing.

1 hour ahead:
• Roast Green Beans with Sun Dried Tomatoes
• Prepare Chipotle Smashed Sweet Potatoes
• Assemble Citrus-Walnut Salad.
• Prepare bar with drink ingredients.

last minute:
• Assemble crostinis.
• Carve turkey, and garnish dishes, if desired.
• Serve guests Sparkling Sippers.

---

editor's favorite

White Bean–and–Black Olive Crostini

Makes about 3 dozen
Hands-on Time: 20 min. **Total Time:** 28 min.

1 (8.5-oz.) French bread baguette, cut diagonally into ¼-inch slices
Olive oil cooking spray
1 (15.5-oz.) can cannellini beans, drained and rinsed
¼ cup olive oil
¼ tsp. salt
¼ tsp. pepper
½ cup pitted kalamata olives, coarsely chopped
½ cup diced jarred roasted red bell peppers
1 Tbsp. olive oil
Garnish: torn basil leaves

1. Preheat oven to 425°. Arrange bread slices on a baking sheet, and coat with cooking spray. Sprinkle with desired amount of salt and pepper. Bake 8 minutes or until toasted.
2. Process beans and next 3 ingredients in a food processor until smooth, stopping to scrape down sides as needed. Toss together olives, roasted red bell peppers, and olive oil. Spread bean mixture on toasted bread slices, and dollop with olive mixture. Garnish, if desired.

test-kitchen secret

Toast the bread for the crostini 1 day ahead; store crostini at room temperature in an airtight container.

Sparkling Sipper

One bottle of Prosecco yields about 6 servings for this recipe, so buy at least 2 bottles for a larger crowd. (Pictured on page 74)

Makes 1 serving
Hands-on Time: 10 min. **Total Time:** 10 min., including simple syrup

1. Fill a 10-oz. glass with ice. Add Prosecco, filling ¾ full. Top with 1 Tbsp. Campari and 2 Tbsp. Fast Simple Syrup (below). Garnish with kumquats and lime slices, if desired. Serve immediately.

Fast Simple Syrup: Bring equal parts sugar and water to a boil in a medium saucepan. Boil, stirring often, 1 minute or until sugar is dissolved. Remove from heat; cool completely. You can also find bottled simple syrup, such as Stirrings, in larger supermarkets.

quick & easy

Citrus-Walnut Salad

Makes 8 servings
Hands-on Time: 15 min. **Total Time:** 30 min., including vinaigrette

- ½ cup walnut pieces
- 8 heads Belgian endive (about 2¼ lb.)
- ½ cup firmly packed fresh parsley leaves
- Cumin-Dijon Vinaigrette
- 2 red grapefruits, peeled and sectioned

1. Preheat oven to 350°. Bake walnuts in a single layer in a shallow pan 6 to 8 minutes or until toasted and fragrant, stirring halfway through.
2. Remove and discard outer leaves of endive. Rinse endive with cold water, and pat dry. Cut each endive head diagonally into ¼-inch-thick slices, and place in a serving bowl. Add walnuts, parsley leaves, and desired amount of vinaigrette; gently toss to coat. Top with grapefruit. Serve with any remaining vinaigrette.

Citrus-Walnut Salad

Cumin-Dijon Vinaigrette

Makes ¾ cup
Hands-on Time: 10 min. **Total Time:** 10 min.

- ½ cup extra virgin olive oil
- 3 Tbsp. white wine vinegar
- 2 Tbsp. Dijon mustard
- ¼ tsp. ground cumin
- ¼ tsp. salt
- ¼ tsp. sugar

1. Whisk together all ingredients. Serve with salad.

quick & easy

Roasted Green Beans with Sun-dried Tomatoes

Makes 8 to 10 servings
Hands-on Time: 15 min. **Total Time:** 27 min.

1½	lb. fresh green beans, trimmed
½	cup sun-dried tomatoes in oil, chopped
⅓	cup pine nuts
3	Tbsp. butter, melted
3	Tbsp. olive oil
1	tsp. salt
½	tsp. pepper

1. Preheat oven to 425°. Toss together all ingredients. Place mixture on an 18- x 12-inch jelly-roll pan. Bake 12 to 15 minutes or to desired degree of doneness, stirring twice.

Roasted Green Beans with Sun-dried Tomatoes; Chipotle Smashed Sweet Potatoes

Roasted Brussels Sprouts with Sun-dried Tomatoes: Substitute 2 lb. fresh Brussels sprouts for 1½ lb. green beans. Remove any discolored leaves from Brussels sprouts, cut off stem ends, and halve sprouts. Toss together all ingredients except sun-dried tomatoes. Bake at 425° for 25 to 30 minutes or until golden and tender, stirring once halfway through and adding sun-dried tomatoes during the last 5 minutes of baking time.

Chipotle Smashed Sweet Potatoes

Chipotle peppers are smoked jalapeños canned in adobo sauce and can be found in most grocery stores. They have tremendous flavor and a lot of heat—a little goes a long way, so add carefully.

Makes 8 servings
Hands-on Time: 25 min. **Total Time:** 30 min.

3	lb. fresh sweet potatoes, peeled and chopped
½	cup butter, cut into pieces
1	to 2 Tbsp. minced canned chipotle peppers in adobo sauce
¼	cup heavy cream
	Salt to taste

1. Bring sweet potatoes and salted water to cover to a boil in a Dutch oven over high heat. Reduce heat to medium, and simmer 10 to 15 minutes or until potatoes are tender. Drain, reserving ½ cup water.
2. Return potatoes to Dutch oven. Add butter, minced peppers, and cream; mash with a potato masher, adding reserved water, a little at a time, for desired consistency. Season with salt to taste. Transfer to a serving bowl.

party pointer

Use plates with vibrant colors that fit the holiday such as red, green, or even gold to create a festive tone for your gathering.

Roasted Turkey Stuffed with Hazelnut Dressing

Roasted Turkey Stuffed with Hazelnut Dressing

Kosher salt allows you to control the saltiness better than regular table salt. The pepper and herbs in the brine solution also help infuse a lot of flavor.

Makes 10 to 12 servings
Hands-on Time: 55 min. **Total Time:** 6 hr., 53 min., plus 2 days for chilling turkey

Turkey
- 1 (18- to 20-lb.) whole fresh turkey*
- 3 cups firmly packed dark brown sugar
- 1 cup kosher salt
- 1 (18- to 20-qt.) food-safe plastic container
- 4 cups hot water
- 4 cups ice cubes
- ¼ cup black peppercorns
- 1 (1-oz.) package fresh thyme
- 6 qt. cold water

Hazelnut Dressing
- 1½ cups coarsely chopped hazelnuts or pecans
- 1½ cups butter
- 2 medium-size yellow onions, chopped
- 8 celery ribs, chopped
- 16 cups assorted day-old bread cubes (such as pumpernickel, sourdough, rustic white, and wheat; about 3 loaves)
- Salt and pepper to taste

Remaining Ingredients
- Wooden picks
- Kitchen string
- 3 Tbsp. olive oil
- 1 Tbsp. kosher salt
- 2 tsp. pepper
- 2 cups water

1. Prepare Turkey: Remove giblets and neck. Combine dark brown sugar and kosher salt in plastic container. Add 4 cups hot water to container; stir until sugar and salt dissolve. Add ice cubes, peppercorns, and thyme; place turkey in brine. Add cold water to cover (about 6 qt.). Weight turkey down using a cast-iron lid, if necessary. Cover and chill 48 hours.

2. Prepare Hazelnut Dressing: Preheat oven to 350°. Bake hazelnuts in a single layer in a shallow pan 8 to 10 minutes or until toasted and fragrant, stirring halfway through.

3. Melt butter in a large Dutch oven over medium-high heat. Add onions and celery, and sauté 10 to 12 minutes or until tender. Add bread cubes and hazelnuts; stir to coat. Season with salt and pepper to taste. Let cool completely (about 1 hour).

4. Remove turkey from brine; discard brine. Place turkey, breast side down, on a work surface, and spoon 4 to 5 cups dressing into neck cavity, pressing firmly. Replace skin over neck cavity, and secure using wooden picks. Turn turkey over, and spoon remaining dressing into body cavity. Tie ends of legs together with string; tuck wingtips under. Pat turkey dry with paper towels. Brush turkey with 3 Tbsp. olive oil; sprinkle with 1 Tbsp. salt and 2 tsp. pepper. Place turkey, breast side down, on a rack in a large roasting pan. Pour 2 cups water into pan.

5. Bake at 350° for 2 to 2½ hours. Turn turkey over, breast side up. Bake 2 to 2½ hours or until a meat thermometer inserted into thigh registers 180° and center of dressing registers 165°, shielding with aluminum foil during last hour of baking. Let turkey stand 20 minutes before carving.

*Frozen whole turkey, thawed, may be substituted.

Note: Depending on the size of your turkey cavity, you may have leftover dressing. Stir ½ to 1 cup chicken broth into remaining dressing, and place in a lightly greased 11- x 7-inch baking dish. Bake at 350° for 25 to 30 minutes or until thoroughly heated.

test kitchen secret

If using a frozen turkey, start thawing it in a pan in the refrigerator 3 to 4 days before roasting, depending on its size. If turkey overlaps pan rim, tuck a strip of heavy-duty foil along pan sides during roasting to keep fat from dripping over.

Upside-Down Apple Tart

Makes 8 to 10 servings
Hands-on Time: 30 min. **Total Time:** 4 hr., 35 min.

- 1 cup cold butter, cut up
- 2 cups all-purpose flour
- Pinch of salt
- 1¾ cups sugar, divided
- ½ cup ice-cold water
- 1 (3-lb.) package small Granny Smith apples, peeled and quartered
- ½ cup butter, cut up

1. Freeze 1 cup cut-up butter 30 minutes. Pulse cold butter, flour, salt, and ¼ cup sugar in a food processor 7 to 8 times or until mixture resembles coarse meal. Add ½ cup ice-cold water, 1 Tbsp. at a time, and pulse just until mixture comes together and a dough forms. Turn dough out onto a piece of plastic wrap, and shape into a disk. Wrap in plastic wrap, and chill 2 to 24 hours.

2. Gently stir together apples, ½ cup butter, and remaining 1½ cups sugar in a large bowl. Place apple mixture in a 10-inch cast-iron skillet. (Skillet will be very full.) Cook over medium-low heat 1 hour to 1 hour and 15 minutes or until liquid is reduced, thickened, and turns golden, stirring only once every 15 minutes. (Depending on your stovetop, you might need to lower the temperature if mixture begins to scorch on the bottom.)

3. Preheat oven to 425°. Unwrap dough, and turn out onto a lightly floured surface. Roll dough to a 12-inch circle; place over warm apple mixture, tucking edges into sides of skillet.

4. Bake at 425° for 25 minutes or until crust is golden brown and flaky. Let cool 10 minutes. Run a knife around edge of skillet; invert apple tart onto a cutting board or serving plate.

test-kitchen secret

Be sure to use the larger cooking eye on your stovetop when making the apple mixture. Resist the temptation to overstir the apples—stir just once every 15 minutes for even cooking.

Upside-Down Apple Tart

Cornmeal-and-Brown Sugar-Crusted Bacon

easy holiday BRUNCH

menu for 8

Cornmeal-and-Brown Sugar-Crusted Bacon
Grits-and-Greens Breakfast Bake
Streusel Coffee Cake
Coffee-Milk Punch

3 days ahead:
• Prepare Simple Collard Greens; cover and chill.

1 day ahead:
• Make Streusel Coffee Cake, wrap in foil, and keep at room temperature. Double recipe, and divide to send as gifts with guests.

1 hour ahead:
• Assemble Grits-and-Greens Breakfast Bake.
• Prepare Cornmeal-and-Brown Sugar-Crusted Bacon.

last minute:
• Prepare Coffee-Milk Punch.

Follow our step-by-step tips, and you'll pull off these recipes with ease and time to spare.

Cornmeal-and-Brown Sugar-Crusted Bacon

For easy cleanup, line jelly-roll pans with aluminum foil.

Makes 8 servings
Hands-on Time: 15 min. **Total Time:** 1 hr.

- ¼ cup plain yellow cornmeal
- 3 Tbsp. brown sugar
- 1½ tsp. freshly ground pepper
- 16 thick bacon slices

1. Preheat oven to 400°. Combine first 3 ingredients in a shallow dish. Dredge bacon slices in cornmeal mixture, shaking off excess.
2. Place half of bacon in a single layer on a lightly greased wire rack in a jelly-roll pan. Repeat procedure with remaining bacon, placing on another lightly greased wire rack in a second jelly-roll pan.
3. Bake at 400° for 40 to 45 minutes or until browned and crisp. Let stand 5 minutes.

step-by-step

1. Dredge each bacon slice in cornmeal mixture, shaking off excess.
2. Place bacon on a wire rack in a jelly-roll pan.

Grits-and-Greens
Breakfast Bake

Grits-and-Greens Breakfast Bake

Give yourself a head start—make Simple Collard Greens up to 3 days ahead.

Makes 8 servings
Hands-on Time: 25 min. **Total Time:** 2 hr., 7 min., including greens

  1   tsp. salt
1½   cups uncooked quick-cooking grits
  1   cup (4 oz.) shredded white Cheddar cheese
  3   Tbsp. butter
  ½   cup half-and-half
  ¼   tsp. freshly ground black pepper
  ¼   tsp. ground red pepper
 10   large eggs, divided (not separated)
  3   cups Simple Collard Greens, drained
      Hot sauce (optional)

1. Preheat oven to 375°. Bring salt and 4 cups water to a boil in a large saucepan over medium-high heat; gradually whisk in grits. Reduce heat to medium, and cook, whisking often, 5 to 7 minutes or until thickened. Remove from heat, and stir in cheese and butter.
2. Whisk together half-and-half, next 2 ingredients, and 2 eggs in a medium bowl. Stir half-and-half mixture into grits mixture. Stir in Simple Collard Greens. Pour mixture into a lightly greased 13- x 9-inch baking dish.
3. Bake at 375° for 25 to 30 minutes or until set. Remove from oven.
4. Make 8 indentations in grits mixture with back of a large spoon. Break remaining 8 eggs, 1 at a time, and slip 1 egg into each indentation. Bake 12 to 14 minutes or until eggs are cooked to desired degree of doneness. Cover loosely with aluminum foil, and let stand 10 minutes. Serve with hot sauce, if desired.

party pointer

Breakfast foods aren't just for brunch. Prepare this tasty menu for a laid-back holiday supper.

---

make ahead

Simple Collard Greens

Makes 3 cups
Hands-on Time: 10 min. **Total Time:** 50 min.

  ½   medium-size sweet onion, chopped
  2   Tbsp. olive oil
  1   (16-oz.) package fresh collard greens, washed, trimmed, and chopped
1½   tsp. salt

1. Cook onion in hot oil in a large Dutch oven over medium heat, stirring occasionally, 10 minutes or until tender. Add collard greens, salt, and 3 cups water. Bring to a boil; reduce heat, and simmer 30 minutes or until tender.

step-by-step

1. Slowly whisk grits into boiling water to prevent lumps from forming.
2. Make 8 indentations in casserole using the back of a spoon.
3. Break eggs and pour each egg, 1 at a time, into each indentation.

Streusel Coffee Cake

Makes 8 to 10 servings
Hands-on Time: 20 min. **Total Time:** 1 hr., 25 min., including topping

- ½ cup butter, softened
- 1 (8-oz.) package cream cheese, softened
- 1¼ cups sugar
- 2 large eggs
- 2 cups all-purpose flour
- 2 tsp. baking powder
- ½ tsp. baking soda
- ½ tsp. salt
- ½ cup milk
- 1 tsp. vanilla extract
- ½ tsp. almond extract
- Crumb Topping

1. Preheat oven to 350°. Beat butter and cream cheese at medium speed with an electric mixer until creamy. Gradually add sugar, beating at medium speed until light and fluffy. Add eggs to sugar mixture, 1 at a time, beating just until yellow disappears.

2. Sift together flour and next 3 ingredients; add to butter mixture alternately with milk, beginning and ending with flour mixture. Beat at low speed just until blended after each addition. Stir in vanilla and almond extracts. Pour cake batter into a greased 13- x 9-inch pan; sprinkle with Crumb Topping.

3. Bake at 350° for 35 to 40 minutes or until a wooden pick inserted in center comes out clean. Let cool 20 minutes before serving.

test-kitchen secret

To make coffee cake 1 day ahead, just bake, cool completely, and wrap in aluminum foil.

Crumb Topping

Makes about 1½ cups
Hands-on Time: 10 min. **Total Time:** 10 min.

- ½ cup all-purpose flour
- ½ cup sugar
- ½ cup coarsely chopped pecans
- ¼ cup butter

1. Stir together flour, sugar, and pecans in a bowl. Cut in butter with a pastry blender or fork until mixture resembles small peas.

quick & easy

Coffee-Milk Punch

Makes 9 cups
Hands-on Time: 15 min. **Total Time:** 15 min.

- 6 cups strong brewed hot coffee
- ½ cup hot fudge topping
- ¼ cup sugar
- 2 cups half-and-half
- 1 cup coffee liqueur
- 1 Tbsp. vanilla extract

1. Whisk together hot coffee, fudge topping, and sugar in a large Dutch oven until smooth. Add half-and-half and remaining ingredients, stirring until blended. Bring mixture to a simmer over medium-high heat. Serve immediately, or let cool, cover, and chill 1 to 24 hours, and serve over ice.

Coffee-Milk Punch

MAKE-AHEAD
party

menu for 12

Bourbon Slushies
Stir-and-Bake Spoon Rolls
Parmesan Cheese Bites
Sausage-Tortellini Soup or Lemon-Chicken Soup
Classic Lasagna
Cheesecake Squares

2 months ahead:
• Prepare and freeze Parmesan Cheese Bites in zip-top freezer bags.
• Prepare Sausage-Tortellini Soup without pasta; cool and freeze in plastic containers.
• Prepare Lemon-Chicken Soup; cool and freeze in plastic containers.
• Prepare lasagna by lining the dish with foil. Assemble lasagna, and freeze; then remove it from dish, wrap completely in foil, and freeze.

2 weeks ahead:
• Bake Stir-and-Bake Spoon Rolls; cool and freeze in zip-top freezer bags. Great gift idea: Double recipe and make second batch as Miniature Spoon Rolls to send home with guests.

5 hours ahead:
• Thaw lasagna. Return it to baking dish, and bake.

1 hour ahead:
• Place frozen soup in Dutch oven, and cook at low heat, stirring occasionally, until warm.

last minute:
• Plate and garnish, if desired.

---

make ahead

Bourbon Slushies

Makes about 4 qt.
Hands-on Time: 10 min. **Total Time:** 9 hr., 10 min.

1 (64-oz.) container pineapple juice
1 (12-oz.) can frozen lemonade concentrate, thawed
1 (12-oz.) can frozen limeade concentrate, thawed
1½ cups bourbon*
¼ cup maraschino cherry juice
Garnish: maraschino cherries

1. Stir together first 4 ingredients and 1 cup water. Divide mixture into 2 (1-gal.) zip-top plastic freezer bags; seal and freeze 8 hours.
2. Remove from freezer, and let stand 1 hour or until softened and beginning to melt. Using hands, squeeze bags until mixture is slushy. Spoon 2 cups mixture into each serving glass. Top each with 2 tsp. cherry juice. (Do not stir.) Serve immediately. Garnish, if desired.

*Lemon-lime soft drink may be substituted for bourbon.

test-kitchen secret

Assemble the base mixture for this drink, and pop it in the freezer. When serving, don't stir. The cherry juice will drip down to the bottom of the glass, producing colorful layers.

make ahead • freezer friendly

Stir-and-Bake Spoon Rolls

Bake these easy rolls and freeze in zip-top plastic freezer bags for up to 2 weeks.

Makes 2 dozen
Hands-on Time: 15 min. **Total Time:** 28 min.

- 1 (¼-oz.) envelope active dry yeast
- 2 cups warm water (100° to 110°)
- 4 cups self-rising flour
- ¾ cup butter, melted
- ¼ cup sugar
- 1 large egg, lightly beaten

1. Preheat oven to 400°. Combine yeast and 2 cups warm water in a large bowl; let stand 5 minutes. Stir in flour and remaining ingredients until blended. Spoon batter into 2 greased (12-cup) muffin pans. Bake for 13 minutes or until golden.

Miniature Spoon Rolls: Spoon batter into 2 greased (24-cup) miniature muffin pans*. Bake at 400° for 9 minutes or until golden. Makes 4 dozen. Hands-on Time: 15 min.; Total Time: 24 min.

*4 (12-cup) miniature muffin pans may be substituted.

Parmesan Cheese Bites

Baked cheese bites may be frozen up to 2 months.

Makes 2 dozen
Hands-on Time: 15 min. **Total Time:** 1 hr., 30 min.

- 1 cup all-purpose flour
- ⅔ cup grated Parmesan cheese
- ¼ tsp. ground red pepper
- ½ cup butter, cut up
- 2 Tbsp. milk

1. Preheat oven to 350°. Combine first 3 ingredients in a medium bowl; cut in butter with a pastry blender or two forks until crumbly. (Mixture will look very dry.) Gently press mixture together with hands, pressing until blended and smooth (about 2 to 3 minutes).

2. Shape dough into 2 (4-inch-long) logs. Wrap in plastic wrap, and chill 1 hour. Cut each log into ¼-inch-thick slices, and place on lightly greased baking sheets. Brush with milk.
3. Bake at 350° for 12 to 15 minutes or until lightly browned.

Parmesan Cheese Squares: Roll out dough into a 10- x 8-inch rectangle on a lightly floured surface. Cut dough into 32 squares using a pastry wheel or knife. Place squares on lightly greased baking sheets; brush with milk, and bake as directed. Makes 32 squares.

Sausage-Tortellini Soup

Prepare this soup through Step 1 to freeze. Reheat the soup before cooking and adding the tortellini.

Makes 4 qt.
Hands-on Time: 38 min. **Total Time:** 1 hr.

- 1½ lb. hot Italian sausage, casings removed*
- 1 medium onion, diced
- 3 garlic cloves, minced
- 2 (15-oz.) cans Italian-style stewed tomatoes
- 1 (16-oz.) bag frozen cut green beans
- 1 (8-oz.) package sliced fresh mushrooms
- 1 (8-oz.) can tomato sauce
- 4 beef bouillon cubes
- 3 carrots, sliced
- 3 medium zucchini, quartered and sliced
- 1 cup dry red wine
- 2 tsp. dried Italian seasoning
- 1 (20-oz.) package refrigerated cheese-filled tortellini
Freshly grated Parmesan cheese

1. Sauté sausage, onion, and garlic in a Dutch oven over medium heat 8 minutes or until sausage crumbles and is no longer pink; drain. Stir in tomatoes, next 8 ingredients, and 10 cups water; bring to a boil. Cover, reduce heat to low, and cook 20 minutes or until carrots are crisp-tender.
2. Cook tortellini according to package directions; drain. Stir into soup just before serving. Serve with freshly grated Parmesan cheese.

*1 lb. turkey Italian sausage may be substituted.

Lemon-Chicken Soup

Makes 5½ qt.
Hands-on Time: 30 min. **Total Time:** 2 hr., 15 min.

6   skin-on, bone-in chicken breasts
2   large onions, chopped
5   celery ribs, chopped
2   garlic cloves, minced
1   tsp. olive oil
1   (1-lb.) package carrots, sliced
4   tsp. lemon zest
2   bay leaves
2   tsp. salt
½   cup loosely packed fresh flat-leaf parsley leaves
Toppings: cooked barley, cooked green beans, lemon slices

1. Bring chicken and water to cover to a boil in a Dutch oven over medium-high heat; reduce heat to low, and simmer 1 hour.
2. Remove chicken, reserving liquid, and let cool 15 minutes. Shred chicken.
3. Pour reserved cooking liquid through a wire-mesh strainer into a bowl, discarding solids; wipe Dutch oven clean. Add water to cooking liquid to equal 10 cups.
4. Sauté onion, celery, and garlic in hot oil in Dutch oven over medium-high heat 5 to 6 minutes or until tender. Add shredded chicken, cooking liquid, carrots, and next 3 ingredients. Cover, reduce heat to medium, and cook 20 minutes or until carrots are tender. Add parsley. Serve with desired toppings.

Lemon-Chicken Soup

make ahead • freezer friendly

Classic Lasagna

Line the dish with foil. Assemble lasagna and freeze; then remove it from the dish, wrap it completely in foil, and freeze. Unwrap the lasagna, and return to dish to bake.

Makes 8 to 10 servings
Hands-on Time: 31 min. **Total Time:** 2 hr., 30 min.

Italian Meat Sauce
2	medium onions, chopped
1	Tbsp. olive oil
4	garlic cloves, minced
1	lb. lean ground beef
1	(14.5-oz.) can basil, garlic, and oregano diced tomatoes
2	(6-oz.) cans tomato paste
1	(8-oz.) can basil, garlic, and oregano tomato sauce
1	bay leaf
1	tsp. dried Italian seasoning
1	tsp. salt
½	tsp. pepper

Lasagna
	Italian Meat Sauce
12	uncooked lasagna noodles
8	cups boiling water
1	Tbsp. olive oil
1	(16-oz.) container ricotta cheese
2	large eggs, lightly beaten
¼	cup grated Parmesan cheese
¼	tsp. salt
¼	tsp. pepper
18	thin part-skim mozzarella cheese slices, divided

1. Prepare Italian Meat Sauce: Sauté onions in hot oil in a 3-qt. skillet over medium-high heat 5 minutes or until tender. Add garlic; sauté 1 minute. Add beef; cook, stirring occasionally, 10 minutes or until beef crumbles and is no longer pink. Stir in diced tomatoes and next 6 ingredients; bring to a boil. Cover, reduce heat, and simmer, stirring occasionally, 30 minutes.
2. Meanwhile, prepare Lasagna: Place noodles in a 13- x 9-inch pan. Carefully pour 8 cups boiling water and olive oil over noodles. Let stand 15 minutes; drain and pat dry.
3. Stir together ricotta cheese and next 4 ingredients.
4. Preheat oven to 350°. Discard bay leaf from sauce. Spoon 2 cups sauce into a lightly greased 13- x 9-inch baking dish. Arrange ⅓ noodles over sauce; top with about ¾ cup ricotta mixture and 6 mozzarella cheese slices. Repeat layers twice.
5. Bake, covered, at 350° for 55 minutes. Uncover and bake 15 minutes or until bubbly. Let stand 10 minutes.

test-kitchen secrets

- Freeze soups in plastic containers up to 2 months ahead. Divide soup into smaller containers for quicker thawing. Place frozen soup in a Dutch oven over very low heat, and cover. Cook, stirring occasionally, until hot. Times will vary with amount of soup, but plan to heat at least 30 to 40 minutes before serving.
- Freeze Parmesan Cheese Bites in a plastic container up to 2 months. Thaw at room temperature 30 minutes.
- Wrap frozen Stir-and-Bake Spoon Rolls loosely in foil to reheat, or make and chill the dough up to a week ahead. Bake just before dinner to fill the house with their mouth-watering aroma.

- Wrap Cheesecake Squares in heavy-duty foil, and place in a zip-top plastic freezer bag. Freeze up to 2 months; thaw at room temperature 2 hours.

Cheesecake Squares

Makes 9 servings
Hands-on Time: 30 min. **Total Time:** 11 hr., 13 min., including crust

Chocolate Crust
1 (8-oz.) package cream cheese, softened
1 (3-oz.) package cream cheese, softened
⅔ cup sugar
6 large eggs
⅓ cup whipping cream
2 tsp. instant coffee granules
9 (1-oz.) semisweet chocolate baking squares
1 Tbsp. plus 1 tsp. vanilla extract
Garnishes: powdered sugar, thawed whipped topping, cocoa powder

1. Prepare Chocolate Crust as directed. Increase oven temperature to 375°.
2. Beat cream cheese and sugar at medium speed with an electric mixer 2 to 3 minutes or until light and fluffy. Add eggs, 1 at a time, beating mixture just until blended after each addition.
3. Microwave whipping cream in a 1-cup microwave-safe measuring cup at HIGH 30 seconds or until very hot. Stir in coffee granules until completely dissolved. Cool coffee mixture slightly.
4. Microwave chocolate in a microwave-safe bowl at HIGH 1 minute. Microwave 1 more minute, stirring at 15-second intervals. Add melted chocolate, vanilla, and coffee mixture to cream cheese mixture. Beat at low speed just until blended. Pour into prepared Chocolate Crust.
5. Bake at 375° for 30 minutes or until edges are firm and center is still soft. Let cool to room temperature (about 1 hour); cover and chill 8 hours. Cut into squares. Garnish, if desired.

Chocolate Crust

Makes 1 (9-inch) crust
Hands-on Time: 18 min. **Total Time:** 1 hr., 11 min.

⅓ cup butter
2 (1-oz.) semisweet chocolate baking squares
1⅓ cups fine, dry breadcrumbs
⅓ cup sugar

Cheesecake Squares

1. Preheat oven to 350°. Stir together butter and chocolate in a medium-size heavy saucepan over low heat, and cook, stirring often, 3 to 5 minutes or until chocolate is melted. Remove from heat, and stir in breadcrumbs and ⅓ cup sugar until well blended. Press mixture onto bottom of a lightly greased 9-inch square pan.
2. Bake mixture at 350° for 8 minutes. Cool on a wire rack 15 minutes. Chill 30 minutes before using.

Sparkling Cranberry Cocktails;
Mini Manchego-Tomato Chutney
Tartlets (recipe on page 96)

COMPANY'S
coming

2 weeks ahead:
• Prepare cranberry syrup for Sparkling Cranberry Cocktails; store in airtight container in refrigerator.

1 day ahead:
• Prepare lentils and onion mixture; cool and store in airtight container in refrigerator.
• Prepare Chestnut Soup; cool and store in airtight container in refrigerator.
• Prepare Mustard Vinaigrette; store in airtight container in refrigerator.
• Blanch green beans, and store in zip-top plastic freezer bag in refrigerator.

6 hours ahead:
• Prepare Cornish Game Hens.
• Bake croutons.
• Prepare pastry cutouts for dessert; cover and chill for 10 minutes. Bake only the tartlets.

1 hour ahead:
• Prepare Wild Rice Salad.
• Prepare squash, and assemble Butternut Croutons.
• Bring lentil and onion mixture to room temperature.

last minute:
• Assemble Mini Manchego-Tomato Chutney Tartlets.
• Assemble Beluga Lentil Toasts.
• Prepare Green Breans with Shallots and Clementine Zest.
• Assemble Spinach and Celery-Leaf Salad, drizzle vinaigrette before serving.
• Stage everything needed for dessert.
• Plate and garnish, if desired.
• Prepare Sparkling Cranberry Cocktails for guests.

after dinner:
• While guests relax after an amazing meal, assemble and bake pear tartlets for dessert.

make ahead

Sparkling Cranberry Cocktails

Makes 6 servings
Hands-on Time: 10 min. **Total Time:** 1 hr., 30 min.

1   cup sugar
1   (12-oz.) package fresh or thawed frozen cranberries (about 3 cups)
1   (750-milliliter) bottle sparkling white wine, chilled

1. Combine sugar and ½ cup water in a saucepan; bring to a boil, stirring constantly. Boil syrup 30 seconds or until sugar is dissolved. Reserve 18 cranberries. Add remaining cranberries to syrup; cook 30 seconds. Remove from heat; cover and let stand 20 minutes.
2. Pour syrup through a strainer into a bowl; reserve berries for another use. Transfer syrup to airtight container; cover and chill 1 hour. (Syrup can be stored in an airtight container in refrigerator up to 2 weeks.) Place 3 reserved cranberries and 1 Tbsp. cranberry syrup in each glass. Top with chilled sparkling white wine; serve immediately.

Mini Manchego-Tomato Chutney Tartlets

Makes 5 to 6 servings
Hands-on Time: 5 min. **Total Time:** 10 min.

- 1 (1.9-oz.) package frozen mini phyllo pastry shells
- 1 cup finely grated Manchego or Mahón cheese
- 3 to 4 Tbsp. tomato or mango chutney

Garnish: fresh marjoram leaves

1. Preheat oven to 400°. Arrange phyllo shells on a baking sheet. Divide cheese among shells, and top each with a rounded ½ teaspoonful chutney.
2. Bake at 400° for 5 to 8 minutes or until bubbly. Serve immediately. Garnish, if desired.

test-kitchen secret

For these tartlets, we like to use Alecia's Tomato Chutney, an Alabama-made product worth ordering if you can't find it in your grocery store. (Call 205/352-4900 or visit aleciaschutney. com.) Mango chutney is a relatively close alternative to this zesty preserve.

Beluga Lentil Toasts

make ahead

Beluga Lentil Toasts

The lentils and onions can be prepared up to 1 day in advance, but be sure to bring the mixtures to room temperature before serving.

Makes 8 to 10 servings
Hands-on Time: 20 min. **Total Time:** 2 hr., 38 min.

- 1½ cups low-sodium chicken broth
- ¾ cup uncooked Beluga lentils, rinsed and sorted
- 1 bay leaf
- 1 fresh thyme sprig
- 1 Tbsp. fresh lemon juice
- ½ tsp. freshly ground pepper
- 4 Tbsp. sherry vinegar, divided
- 2 tsp. kosher salt, divided
- 2 Tbsp. extra virgin olive oil
- 1 Tbsp. Meyer lemon oil
- 2 Tbsp. unsalted butter
- 2 medium-size red onions, thinly sliced (about 6 cups)
- 3 Tbsp. crème de cassis

Melba toast rounds
- ½ cup crème fraîche

1. Bring first 4 ingredients to a boil in a large saucepan. Cover, reduce heat, and simmer, stirring occasionally, 20 to 30 minutes or until lentils are tender. Drain, discarding bay leaf and thyme sprig. Transfer lentils to a bowl, and cool to room temperature (about 20 minutes).
2. Whisk together lemon juice, pepper, 2 Tbsp. vinegar, and 1 tsp. kosher salt in a small bowl. Gradually whisk in olive oil and lemon oil until blended. Pour over cooled lentils; sprinkle with salt and pepper to taste. Cover lentil mixture, and chill.
3. Melt butter in a large skillet over low heat. Add onions and remaining 1 tsp. kosher salt, and cook over low heat, stirring occasionally, 45 to 50 minutes or until onions are caramelized. Transfer onions to a bowl. Add remaining 2 Tbsp. vinegar to skillet, stirring to loosen particles from bottom of skillet. Pour hot vinegar over onions; add crème de cassis, and stir until blended. Let cool 10 minutes.
4. Top toast rounds with crème fraîche (about ¼ tsp. each), and top with lentils and caramelized onions.

Chestnut Soup

Makes 6 to 8 servings
Hands-on Time: 20 min. **Total Time:** 1 hr., 20 min.

2   Tbsp. butter
1   large yellow onion, diced
1   celery rib, diced
2   (7.4-oz.) jars whole roasted chestnuts, coarsely
    chopped
¼   cup Marsala
1   (32-oz.) container chicken broth
¼   cup heavy cream
1   tsp. kosher salt
¼   to ½ tsp. freshly ground white pepper
⅛   tsp. freshly grated nutmeg
Garnishes: crème fraîche, chopped roasted chestnuts,
    cracked black pepper

1. Melt butter in a large saucepan; add onion and celery, and sauté 4 to 6 minutes or until tender. Add chopped chestnuts, and sauté 2 minutes. (Remove a few chestnut pieces for garnish, if desired.) Add Marsala, and stir to loosen particles from bottom of pan. Add chicken broth and next 3 ingredients. Bring to a boil, reduce to medium-low heat, and simmer, uncovered, 20 minutes. Let soup cool 15 minutes.
2. Process soup in a blender, in batches, until smooth. Return to saucepan, stir in nutmeg, and bring to a simmer. Cook until thoroughly heated. Garnish, if desired.

Chestnut Soup

Spinach and Celery-Leaf Salad with Mustard Vinaigrette

With tender texture and delicate flavor, celery leaves make a great addition to salads. Here, they pair well with apples, mustard, and pungent cheese.

Makes 6 servings
Hands-on Time: 20 min. **Total Time:** 30 min.

- 2 Tbsp. minced shallot (about ½ large shallot)
- 2 Tbsp. sherry vinegar
- ⅛ tsp. salt
- ¼ cup extra virgin olive oil
- 2 tsp. country-style Dijon mustard
- 4 cups fresh baby spinach
- 2 cups arugula
- 1 cup loosely packed celery leaves
- 1 Braeburn or other semi-tart apple, diced (about 2 cups)
- 4 oz. Gorgonzola cheese, crumbled

1. Combine first 3 ingredients in a small bowl, and let stand 10 minutes. Gradually add olive oil and mustard, whisking until blended.
2. Combine spinach, arugula, and celery leaves in a large bowl. Add apple and cheese. Drizzle salad with vinegar mixture, gently toss, and serve immediately.

Note: We tested with Grey Poupon Country Dijon Mustard.

Spinach and Celery-Leaf Salad with Mustard Vinaigrette

make ahead

Green Beans with Shallots and Clementine Zest

This side dish takes minimal effort. Blanch, shock, drain, and chill the beans up to a day in advance, then sauté to serve.

Makes 6 servings
Hands-on Time: 20 min. **Total Time:** 50 min.

- 1½ lb. fresh green beans, trimmed and halved
- 1 Tbsp. unsalted butter
- 1 Tbsp. olive oil
- 3 small shallots, thinly sliced (about ½ cup)
- 2 tsp. clementine zest (about 2 clementines)
- 1 tsp. kosher salt
- ¼ tsp. freshly ground pepper

1. Cook green beans in boiling salted water to cover in a 4½- to 5-qt. stockpot over high heat 3 to 5 minutes or until crisp-tender; drain. Plunge into ice water to stop the cooking process; drain. Cover and chill 30 minutes or up to 1 day.
2. Melt butter with olive oil in a skillet over medium-high heat; add shallots and 1 tsp. zest, and sauté 1 to 1½ minutes or until translucent and soft. Add beans, kosher salt, and pepper. Sauté 30 seconds or until beans are thoroughly heated. Transfer beans to a serving platter. Sprinkle with remaining clementine zest. Serve immediately.

test-kitchen secret

Heat your serving platter in a warm oven or in a sink of hot water while you sauté.

Try these tried-and-true recipes for a memorable meal.

Wild Rice Salad

Most varieties of cooked whole grains can be tossed in a marinade and served warm or at room temperature, making them an ideal buffet side dish. If you think the amount of rosemary in this recipe seems like overkill, just wait until you taste it. A quick fry in oil tames the herb's pungent flavor.

Makes 6 to 8 servings
Hands-on Time: 20 min. **Total Time:** 1 hr., 10 min.

1½ cups uncooked long-grain brown rice
⅔ cup uncooked wild rice
½ cup pine nuts
3 (4-inch) rosemary sprigs
½ cup olive oil
Pinch of kosher salt
⅓ cup dried cranberries
2 Tbsp. sherry vinegar
1 tsp. kosher salt
¼ tsp. freshly ground pepper
2 tsp. honey
3 green onions, finely sliced (about ½ cup)

1. Prepare long-grain brown rice and wild rice according to package directions.

2. Meanwhile, heat ½ cup pine nuts in a small skillet over medium-low heat, stirring often, until toasted and fragrant. Remove from skillet.

3. Cook rosemary in hot oil in skillet over medium heat 1 minute, turning with tongs halfway through. Transfer to a paper towel–lined plate to drain, and sprinkle with a pinch of kosher salt. Let oil cool. Reserve ¼ cup oil.

4. Combine cranberries and next 3 ingredients in a small bowl. Let stand 15 minutes. Whisk in honey and reserved ¼ cup rosemary oil.

5. Combine brown rice, wild rice, pine nuts, and green onions in a large bowl. Crush fried rosemary, and sprinkle over rice mixture. Add cranberry mixture, and toss to combine.

6. Let salad cool 30 minutes before serving, or cover with plastic wrap, and chill up to 1 day. Let chilled salad stand at room temperature 15 minutes before serving.

test-kitchen secret

Test the readiness of the oil with 1 rosemary leaf (needle). It should start to sizzle. If not, wait a few seconds and test again.

Cornish Game Hens with
Butternut Croutons

Cornish Game Hens with Butternut Croutons

Generally, 1-lb. hens are the perfect single-serving size.
In this recipe, all 6 birds can be cooked on a baking sheet.
Serve the dish family style (on a large platter), or plate hens
individually. Either way, be sure to warm your serving
dishes in advance.

Makes 6 servings
Hands-on Time: 30 min. **Total Time:** 2 hr., 25 min.,
including croutons

  Wooden picks
  6 (1- to 1½-lb.) Cornish game hens, rinsed and
      patted dry
4½ tsp. salt, divided
  2 tsp. freshly ground pepper, divided
  2 clementines, unpeeled and quartered
  6 fresh sage leaves
  Kitchen string
  3 Tbsp. butter, softened
  Butternut Croutons, warm

1. Preheat oven to 450°. Soak wooden picks in water to
cover 30 minutes.
2. Meanwhile, season each hen cavity with ½ tsp. salt and
¼ tsp. pepper, and insert 1 clementine quarter.
3. Loosen and lift skin from hen breasts with fingers,
without totally detaching skin.
4. Place 1 sage leaf under skin of each hen. Carefully
replace skin, and secure using wooden picks. Tie ends of
legs together with string; tuck wingtips under.
5. Arrange hens, tail to tail in 2 rows, on a jelly-roll pan.
Rub hens with butter, and sprinkle with remaining 1½ tsp.
salt and ½ tsp. pepper.
6. Bake at 450° for 45 to 50 minutes or until golden
brown and a meat thermometer inserted into thickest
portion of thigh registers 165°. Transfer hens to a serving
platter, and cover loosely with heavy-duty aluminum
foil. Let stand 5 minutes before serving. Serve with warm
Butternut Croutons.

Butternut Croutons

Makes 6 servings
Hands-on Time: 35 min. **Total Time:** 1 hr., 5 min.

 3 cups (¾-inch) cubed fresh peasant-style bread
1½ lb. butternut squash, peeled and cut into ½-inch
    pieces (about 4 cups)
 10 shallots, quartered (about 9 to 10 oz.)
1½ Tbsp. dark brown sugar
 3 Tbsp. olive oil
1½ tsp. salt
 ¾ tsp. freshly ground white pepper
 2 Tbsp. chopped fresh sage

1. Preheat oven to 400°. Bake bread cubes on a baking
sheet 10 to 12 minutes or until lightly browned and
toasted. Let cool. Increase oven temperature to 450°.
2. Mound squash and shallots in center of a lightly greased
jelly-roll pan. Whisk together sugar and next 3 ingredients
in a small bowl. Pour over squash and shallots, and toss
to coat. Spread vegetables in a single layer in jelly-roll pan,
using 2 pans if necessary.
3. Bake at 450° for 20 minutes or until tender, stirring
halfway through. Toss warm squash mixture with croutons
and sage in a bowl.

Individual Pear Tartlets

Wow your guests with this amazing dessert that only looks
complicated. Credit for using puff pastry in this way goes
to dessert maven Gale Gand, who made an apple version of
this years ago on television.

Makes 6 servings
Hands-on Time: 30 min. **Total Time:** 1 hr., 12 min.

 12 wooden picks
 3 Tbsp. all-purpose flour
 ½ (17.3-oz.) package frozen puff pastry sheets, thawed
 Parchment paper
 6 Tbsp. light brown sugar
 4 Tbsp. butter, melted
 1 Tbsp. fresh lemon juice
 ½ tsp. ground cinnamon
 ⅛ tsp. ground allspice
 5 to 6 Bosc pears (about 10 oz. each), peeled, halved
    lengthwise, and cut crosswise into ⅛-inch slices
 Garnishes: sweetened whipped cream, freshly grated
    nutmeg

1. Preheat oven to 400°. Soak wooden picks in water to
cover 30 minutes.
2. Meanwhile, lightly dust work surface with 3 Tbsp. flour;
roll out 1 puff pastry sheet to ⅛-inch thickness. Cut into
6 (4-inch) rounds. Cut additional seasonal shapes, such as
leaves or stars, from scraps, if desired. Transfer rounds to
a parchment-lined jelly-roll pan. Transfer seasonal shapes
to a second parchment-lined jelly-roll pan. Chill pastry
10 minutes or until ready to assemble.
3. Bake rounds at 400° for 7 minutes. (Do not prebake
additional shapes.)
4. Stir together brown sugar and next 4 ingredients in a
large bowl. Carefully stir in pear slices.
5. Arrange pear slices in concentric circles on rounds.
When each round is stacked about 2 inches high, insert
2 presoaked wooden picks into top of each tartlet to secure
slices. Drizzle with any remaining sugar mixture.
6. Bake tartlets and shapes at 400° for 15 minutes or until
shapes are puffed and golden brown. Transfer shapes to a
wire rack, and let cool completely. Bake tartlets 10 more
minutes or until golden brown and slightly caramelized.
Transfer tarts to dessert plates. Serve immediately with
baked pastry shapes. Garnish, if desired.

Individual Pear Tartlets

all-time favorite RECIPES

One-Dish Blackberry French Toast

BREAKFAST
anytime

make ahead

One-Dish Blackberry French Toast

Mix up this dish in 30 minutes the night before for a stress-free meal the next day.

Makes 8 to 10 servings
Hands-on Time: 21 min. **Total Time:** 8 hr., 51 min.

- 1 cup blackberry jam
- 1 (12-oz.) French bread loaf, cut into 1½-inch cubes
- 1 (8-oz.) package ⅓-less-fat cream cheese, cut into 1-inch cubes
- 4 large eggs
- 2 cups half-and-half
- 1 tsp. ground cinnamon
- 1 tsp. vanilla extract
- ½ cup firmly packed brown sugar
- Toppings: maple syrup, whipped cream

1. Cook jam in a small saucepan over medium heat 1 to 2 minutes or until melted and smooth, stirring once.
2. Place half of bread cubes in bottom of a lightly greased 13- x 9-inch baking dish. Top with cream cheese cubes, and drizzle with melted jam. Top with remaining bread cubes.
3. Whisk together eggs and next 3 ingredients. Pour over bread mixture. Sprinkle with brown sugar. Cover tightly, and chill 8 to 24 hours.
4. Preheat oven to 325°. Bake, covered, 20 minutes. Uncover and bake 10 to 15 minutes more or until bread is golden brown and egg mixture is set. Serve with desired toppings.

make ahead

Cinnamon Roll Bake

Makes 6 to 8 servings
Hands-on Time: 15 min. **Total Time:** 5 hr., 20 min.

- 3 egg yolks*
- 2 large eggs*
- 2 cups milk
- 2 Tbsp. sugar
- 1 tsp. ground cinnamon
- 1 tsp. vanilla extract
- ¼ tsp. salt
- 1 (16-oz.) package frozen cinnamon rolls
- ½ cup golden raisins
- 2 Tbsp. butter, cut into ¼-inch cubes

1. Whisk together first 7 ingredients until blended.
2. Break apart cinnamon rolls, and chop. Place in a lightly greased 11- x 7-inch baking dish.
3. Toss raisins with rolls in dish. Pour egg mixture over top; dot with butter. Cover and chill 4 to 24 hours.
4. Preheat oven to 325°. Bake casserole 55 minutes to 1 hour or until set and golden. Let stand 5 minutes before serving.

*1 cup egg substitute may be substituted for egg yolks and whole eggs.

Note: We tested with Sister Schubert's Cinnamon Yeast Rolls.

Orange-Apricot Bake: Substitute ⅛ tsp. ground nutmeg for 1 tsp. cinnamon, 1 (16-oz.) package orange yeast rolls for cinnamon rolls, and ½ cup chopped dried apricots for raisins. Proceed with recipe as directed.

Italian Bread Pudding

make ahead

Italian Bread Pudding

Makes 6 servings
Hands-on Time: 15 min. **Total Time:** 5 hr., 15 min.

5	large eggs*
1	cup milk
1½	tsp. Dijon mustard
1	tsp. dried basil
¾	tsp. salt
⅛	to ¼ tsp. ground red pepper
1	(9.5-oz.) package frozen mozzarella-and-Monterey Jack cheese Texas toast, chopped
3	plum tomatoes, seeded and chopped (about 1¼ cups)
8	fully cooked bacon slices, chopped
1	cup grated Cheddar cheese

Garnish: fresh basil leaves

1. Whisk together first 6 ingredients until blended.
2. Layer half of Texas toast in a lightly greased 11- x 7-inch baking dish; sprinkle toast with half each of tomatoes, bacon, and cheese. Repeat layers once. Pour egg mixture over toast and cheese.
3. Cover and chill 4 to 24 hours.
4. Preheat oven to 325°. Bake casserole 50 to 55 minutes or until center is set. Let stand 5 minutes before serving. Garnish, if desired.

*1¼ cups egg substitute may be substituted.

Note: We tested with Pepperidge Farm Mozzarella and Monterey Jack Texas Toast.

Texas Toast Bread Pudding: Omit dried basil, tomatoes, and bacon. Proceed with recipe as directed.

Sausage Roll Casserole: Omit dried basil, tomatoes, and bacon. Increase cheese to 1½ cups. Substitute 1 (18-oz.) package frozen sausage wrap rolls for Texas toast. Break apart sausage rolls; cut each roll crosswise into thirds, cutting across sausage. Proceed with recipe as directed.

Note: We tested with Sister Schubert's Sausage Wrap Rolls.

make ahead

Ham-and-Cheese Croissant Casserole

You can substitute leftover baked ham for chopped ham in this dish. Nutmeg is optional but adds a subtle touch of spice.

Makes 6 servings
Hands-on Time: 15 min. **Total Time:** 9 hr., 15 min.

- 3 (5-inch) large croissants
- 1 (8-oz.) package chopped cooked ham
- 1 (5-oz.) package shredded Swiss cheese
- 6 large eggs
- 1 cup half-and-half
- 1 Tbsp. dry mustard
- 2 Tbsp. honey
- ½ tsp. salt
- ½ tsp. pepper
- ¼ tsp. ground nutmeg (optional)

1. Cut croissants in half lengthwise; cut each half into 4 to 5 pieces. Place croissant pieces in a lightly greased 10-inch deep-dish pie plate. Top with ham and cheese.
2. Whisk together eggs, next 5 ingredients, and, if desired, nutmeg in a large bowl.
3. Pour egg mixture over ham mixture in pie plate, pressing croissants down to submerge in egg mixture. Cover tightly, and chill 8 to 24 hours.
4. Preheat oven to 325°. Bake, covered, 35 minutes. Uncover and bake 25 to 30 minutes or until browned and set. Let stand 10 minutes before serving.

party pointer

If you need to keep this casserole warm while you open presents, cover it with foil and put it in a 200° oven.

Cheddar Cheese Grits Casserole

Makes 6 servings
Hands-on Time: 15 min. **Total Time:** 55 min.

- 4 cups milk
- ¼ cup butter
- 1 cup uncooked quick-cooking grits
- 1 large egg, lightly beaten
- 2 cups (8 oz.) shredded sharp Cheddar cheese
- 1 tsp. salt
- ½ tsp. pepper
- ¼ cup grated Parmesan cheese

1. Preheat oven to 350°. Bring milk just to a boil in a large saucepan over medium-high heat; gradually whisk in butter and grits. Reduce heat, and simmer, whisking constantly, 5 to 7 minutes or until grits are done. Remove from heat.
2. Stir in egg and next 3 ingredients. Pour into a lightly greased 11- x 7-inch baking dish. Sprinkle with grated Parmesan cheese.
3. Bake, covered, at 350° for 35 to 40 minutes or until mixture is set. Serve immediately.

Cheddar Cheese Grits Casserole

Hot Tomato Grits

editor's favorite

Hot Tomato Grits

Makes 6 servings
Hands-on Time: 40 min. **Total Time:** 40 min.

2	bacon slices, chopped
2	(14½-oz.) cans chicken broth
½	tsp. salt
1	cup uncooked quick-cooking grits
2	large tomatoes, peeled and chopped
2	Tbsp. canned chopped green chiles
1	cup (4 oz.) shredded Cheddar cheese

Garnishes: chopped fresh parsley, shredded
  Cheddar cheese

1. Cook bacon in a heavy saucepan over medium-high heat 8 to 10 minutes or until crisp. Remove bacon, reserving drippings in pan. Drain bacon on paper towels.
2. Gradually add chicken broth and salt to hot drippings in pan; bring to a boil. Stir in grits, tomatoes, and green chiles; return to a boil, stirring often. Reduce heat, and simmer, stirring often, 15 to 20 minutes.
3. Stir in Cheddar cheese until melted. Top with chopped bacon. Garnish, if desired. Serve immediately.

Two-Cheese Grits

Makes 4 servings
Hands-on Time: 15 min. **Total Time:** 15 min.

1   tsp. salt
1   cup uncooked quick-cooking grits
1   cup (4 oz.) shredded Cheddar cheese
½   cup (2 oz.) shredded Parmesan cheese
2   Tbsp. butter
Pepper to taste

1. Bring 4 cups water and 1 tsp. salt to a boil in a 3-qt. saucepan. Whisk in grits; reduce heat to medium-low, and cook 5 to 6 minutes or until tender. Remove from heat, and stir in Cheddar cheese, Parmesan cheese, and butter. Sprinkle with pepper to taste.

Pam-Cakes with Buttered Honey Syrup

Use a light hand when stirring the batter; overmixing will cause a rubbery texture. When using a griddle to cook pancakes, set the temperature dial to 350°.

Makes about 16 (4-inch) pancakes
Hands-on Time: 34 min. **Total Time:** 39 min., including syrup

1¾   cups all-purpose flour
2   tsp. sugar
1½   tsp. baking powder
1   tsp. baking soda
1   tsp. salt
2   cups buttermilk
2   large eggs
¼   cup butter, melted
Buttered Honey Syrup

1. Combine flour and next 4 ingredients in a large bowl. Whisk together buttermilk and eggs.
2. Gradually stir buttermilk mixture into flour mixture. Gently stir in butter. (Batter will be lumpy.)

3. Pour about ¼ cup batter for each pancake onto a hot buttered griddle or large nonstick skillet. Cook pancakes 3 to 4 minutes or until tops are covered with bubbles and edges look dry and cooked. Turn and cook 3 to 4 minutes or until golden brown. Place pancakes in a single layer on a baking sheet, and keep warm in a 200° oven up to 30 minutes. Serve with Buttered Honey Syrup.

Buttered Honey Syrup

Makes about ¾ cup
Hands-on Time: 5 min. **Total Time:** 5 min.

⅓   cup butter
½   cup honey

1. Melt butter in a small saucepan over medium-low heat. Stir in honey, and cook 1 minute or until warm.

Note: Buttered Honey Syrup cannot be made ahead. The heated honey will crystallize when cooled and will not melt if reheated.

Pam-Cakes with Buttered Honey Syrup

Praline-Pecan
French Toast

Praline-Pecan French Toast

The twist: A short-order breakfast special gets an easy hands-off finish in the oven.

Makes 8 to 10 servings
Hands-on Time: 20 min. **Total Time:** 8 hr., 55 min.

- 1 (16-oz.) French bread loaf
- 1 cup firmly packed light brown sugar
- ⅓ cup butter, melted
- 2 Tbsp. maple syrup
- ¾ cup chopped pecans
- 4 large eggs, lightly beaten
- 1 cup 2% reduced-fat milk
- 2 Tbsp. granulated sugar
- 1 tsp. ground cinnamon
- 1 tsp. vanilla extract

1. Cut 10 (1-inch-thick) slices of bread. Reserve remaining bread for another use.
2. Stir together brown sugar and next 2 ingredients; pour into a lightly greased 13- x 9-inch baking dish. Sprinkle with chopped pecans.
3. Whisk together eggs and next 4 ingredients. Arrange bread slices over pecans; pour egg mixture over bread. Cover and chill 8 hours.
4. Preheat oven to 350°. Bake bread 35 to 37 minutes or until golden brown. Serve immediately.

Use French bread with soft crust because it's easier to cut.

Apricot-Stuffed French Toast

Makes 6 servings
Hands-on Time: 55 min. **Total Time:** 1 hr., 30 min., including syrup

- 1 (8-ounce) package cream cheese, softened
- ⅓ cup chopped dried apricot halves
- 2 tablespoons sugar
- 1 (16-ounce) loaf Italian bread
- 4 large eggs
- 1½ cups half-and-half
- 1 teaspoon vanilla extract
- Apricot Syrup (optional)

1. Beat first 3 ingredients at medium speed with an electric mixer until light and fluffy.
2. Cut ends from bread. Cut bread into 6 slices; cut a pocket through top crust of each slice. Stuff each slice evenly with cream cheese mixture; place stuffed bread in a lightly greased 13- x 9-inch dish.
3. Whisk together eggs, half-and-half, and vanilla; pour mixture over bread slices. Cover and chill 30 minutes, turning once.
4. Cook stuffed bread slices on a lightly greased griddle over medium-high heat 3 minutes on all 4 sides or until golden. Serve with Apricot Syrup, if desired.

Apricot Syrup

Makes 1½ cups
Hands-on Time: 1 min. **Total Time:** 2 min.

- 1 (10-oz.) jar no-sugar-added apricot spread
- ½ cup maple syrup
- 1 tsp. ground ginger

1. Stir together all ingredients in a glass bowl. Microwave mixture at HIGH 1 minute.

Praline Pull-Apart Bread

Makes 12 servings
Hands-on Time: 15 min. **Total Time:** 9 hr., 25 min.

1	cup granulated sugar
4	tsp. ground cinnamon, divided
1	(2-lb.) package frozen bread roll dough
½	cup butter, melted
1	cup chopped pecans
¾	cup whipping cream
¾	cup firmly packed brown sugar

1. Stir together granulated sugar and 3 tsp. cinnamon. Coat each roll in butter; dredge rolls in sugar mixture. Arrange in a lightly greased 10-inch tube pan; sprinkle with pecans. Cover and chill 8 to 18 hours.
2. Preheat oven to 325°. Beat whipping cream at high speed with an electric mixer until soft peaks form; stir in brown sugar and remaining 1 tsp. cinnamon. Pour whipped mixture over dough. Place pan on an aluminum foil–lined baking sheet.
3. Bake at 325° for 1 hour or until golden brown. Cool on a wire rack 10 minutes; invert onto a serving plate, and drizzle with any remaining glaze in pan.

Note: We tested with Rhodes White Dinner Rolls.

test-kitchen secret

Don't skip the quick step of beating the cream before stirring in the brown sugar—that's the secret to the smooth texture of the caramel-flavored sauce.

Biscuit Beignets

Makes 4 to 6 servings
Hands-on Time: 11 min. **Total Time:** 11 min.

1	(12-oz.) can refrigerated buttermilk biscuits
	Vegetable oil
	Garnish: powdered sugar

1. Separate biscuits into individual rounds, and cut into quarters. Pour oil to a depth of 2 inches into a Dutch oven, heat over medium heat to 350°. Fry biscuit quarters, in batches, 1 to 1½ minutes on each side or until golden. Drain on paper towels, and dust generously with powdered sugar. Serve immediately.

Cornmeal-Cranberry Muffins

You can freeze these muffins in zip-top plastic freezer bags. Thaw them at room temperature, or microwave frozen muffins at HIGH 15 to 30 seconds.

Makes 1 dozen
Hands-on Time: 15 min. **Total Time:** 50 min.

1⅓	cups all-purpose flour
¾	cup sugar
½	cup yellow cornmeal
2	tsp. baking powder
¾	cup buttermilk
¼	cup orange juice
3	Tbsp. butter, melted
1	egg, lightly beaten
1	cup cranberries
	Paper baking cups
	Cooking spray

1. Preheat oven to 425°. Stir together first 4 ingredients in a large bowl; make a well in center of mixture.
2. Add buttermilk and next 3 ingredients, and stir just until dry ingredients are moistened. Fold in cranberries.
3. Place paper baking cups in 1 (12-cup) muffin pan, and coat with cooking spray; spoon batter into cups, filling two-thirds full.
4. Bake at 425° for 20 minutes or until lightly browned and a wooden pick inserted in center comes out clean. Remove muffins from pans to wire racks; let cool 15 minutes. Serve warm or at room temperature.

Praline Pull-Apart Bread

Cornmeal-Cranberry Muffins

Biscuit Beignets

crowd-pleasing party
STARTERS

editor's favorite

Blue Cheese–Bacon Dip

Makes 12 to 15 servings
Hands-on Time: 36 min. **Total Time:** 56 min.

3 Tbsp. chopped walnuts
7 bacon slices, chopped
2 garlic cloves, minced
2 (8-oz.) packages cream cheese, softened
⅓ cup half-and-half
4 oz. crumbled blue cheese
2 Tbsp. chopped fresh chives
Garnish: chopped fresh chives
Grape clusters, assorted crackers

1. Preheat oven to 350°. Bake walnuts in single layer in a shallow pan 6 to 8 minutes or until toasted and fragrant, stirring after 3 minutes.
2. Cook bacon in a skillet over medium-high heat, stirring often, 10 minutes or until crisp. Remove bacon, and drain on paper towels, reserving 1 Tbsp. drippings in skillet. Add minced garlic to hot drippings, and sauté 1 minute.
3. Beat cream cheese at medium speed with an electric mixer until smooth. Add half-and-half, beating until combined. Stir in bacon, garlic, blue cheese, and chives. Spoon mixture into 4 (1-cup) baking dishes or 1 (1-qt.) baking dish.
4. Bake at 350° for 20 minutes or until golden and bubbly. Sprinkle with walnuts. Garnish, if desired. Serve dip with grape clusters and assorted crackers.

Blue Cheese–Bacon Dip

Goat Cheese–Bacon Dip: Substitute pecans for walnuts, goat cheese for blue cheese, and 2 tsp. chopped fresh thyme for 2 Tbsp. chives. Serve with pear slices, toasted baguette slices, and assorted crackers.

Cheddar Cheese–Bacon Dip: Substitute pecans for walnuts, shredded sharp Cheddar cheese for blue cheese, and chopped fresh parsley for chives. Add ⅛ to ¼ tsp. ground red pepper, if desired. Serve with apple slices and assorted crackers.

Baked Tex-Mex Pimiento Cheese Dip

You can also bake the mixture in 2 (1-qt.) baking dishes.

Makes about 4 cups
Hands-on Time: 15 min. **Total Time:** 35 min.

- 1½ cups mayonnaise
- ½   (12-oz.) jar roasted red bell peppers, drained and chopped
- ¼   cup chopped green onions
- 1   jalapeño pepper, seeded and minced
- 1   (8-oz.) block extra-sharp Cheddar cheese, shredded
- 1   (8-oz.) block pepper Jack cheese, shredded
- Garnish: fresh cilantro leaves
- Serve with: French bread cubes

1. Preheat oven to 350°. Stir together first 4 ingredients in a large bowl; stir in cheeses. Spoon mixture into a lightly greased 2-qt. baking dish.
2. Bake at 350° for 20 to 25 minutes or until cheese dip is golden and bubbly. Garnish, if desired. Serve with French bread cubes.

make ahead

Colby–Pepper Jack Cheese Dip

Prepare up to a day ahead; cover and chill in an airtight container, and bake just before serving.

Makes 10 servings
Hands-on Time: 15 min. **Total Time:** 45 min.

- 1   (8-oz.) package cream cheese, softened
- ⅔   cup sour cream
- ⅓   cup mayonnaise
- 1   tbsp. finely chopped canned chipotle pepper in adobo sauce
- 2   tsp. chili powder
- 2   cups chopped cooked chicken
- 2   cups (8 oz.) shredded Colby-Jack cheese blend
- 1   (4-oz.) can chopped green chiles
- 4   green onions, finely chopped
- 2   jalapeño peppers, seeded and minced
- ¼   cup chopped fresh cilantro
- Garnish: fresh cilantro sprig
- Tortilla and sweet potato chips

1. Preheat oven to 350°. Stir together first 5 ingredients in a large bowl until smooth. Stir in chicken and next 5 ingredients until blended. Spoon cheese mixture into a lightly greased 8-inch square baking dish.
2. Bake at 350° for 30 minutes or until bubbly. Spoon into a serving bowl. Garnish, if desired. Serve with tortilla and sweet potato chips.

test-kitchen secrets

In a hurry? Try these Test Kitchen–approved ready-made dips and salsa available from whole-sale clubs and grocery stores.
- Sabra Roasted Pine Nut Hummus
- Chef Solutions Heat & Eat Spinach Artichoke Dip
- Garden Fresh Gourmet Jack's Special Salsa
- Others we liked: Boursin Garlic & Fine Herbs Gournay Cheese, Hannah Tzatziki Yogurt Dip, and Wholly Guacamole.

Sausage, Bean, and Spinach Dip

1. Preheat oven to 375°. Cook onion, pepper, and sausage in a large skillet over medium-high heat, stirring often, 8 to 10 minutes or until meat crumbles and is no longer pink. Drain. Stir in garlic and thyme; cook 1 minute. Stir in wine; cook 2 minutes or until liquid has almost completely evaporated.
2. Add cream cheese, and cook, stirring constantly, 2 minutes or until cream cheese is melted. Stir in spinach and salt, and cook, stirring constantly, 2 minutes or until spinach is wilted. Gently stir in beans. Pour mixture into a 2-qt. baking dish; sprinkle with Parmesan cheese.
3. Bake at 375° for 18 to 20 minutes or until golden brown. Serve dip with corn chip scoops, bell pepper strips, and pretzel rods.

make ahead

Muffuletta Dip

Parmesan cheese helps hold ingredients together.

Makes about 4 cups
Hands-on Time: 10 min. **Total Time:** 1 hr., 10 min.

1	cup Italian olive salad, drained
1	cup diced salami (about 4 oz.)
¼	cup grated Parmesan cheese
¼	cup chopped pepperoncini salad peppers
1	(2¼-oz.) can sliced black olives, drained
4	oz. provolone cheese, diced
1	celery rib, finely chopped
½	red bell pepper, chopped
1	Tbsp. olive oil
¼	cup chopped fresh parsley

French bread crostini

1. Stir together first 9 ingredients. Cover and chill 1 to 24 hours before serving. Stir in parsley just before serving. Serve with French bread crostini. Store leftovers in refrigerator up to 5 days.

Note: We tested with Boscoli Italian Olive Salad.

Sausage, Bean, and Spinach Dip

Makes: about 6 cups
Hands-on Time: 25 min. **Total Time:** 45 min.

1	sweet onion, diced
1	red bell pepper, diced
1	(1-lb.) package hot ground pork sausage
2	garlic cloves, minced
1	tsp. chopped fresh thyme
½	cup dry white wine
1	(8-oz.) package cream cheese, softened
1	(6-oz.) package fresh baby spinach, coarsely chopped
¼	tsp. salt
1	(15-oz.) can pinto beans, drained and rinsed
½	cup (2 oz.) shredded Parmesan cheese

Corn chip scoops, red bell pepper strips, pretzel rods

Caption: Sausage, Bean, and Spinach Dip

test-kitchen secret

You can also serve this versatile recipe with crackers over a block of cream cheese, or toss leftovers in a Caesar salad.

Muffuletta Dip

Warm Turnip Green Dip

To make the dish spicier, offer guests several brands of hot sauce on the side.

Makes 4 cups
Hands-on Time: 15 min. **Total Time:** 40 min.

- 5   bacon slices, chopped
- ½   medium-size sweet onion, chopped
- 2   garlic cloves, chopped
- ¼   cup dry white wine
- 1   (16-oz.) package frozen chopped turnip greens, thawed
- 12 oz. cream cheese, cut into pieces
- 1   (8-oz.) container sour cream
- ½   tsp. dried crushed red pepper
- ¼   tsp. salt
- ¾   cup freshly grated Parmesan cheese
- Garnish: dried crushed red pepper
- Assorted crackers, flatbread, and gourmet wafers

1. Preheat oven to broil. Cook bacon in a Dutch oven over medium-high heat 5 to 6 minutes or until crisp; remove bacon, and drain on paper towels, reserving 1 Tbsp. drippings in Dutch oven.

Warm Turnip Green Dip

2. Sauté onion and garlic in hot drippings 3 to 4 minutes. Add wine, and cook 1 to 2 minutes, stirring to loosen particles from bottom of Dutch oven. Stir in turnip greens, next 4 ingredients, and ½ cup Parmesan cheese. Cook, stirring often, 6 to 8 minutes or until cream cheese is melted and mixture is thoroughly heated. Transfer to a lightly greased 1½-qt. baking dish. (Make certain that you use a broiler-safe baking dish.) Sprinkle with remaining ¼ cup Parmesan cheese.
3. Broil 6 inches from heat 4 to 5 minutes or until cheese is lightly browned. Sprinkle with bacon. Garnish, if desired. Serve with assorted crackers, flatbread, and wafers.

> ### *make-ahead tip*
> To make ahead, prepare recipe as directed through Step 2. Cover and chill 8 hours. Bake, covered with aluminum foil, at 350° for 30 minutes. Uncover and bake 30 minutes more. Sprinkle with bacon. Serve with assorted crackers and chips.

Hot Crab Dip

Combine fresh crabmeat with cream cheese, sour cream, and Cheddar cheese for a rich and creamy seafood dip. For a lighter version, use reduced-fat cream cheese and light sour cream.

Makes 6 servings
Hands-on Time: 15 min. **Total Time:** 50 min.

- 2   (8-oz.) packages cream cheese, softened
- 1   (8-oz.) container sour cream
- ¼   cup mayonnaise
- 1   Tbsp. Worcestershire sauce
- 1   Tbsp. lemon juice
- 1   tsp. dry mustard
- ¼   tsp. garlic salt
- 1   lb. fresh crabmeat, drained and picked
- 1   cup (4 oz.) shredded Cheddar cheese
- Garnish: chopped fresh parsley
- Crackers or toasted French bread rounds

1. Preheat oven to 350°. Combine first 7 ingredients, stirring until blended. Fold in crabmeat.
2. Spoon mixture into an 11- x 7-inch baking dish; sprinkle evenly with Cheddar cheese.
3. Bake at 350° for 35 minutes or until bubbly. Garnish, if desired. Serve immediately with crackers or toasted French bread rounds.

Loaded Baked Potato Dip

Layered Lima Bean Dip

Makes 4 cups
Hands-on Time: 25 min. **Total Time:** 3 hr., 45 min., including mash

- 2 cups plain low-fat yogurt
- ½ (10-oz.) whole wheat French bread baguette
- Olive oil cooking spray
- ½ tsp. freshly ground pepper
- 1 small cucumber, seeded and diced
- ¼ tsp. salt
- Lima Bean Mash
- ¼ cup (1 oz.) freshly grated 1.5% reduced-fat sharp Cheddar cheese
- 1 medium tomato, seeded and diced (about ½ cup)
- 3 cooked bacon slices, crumbled
- Assorted vegetable slices

1. Preheat oven to 350°. Line a fine wire-mesh strainer with 1 coffee filter. Place strainer over a bowl; spoon yogurt into strainer. Cover yogurt with plastic wrap, and chill 2 hours.
2. Cut baguette into ¼-inch slices; place on a baking sheet. Lightly coat 1 side of bread with cooking spray; sprinkle with pepper. Bake at 350° for 8 to 10 minutes or until toasted.
4. Spoon yogurt into a bowl, discarding strained liquid. (Yogurt will be thick.) Stir in cucumber and salt.
5. Spread Lima Bean Mash on bottom of a 9-inch deep-dish pie plate. Spread yogurt mixture over Lima Bean Mash. Top with cheese, tomato, and bacon. Serve with assorted vegetable slices.

Lima Bean Mash

Makes 1½ cups
Hands-on Time: 10 min. **Total Time:** 1 hr., 10 min.

- 2 cups frozen baby lima beans
- 2 garlic cloves, chopped
- ¼ tsp. kosher salt
- 1 Tbsp. olive oil
- ½ tsp. lemon zest
- 2 tsp. fresh lemon juice

1. Combine lima beans, garlic, kosher salt, and 1 cup water in a medium saucepan. Bring to a boil over medium heat. Cover, reduce heat to low, and cook 15 minutes. Remove from heat, and let cool 15 minutes. Drain, reserving ¼ cup liquid.
2. Process mixture, reserved liquid, olive oil, and remaining ingredients in a food processor 30 seconds or until smooth. Cover and chill 30 minutes to 1 hour. Store in an airtight container up to 3 days.

make ahead

Loaded Baked Potato Dip

We baked frozen waffle fries extra-crispy for our dippers.

Makes about 4 cups
Hands-on Time: 15 min. **Total Time:** 1 hr., 25 min.

- 1 (2.1-oz.) package fully cooked bacon slices
- 1 (16-oz.) container sour cream
- 2 cups (8 oz.) freshly shredded sharp Cheddar cheese
- ⅓ cup sliced fresh chives
- 2 tsp. hot sauce
- Garnishes: cooked, crumbled bacon; sliced fresh chives; freshly cracked pepper
- Waffle fries

1. Microwave bacon according to package directions until crisp; drain on paper towels. Cool 10 minutes; crumble. Stir together bacon and next 4 ingredients. Cover and chill 1 to 24 hours before serving. Garnish, if desired. Serve with crispy, warm waffle fries. Store leftovers in refrigerator up to 7 days.

Warm Artichoke-Shrimp Dip

Warm Artichoke-Shrimp Dip

Serve half of dip first, keeping remaining half warm in saucepan.

Makes about 4 cups
Hands-on Time: 15 min. **Total Time:** 15 min.

2   (14-oz.) cans artichoke hearts, drained and chopped
1   cup freshly grated Parmesan cheese
¾   cup mayonnaise
½   cup fine, dry breadcrumbs
2   garlic cloves, minced
2   Tbsp. lemon juice
½   lb. peeled, cooked shrimp, chopped
Garnishes: lemon zest; peeled, cooked shrimp
Pita crackers, breadsticks

1. Combine artichoke hearts and next 5 ingredients in a large saucepan. Cook over medium heat, stirring often, 4 to 5 minutes or until thoroughly heated. Stir in shrimp. Transfer to a serving bowl. Garnish, if desired. Serve with pita crackers and breadsticks.

Southwest–White Bean Spread

This recipe stands out when paired with sun-dried tomato pita chips.

Makes about 1¼ cups
Hands-on Time: 10 min. **Total Time:** 2 hr., 40 min.

1   garlic clove
1   (15.5-oz.) can cannellini or great Northern beans, rinsed and drained
⅓   cup loosely packed fresh cilantro leaves
3   Tbsp. fresh lime juice
2   Tbsp. olive oil
½   tsp. ground cumin
Salt to taste
Pita chips, sliced cucumbers, olives

1. Pulse garlic, next 5 ingredients, and 2 Tbsp. water in a food processor 3 or 4 times or until combined; process 1 to 2 minutes or until smooth, stopping to scrape down sides. Add salt to taste. Cover and chill at least 2 hours or up to 3 days. Let stand at room temperature 30 minutes before serving. Drizzle with additional olive oil, if desired. Serve with pita chips, sliced cucumbers, and olives.

Smoky Southwestern Spread: Prepare recipe as directed, adding 1½ Tbsp. chopped chipotle peppers in adobo sauce to mixture in food processor before pulsing. Chill as directed.

Green Chile Spread: Prepare recipe as directed, omitting water and adding 1 (4-oz.) can chopped green chiles to mixture in food processor before pulsing. Chill as directed.

Pickled Jalapeño Spread: Prepare recipe as directed, adding 1 Tbsp. chopped pickled jalapeño pepper slices to mixture in food processor before pulsing. Chill as directed.

make ahead • freezer friendly

Beer-Cheese Spread

This recipe makes a lot, but it can be frozen for up to a month. It fits perfectly into 4 (10-oz.) ramekins.

Makes 5 cups
Hands-on Time: 15 min. **Total Time:** 2 hr., 15 min.

1   (2-lb.) block sharp Cheddar cheese, shredded
1   small onion, minced
2   garlic cloves, minced
½   tsp. hot sauce
¼   tsp. ground red pepper
1   (12-oz.) bottle amber beer, at room temperature
Salt and pepper to taste
Garnish: thyme sprig

1. Beat together first 5 ingredients at low speed with a heavy-duty electric stand mixer until blended. Gradually add beer, beating until blended after each addition. Beat at medium-high speed 1 minute or until blended and creamy. Season dip with salt and pepper to taste. Cover and chill 2 hours. Garnish, if desired. Store in an airtight container in refrigerator up to 2 weeks.

Note: We tested with Abita Amber Beer. This spread can be frozen up to 1 month; thaw overnight in refrigerator.

test-kitchen secret

Try this yummy spread over French fries, hot dogs, or chili.

Feta Spread (Htipiti)

Not only does this deliciously sharp dip make a great starter for the Christmas feast, but it also pairs beautifully with lamb.

Makes 1 cup
Hands-on Time: 10 min. **Total Time:** 2 hr., 10 min.

- 8   oz. crumbled feta cheese
- 2   Tbsp. olive oil
- 1   Tbsp. lemon juice
- 1   tsp. finely chopped pepperoncini salad peppers
- 1   tsp. minced garlic
- 1   tsp. chopped fresh oregano
- ¼   to ½ tsp. dried crushed red pepper
- ⅛   tsp. black pepper
- Garnishes: dried crushed red pepper, olive oil
- Crostini, pita chips

1. Place all ingredients in a food processor and pulse 6 to 8 times or until combined, stopping to scrape down sides. Cover and chill 2 hours before serving. Store in refrigerator up to 3 days. Garnish with dried crushed red pepper and olive oil, if desired. Serve with crostini and pita chips.

Note: To serve as a sauce, prepare as directed, processing mixture 3 to 4 minutes. Serve immediately.

Roasted Garlic–Edamame Spread

This is delicious on toasted crostini topped with fresh basil. It also works well as a sandwich spread and can be made up to 3 days ahead.

Makes about 2½ cups
Hands-on Time: 15 min. **Total Time:** 50 min.

- 1   garlic bulb
- 1   Tbsp. olive oil
- 2   cups fully cooked, shelled edamame (green soybeans)*
- ½   cup ricotta cheese
- ¼   cup chopped fresh basil
- 2   Tbsp. lemon juice
- ¼   cup olive oil
- 1   tsp. kosher salt
- ½   tsp. freshly ground pepper
- Assorted fresh vegetables

1. Preheat oven to 425°. Cut off pointed end of garlic; place garlic on a piece of aluminum foil, and drizzle with 1 Tbsp. olive oil. Fold foil to seal. Bake 30 minutes; let cool 5 minutes. Squeeze pulp from garlic cloves into a bowl.
2. Process edamame in a food processor 30 seconds or until smooth, stopping to scrape down sides. Add roasted garlic, ricotta, basil, and lemon juice; pulse 2 to 3 times or until blended.
3. With processor running, pour ¼ cup oil through food chute in a slow, steady stream, processing until smooth. Stir in salt and pepper. Serve with assorted fresh vegetables.

*2 cups uncooked, frozen, shelled edamame (green soybeans) may be substituted. Prepare edamame according to package directions. Plunge into ice water to stop the cooking process; drain. Proceed with recipe as directed.

Roasted Garlic–Lima Bean Spread: Substitute 2 cups frozen lima beans for shelled edamame. Prepare lima beans according to package directions. Proceed with recipe as directed.

Smoked Trout–and–Horseradish Spread

Transform leftovers into crostini by topping toasted French bread rounds with this creamy spread and a sprinkle of finely diced apples and toasted pecans.

Makes 2 cups
Hands-on Time: 10 min. **Total Time:** 10 min.

- 8   oz. smoked trout
- 1   (8-oz.) package cream cheese, softened
- 2   green onions, sliced
- ¼   cup loosely packed fresh parsley leaves
- 5   tsp. horseradish
- 1   Tbsp. chopped fresh dill
- 1   tsp. lemon zest
- 2   tsp. lemon juice
- ½   tsp. freshly ground pepper
- ¼   tsp. salt
- Garnish: lemon slices
- Granny Smith apple slices, celery sticks, flatbread crackers

1. Remove and discard skin and bones from trout, if necessary. Flake trout into small pieces.

2. Pulse cream cheese and next 8 ingredients in a food processor 7 to 8 times or until combined, stopping to scrape down sides as needed. Stir in flaked trout pieces. Transfer to a serving dish. Serve immediately, or cover and chill up to 2 days. If chilled, let stand 30 minutes at room temperature before serving. Garnish, if desired. Serve with apple slices, celery sticks, and flatbread crackers.

Smoked Salmon–and–Horseradish Spread: Substitute 2 (4-oz.) packages smoked salmon, finely chopped, for trout. Omit Step 1. Proceed with recipe as directed.

test-kitchen secret

Keep sliced apples or pears from browning by tossing them with lemon-lime soda. It works just like lemon juice but without the sour taste. The citric acid in the soda will keep the fruit looking fresh.

Smoked Trout–and–Horseradish Spread

Warm Brie with Ginger-Citrus Glaze

Makes 6 to 8 servings
Hands-On Time: 10 min. **Total Time:** 17 min.

  1 (8-oz.) Brie round
  ¼ cup ginger preserves*
  1 Tbsp. honey
  2 tsp. apple cider vinegar
1½ tsp. orange zest
  ½ tsp. chopped fresh rosemary
  ¼ tsp. salt
  ¼ tsp. freshly ground pepper
     Assorted crackers, fresh fruit

1. Preheat oven to 400°. Trim and discard rind from top of Brie. Place Brie on a lightly greased baking sheet. Bake 7 to 9 minutes or until cheese is just melted.
2. Meanwhile, microwave ginger preserves and next 6 ingredients in a small microwave-safe glass bowl at HIGH 30 seconds; stir until blended and smooth. Microwave at HIGH 1 minute. Let stand while cheese bakes.
3. Transfer Brie to a serving dish; drizzle warm glaze immediately over Brie. Serve with assorted crackers and fresh fruit.

*¼ cup fig preserves may be substituted.

Note: We tested with Dundee Ginger Preserve.

test-kitchen secret

If you are serving bread with this warm cheese, place slices on the same baking sheet with the Brie. They will toast while the cheese cooks.

Guacamole Mini Parfaits with Caviar

To pull this sophisticated dish together fast, purchase peeled, boiled eggs in the deli or dairy section of your grocery store. Use leftover purchased boiled eggs to make deviled eggs, and top with leftover caviar for an extra-special twist to a Southern favorite.

Makes 6 servings
Hands-On Time: 10 min. **Total Time:** 10 min.

  ½ cup sour cream
  1 medium avocado, diced
  2 Tbsp. minced red onion
2½ tsp. lemon juice
  ¾ tsp. chopped fresh dill
     Salt and pepper to taste
  1 small plum tomato, seeded and finely chopped
  1 large hard-cooked egg, peeled and finely chopped
  1 (2-oz.) jar black caviar, chilled and drained
     Thin breadsticks, assorted crackers

1. Spoon sour cream into a 1-qt. zip-top plastic bag. Snip 1 corner of bag to make a small hole; pipe sour cream into 6 (2-oz.) shot glasses.
2. Combine avocado and next 3 ingredients in a bowl. Mash with a fork, and season with salt and pepper to taste.
3. Spoon avocado mixture over sour cream in shot glasses. Top each with tomato, egg, and ½ to 1 tsp. caviar. Reserve remaining caviar for another use. Serve parfaits with breadsticks and assorted crackers.

Guacamole Mini Parfaits
with Caviar

Maryland Crab Cakes

Makes 3 dozen
Hands-On Time: 1 hr., 2 min. **Total Time:** 3 hr., 12 min., including sauce

2	lb. fresh lump crabmeat*
½	cup minced green onions
½	cup minced red bell pepper
1	Tbsp. olive oil
½	cup Italian-seasoned breadcrumbs
1	large egg, lightly beaten
½	cup mayonnaise
1	Tbsp. fresh lemon juice
1	tsp. Old Bay seasoning
½	tsp. pepper
Dash of Worcestershire sauce
2	Tbsp. butter
Creamy Caper-Dill Sauce

1. Rinse, drain, and flake crabmeat, being careful not to break up lumps; remove any bits of shell.

2. Sauté green onions and bell pepper in hot oil in a large nonstick skillet 8 minutes or until tender.

3. Stir together green onion mixture, breadcrumbs, and next 6 ingredients. Gently fold in crabmeat. Shape mixture into 36 (1½-inch) patties (about 1 heaping tablespoonful each). Place on an aluminum foil–lined baking sheet; cover and chill 2 to 8 hours.

4. Melt butter in a large nonstick skillet over medium heat. Add patties, and cook, in batches, 3 to 4 minutes on each side or until golden. Drain on paper towels. Keep warm on a wire rack in a jelly-roll pan in a 200° oven. Serve with Creamy Caper-Dill Sauce.

*Regular crabmeat may be substituted.

make-ahead tip

Form patties up to 1 week ahead, and freeze on an aluminum foil–lined baking sheet. Thaw overnight. Cook as directed.

Maryland Crab Cakes

Creamy Caper-Dill Sauce

Find capers on the pickle aisle. They can be stored in the fridge for up to 6 months, undrained, after purchase.

Makes 1¼ cups
Hands-On Time: 10 min. **Total Time:** 10 min.

- ¾ cup mayonnaise
- ½ cup sour cream
- ¼ tsp. lemon zest
- 2 Tbsp. fresh lemon juice
- 1 Tbsp. drained capers
- 2 tsp. chopped fresh dill
- 1 tsp. Dijon mustard
- ¼ tsp. salt
- ¼ tsp. pepper

1. Stir together all ingredients. Store in an airtight container in refrigerator up to 3 days.

Ham-Stuffed Biscuits with Mustard Butter

Makes 5 dozen
Hands-on Time: 1 hr. **Total Time:** 2 hr., 22 min., including butter

- 1 (¼-oz.) envelope active dry yeast
- ½ cup warm water (100° to 110°)
- 2 cups buttermilk
- 5½ cups all-purpose flour
- 1½ Tbsp. baking powder
- 1½ tsp. salt
- ½ tsp. baking soda
- ¼ cup sugar
- ¾ cup shortening
  Mustard Butter
- 2 lb. thinly sliced cooked ham

1. Combine yeast and ½ cup warm water in a 4-cup liquid measuring cup, and let mixture stand 5 minutes. Stir in buttermilk.
2. Combine flour and next 4 ingredients in a large bowl; cut in shortening with a pastry blender or fork until mixture resembles coarse meal. Add buttermilk mixture, stirring with a fork just until dry ingredients are moistened.

3. Turn dough out onto a well-floured surface, and knead 4 to 5 times.
4. Roll dough to ½-inch thickness; cut with a 2-inch round cutter, and place on lightly greased baking sheets. Cover and let rise in a warm place (85°), free from drafts, 1 hour.
5. Bake at 425° for 10 to 12 minutes or until golden. Split each biscuit, and spread evenly with Mustard Butter. Top with slices of cooked ham, and serve.

Mustard Butter

Makes about 1 cup
Hands-on Time: 5 min. **Total Time:** 5 min.

- 1 cup butter, softened
- 2 Tbsp. minced sweet onion
- 2 Tbsp. spicy brown mustard

1. Stir together all ingredients until blended.

party pointer

If you want to entertain a crowd but find that you're short on time this holiday season, bake frozen tea biscuits instead of making the biscuits from scratch. Have guests dress biscuits with flavored butter and mustard blends.

Instant Italian Cheese Tray

Instant Italian Cheese Tray

Make a ho-hum cheese tray spectacular with simple, yet unexpected additions. For example, one large wedge of cheese looks like you splurged, but it's actually less expensive than offering several smaller choices.

Makes 8 servings
Hands-On Time: 10 min. **Total Time:** 26 min., including Fennel-Olive Sauté

Warm Fennel-Olive Sauté
1   (8-oz.) wedge fontina cheese
2   Fuyu persimmons, sliced
¼   lb. thinly sliced prosciutto
Sliced ciabatta bread

1. Arrange all ingredients on a large serving platter or cutting board.

Warm Fennel-Olive Sauté

Makes 12 servings
Hands-On Time: 10 min. **Total Time:** 16 min.

1   lemon
1   tsp. minced garlic
¾   tsp. fennel seeds
½   tsp. dried crushed red pepper
⅓   cup extra virgin olive oil
1½ cups mixed olives
8   pickled okra, cut in half lengthwise
1   fennel bulb, cored and sliced
½   cup lightly salted roasted almonds

1. Remove lemon peel in strips using a vegetable peeler, reserving lemon for another use.
2. Sauté lemon peel, garlic, fennel seeds, and red pepper in hot oil in a large skillet over medium heat 1 minute. Add olives and next 3 ingredients, and cook, stirring occasionally, 5 to 7 minutes or until fennel is crisp-tender. Transfer to a shallow serving dish.

Andouille with Smoked Paprika and Red Wine

Makes 8 servings
Hands-On Time: 20 min. **Total Time:** 20 min.

1   lb. andouille sausage, cut into ½-inch rounds*
2   Tbsp. olive oil
1   Tbsp. chopped fresh oregano
2   tsp. minced garlic
¾   tsp. smoked paprika
½   cup dry red wine
Wooden picks

1. Cook andouille sausage rounds in hot olive oil in a large skillet over medium-high heat 3 minutes on each side or until browned.
2. Stir in oregano, garlic, and paprika, and cook 1 minute or until fragrant. Add red wine, and cook, stirring often, 2 to 3 minutes or until wine is reduced and thickened. Transfer to a shallow bowl. Serve with wooden picks.

*Spicy smoked sausage may be substituted.

Goat Cheese–Pesto Crostini

Makes about 6 to 8 appetizer servings
Hands-On Time: 20 min. **Total Time:** 30 min.

1   (8.5-oz.) French bread baguette
½   cup refrigerated pesto
½   (10.5-oz.) package fresh goat cheese
⅓   cup sun-dried tomatoes, drained and cut into thin strips
7   pitted whole Spanish olives, sliced

1. Preheat oven to 375°. Cut baguette into 28 (½-inch-thick) slices, and place on a lightly greased baking sheet. Bake 5 minutes.
2. Spread 1 side of each bread slice with a layer of pesto and a layer of goat cheese. Top half of bread slices with sun-dried tomato strips and remaining half with sliced olives.
3. Bake at 375° for 5 minutes.

Caribbean Cashews

Orange rind adds a fresh citrus note to these simple and tasty spiced nuts.

Makes 2 cups
Hands-On Time: 8 min. **Total Time:** 1 hr., 8 min.

 2 Tbsp. butter
 1 (9.75-oz.) container lightly salted whole cashews
    (about 2 cups)
 2 tsp. orange zest
 2 tsp. Caribbean jerk seasoning
 Wax paper

1. Preheat oven to 350°. Heat butter in an 8-inch cake pan in oven 3 to 4 minutes or until melted; stir in nuts, orange zest, and seasoning.
2. Bake at 350° for 20 minutes, stirring occasionally. Arrange cashews in a single layer on wax paper, and let cool completely (about 40 minutes). Store cashews in an airtight container.

test-kitchen secret

When baking nuts, it's important to spread them out in a flat layer so that they all bake evenly and get crisp. Let the nuts cool completely before storing.

Mock Tea Sangría

Makes 9 cups
Hands-On Time: 25 min. **Total Time:** 2 hr., 30 min.

 1 (10-oz.) package frozen raspberries, thawed
 ⅓ cup sugar
 1 family-size tea bag
 2 cups red grape juice
 1 lemon, sliced
 1 lime, sliced
 1 (16-oz.) bottle orange soft drink, chilled

1. Process raspberries in a blender or food processor until smooth, stopping to scrape down sides. Pour puree through a fine wire-mesh strainer into a large container, discarding raspberry seeds.
2. Bring sugar and 3 cups water to a boil in a saucepan, stirring often. Remove from heat; add tea bag. Cover and steep 5 minutes.
3. Remove tea bag with a slotted spoon, squeezing gently; cool tea mixture slightly. Stir together raspberry puree, tea mixture, grape juice, and lemon and lime slices. Cover and chill 2 to 24 hours. Stir in orange soft drink, and serve immediately over ice.

Frozen Sangría

You'll need 2 (2-gal.) freezer bags for this recipe that makes 24 cups of sangría.

Makes about 1½ gal.
Hands-On Time: 10 min. **Total Time:** 24 hr., 10 min.

 1 gal. sangría
 1 (12-oz.) can frozen limeade, thawed
 1 (2-liter) bottle lemon-lime soft drink
 2 cups sliced oranges, lemons, and limes

1. Place 1 (2-gal.) zip-top plastic freezer bag inside another 2-gal. zip-top plastic freezer bag. Place bags in a large bowl. Combine sangría, limeade, and lemon-lime soft drink in the inside bag. Seal both bags, and freeze 24 hours. (Double bagging helps to avoid spills.)
2. Remove mixture from freezer 1 hour before serving, squeezing occasionally until slushy. Transfer mixture to a 2-gal. container. Stir in fruit.

Kid-Friendly Frozen Sangría: Substitute cranberry juice for sangría.

Warm Spiced Sangría

Makes 11½ cups
Hands-on Time: 10 min. **Total Time:** 2 hr., 40 min.

- 8 black peppercorns
- 6 whole allspice
- 6 whole cloves
- 2 (3-inch) cinnamon sticks
- 3 (3- x 1-inch) orange rind strips
- 3 cups orange juice
- 1½ cups apple cider
- ¾ cup sugar
- 2 (750-milliliter) bottles dry red wine
- ½ cup brandy
- 1 orange, sliced
- 2 small Granny Smith apples, sliced

1. Place peppercorns, allspice, cloves, cinnamon sticks, and orange rind strips on a 5-inch square of cheesecloth. Gather edges of cheesecloth, and tie securely with kitchen string.
2. Combine orange juice, apple cider, sugar, and spice bag in a 6-qt. slow cooker. Cover and cook on HIGH 2 hours. Stir in wine, brandy, orange slices, and apple slices. Cover and cook on LOW 30 minutes or until thoroughly heated. Discard spice bag before serving.

Orange Lady

Makes 2 servings
Hands-On Time: 5 min. **Total Time:** 5 min.

- 6 Tbsp. gin
- ¼ cup orange juice
- 2 Tbsp. powdered sugar
- 3 Tbsp. lemon juice
- 2 Tbsp. orange liqueur
- Crushed ice
- Garnish: orange slices

1. Combine gin, orange juice, powdered sugar, lemon juice, and orange liqueur in a cocktail shaker; fill with crushed ice. Cover with lid, and shake until thoroughly chilled. Remove lid, and strain into 2 chilled glasses. Garnish, if desired. Serve immediately.

Note: We tested with Cointreau for orange liqueur.

Orange Lady

party pointer

Signature cocktails are special drinks selected to correspond with the theme of the party. Typically, they are mixed liquor drinks, but they can also be special beers or non-alcoholic drinks. These beverages may seem like extra work, but their special presentation will add an extra dimension to your festivities.

Peach-Bourbon Sours

(Pictured on page 102)

Makes 6 servings
Hands-on Time: 10 min. **Total Time:** 10 min.

½ cup peach preserves*
½ cup hot water
1 cup plus 2 Tbsp. bourbon or whiskey
3 Tbsp. lemon juice
Garnishes: lemon slices, fresh basil sprigs

1. Whisk together peach preserves and hot water in a glass pitcher until preserves are dissolved. Whisk in bourbon and lemon juice.
2. Fill a cocktail shaker with ice. Add ⅓ of bourbon mixture; cover with lid, and shake until thoroughly chilled. Pour over ice into 2 (8- to 12-oz.) glasses. Repeat procedure with remaining bourbon mixture. Garnish, if desired. Serve drinks immediately.

*Seedless blackberry, apricot, or ginger preserves may be substituted.

party pointer

Add garnishes to complement the preserves flavor you choose. Lemon slices and fresh basil sprigs look great on glasses of Peach-Bourbon Sours, while orange and cranberries are fancy touches to Cranberry Old-Fashioned Cocktail.

Cranberry Old-Fashioned Cocktail

Made with leftover cranberry sauce.

Makes 1 drink
Hands-on Time: 5 min. **Total Time:** 5 min.

1 orange wedge
1 sugar cube
Dash of bitters
Crushed ice
¼ cup bourbon
2 Tbsp. whole-berry cranberry sauce
Club soda
Garnish: orange twist and fresh cranberries

1. Mash orange wedge, sugar cube, and bitters against bottom and sides of a 10-oz. old-fashioned glass using a muddler or wooden spoon. Fill glass with crushed ice. Stir in bourbon, cranberry sauce, and a splash of club soda. Garnish, if desired. Serve immediately.

Cranberry Old-Fashioned Cocktail

Cranberry-Moonshine Cocktail

Makes 1 serving
Hands-on Time: 5 min. **Total Time:** 5 min., plus 3 days and 15 min. for moonshine

- 2 cups ice cubes
- 3 tablespoons Cranberry-Infused Moonshine
- 1 tablespoon orange liqueur
- Blood orange Italian soda, chilled

1. Combine ice cubes, Cranberry-Infused Moonshine, and orange liqueur in a cocktail shaker. Cover with lid, and shake until chilled. Remove lid, and strain into a chilled glass; top with chilled blood orange Italian soda. Serve immediately.

Note: We tested with Grand Marnier orange liqueur and Archer Farms soda.

Cranberry-Infused Moonshine

Pour infused moonshine into decanters, and add fresh cranberries and citrus rind for a pretty look. Use this mixture for our drink recipes only, not straight up or on the rocks.

Makes about 3¼ cups
Hands-on Time: 10 min. **Total Time:** 15 min., plus 3 days for infusing

- 1 cup fresh cranberries
- ¼ cup sugar
- 1 (750-mililiter) bottle moonshine
- 2 (2- x 1-inch) orange rind strips

1. Cook cranberries, sugar, and 3 Tbsp. water in a saucepan over medium heat 5 minutes or until sugar dissolves, liquid begins to turn a light pink color, and cranberries just begin to pop. Let cool slightly (about 10 minutes).
2. Pour mixture into a large glass jar; stir in moonshine and orange rind strips. Let stand at room temperature 3 days.
3. Pour through a fine wire-mesh strainer into a bowl; discard solids. Return moonshine mixture to jar. Store in refrigerator up to 2 months.

Note: We tested with Junior Johnson's Midnight Moon Carolina Moonshine (piedmontdistillers.com).

Cranberry-Moonshine Cocktail

Creamy Sorghum Eggnog

Makes about 12½ cups
Hands-on Time: 5 min. **Total Time:** 5 min.

1 cup bourbon
½ cup sorghum
2 qt. refrigerated eggnog
3 cups milk
Crushed gingersnaps

1. Whisk together bourbon and sorghum. Stir in eggnog and milk. Chill until ready to serve. Sprinkle individual servings with crushed gingersnaps.

Classic Eggnog

Makes about 3 qt.
Hands-on Time: 55 min. **Total Time:** 5 hr., 55 min.

1½ cups sugar
12 large eggs, lightly beaten
4 cups half-and-half
4 cups milk
¼ tsp. salt
½ cup bourbon
½ cup brandy
2 tsp. vanilla extract
2 cups whipping cream
½ tsp. ground nutmeg

1. Gradually add sugar to eggs in a large glass mixing bowl, whisking until blended. Set aside.
2. Stir together half-and-half, milk, and salt in a Dutch oven over medium-low heat. Cook, stirring occasionally, 12 to 15 minutes or just until mixture begins to bubble around edges of pan. (Do not boil.)
3. Gradually stir half of hot milk mixture into egg mixture. Stir combined milk and egg mixture into remaining hot milk mixture in Dutch oven.
4. Cook mixture over medium-low heat, stirring constantly, until mixture slightly thickens and a thermometer registers 160° (about 25 to 30 minutes). Remove from heat, and stir 1 minute. Pour mixture through a fine wire-mesh strainer into a serving bowl. Stir in bourbon, brandy, and vanilla; let cool 1 hour. Cover and chill at least 4 hours.
5. Beat whipping cream at high speed with an electric mixer until soft peaks form. Fold whipped cream into chilled eggnog, and sprinkle with nutmeg.

Grown-up Frappés

Makes 3 cups
Hands-on Time: 10 min. **Total Time:** 10 min.

2 cups vanilla ice cream
⅔ cup milk
⅓ cup crème de cacao
9 miniature or 3 (1.4-oz.) chocolate-covered peppermint patties, chopped

1. Process ice cream, milk, crème de cacao, and chopped peppermint patties, in a blender until smooth.

Peppermint Patty Frappés

Makes 3 cups
Hands-on Time: 10 min. **Total Time:** 10 min.

2 cups vanilla ice cream
1 cup milk
9 miniature or 3 (1.4-oz.) chocolate-covered peppermint patties, chopped

1. Process ice cream, milk, and chocolate-covered peppermint patties, chopped, in a blender until smooth.

Note: We tested with York Peppermint Patties.

party pointers

3 Ways To Serve a Frappé

- Black Bottom: Pour chocolate fudge shell topping into frozen glasses.
- Sparkly: Dip rims of glasses in warm hot fudge topping; sprinkle with crushed peppermints.
- Spiked: Sweeten whipping cream with crème de cacao instead of sugar.

Peppermint Patty Frappés,
Grown-up Frappés, and Milk
Chocolate–Peppermint Bark
(recipe on page 230)

Cherries Jubilee–Black
Pepper Glazed Ham

merry MAIN DISHES

editor's favorite

Cherries Jubilee–Black Pepper Glazed Ham

We baked this ham at a low temperature—275°—which made it juicier and more tender than a higher temperature would have yielded.

Makes 10 servings
Hands-on Time: 30 min. **Total Time:** 4 hr., 45 min.

- 1 (10- to 12-lb.) smoked, ready-to-cook, bone-in ham
- 1 (14-oz.) can low-sodium chicken broth
- 2¼ cups cherry preserves (about 2 [12-oz.] jars)
- ¾ cup brandy
- ¼ cup cider vinegar
- 1 Tbsp. freshly ground pepper
- 3 Tbsp. whole grain mustard
- 3 Tbsp. cane syrup
- Whole grain Dijon mustard
- Garnishes: fresh cherries, fresh sage sprigs

1. Remove skin from ham, and trim fat to ¼-inch thickness. Make shallow cuts in fat 1 inch apart in a diamond pattern. Place ham in an aluminum foil–lined roasting pan; add broth to pan.
2. Stir together preserves and next 5 ingredients in a saucepan; bring to a boil over medium-high heat, stirring constantly. Reduce heat to medium-low; simmer, stirring constantly, 5 minutes or until mixture is slightly reduced. Cover and chill half of cherry mixture until ready to serve. Brush ham with remaining half of cherry mixture.
3. Bake ham at 275° on lower oven rack 4 hours to 4 hours and 30 minutes or until a meat thermometer inserted into thickest portion registers 148°, basting with cherry mixture every 30 minutes. Let ham stand 15 minutes before slicing.
4. If desired, reheat reserved chilled cherry mixture. Serve ham with reserved cherry mixture and mustard. Garnish, if desired.

Lela's Baked Ham

Choose the size ham that best suits your family. Bake it 20 minutes per pound and 20 more minutes once you add the second layer of glaze. Sop up the drippings with warm rolls.

Makes 8 to 10 servings
Hands-on Time: 20 min. **Total Time:** 3 hr., 40 min.

- 1 (8-lb.) smoked, ready-to-cook, bone-in ham
- 1 cup firmly packed light brown sugar
- 2 Tbsp. cola soft drink
- 1 Tbsp. yellow mustard
- Garnish: fresh sage sprigs

1. Preheat oven to 350°. If necessary, trim skin or excess fat from ham. Stir together light brown sugar and next 2 ingredients in a small bowl. Brush half of glaze over ham. Wrap ham tightly with heavy-duty aluminum foil. Place in a foil-lined 13- x 9-inch pan.
2. Bake ham at 350° for 2 hours and 40 minutes or until a meat thermometer inserted into ham registers 148°. Uncover ham, and brush with remaining glaze. Bake, uncovered, 20 to 30 minutes or until lightly browned. Transfer to a serving dish; let stand 20 minutes. Skim fat from pan drippings, and serve drippings with ham. Garnish, if desired.

test-kitchen secret

How To Carve a Ham the Easy Way

1. Look for knife sets you can sharpen, or choose sets from cutlery makers such as Wüsthof.
2. A ham has three sections, each wrapped in a thin layer of fat. Cut sections away from the bone—largest to smallest—by following the fat lines.
3. Place each section of the ham, cut side down, on a cutting board. For the juiciest slices and most flavorful taste, slice the sections thinly.

Honey-Bourbon
Glazed Ham

Honey-Bourbon Glazed Ham

Makes 15 servings
Hands-on Time: 20 min. **Total Time:** 3 hr. , 20 min.

 1   (9¼-lb.) fully cooked, bone-in ham
 40 whole cloves
 ½   cup firmly packed light brown sugar
 ½   cup honey
 ½   cup bourbon
 ⅓   cup Creole mustard
 ⅓   cup molasses

1. Preheat oven to 350°. Remove skin from ham, and trim fat to ¼-inch thickness. Make shallow cuts in fat 1 inch apart in a diamond pattern; insert cloves in centers of diamonds. Place ham in an aluminum foil–lined 13- x 9-inch pan.

2. Stir together brown sugar and next 4 ingredients; spoon over ham.

3. Bake at 350° on lowest oven rack 2 hours and 30 minutes, basting with pan juices every 30 minutes. Shield ham with foil after 1 hour to prevent excessive browning. Remove ham from oven, and let stand 30 minutes.

Honey-Bourbon Boneless Glazed Ham:

Substitute 1 (4-lb.) smoked, fully cooked boneless ham for bone-in ham. Reduce cloves to 3 (do not insert into ham). Stir together brown sugar mixture as directed in Step 2; stir in cloves. Place ham in a foil-lined 13- x 9-inch pan. Pour sauce over ham. Bake as directed, reducing bake time to 1 hour and basting every 30 minutes. Makes 10 servings. Hands-on Time: 10 min.; Total Time: 1 hr., 10 min.

Pork Loin Roast with Carolina Apple Compote

Makes 8 to 10 servings
Hands-on Time: 1 hr., 26 min. **Total Time:** 4 hr., 41 min.

3	garlic cloves, minced
3	tsp. dried Italian seasoning
2	tsp. salt
½	tsp. pepper
1	(3-lb.) boneless pork loin roast
2	tsp. canola oil
2	lb. Gala apples, unpeeled
1	Tbsp. lemon juice
1	cup apple cider
5	Tbsp. sugar
2½	tsp. orange zest
½	tsp. ground cinnamon
	Pinch of ground cloves
1	Tbsp. butter

1. Combine first 4 ingredients. Rub mixture on all sides of pork roast. Tie pork with kitchen string, securing at 1-inch intervals. Cover and chill 2 hours.

2. Preheat oven to 375°. Brown roast in hot oil in a large skillet over medium-high heat 2 to 4 minutes on all sides. Place pork on a lightly greased rack in an aluminum foil–lined roasting pan.

3. Bake at 375° for 1 hour or until a meat thermometer inserted into thickest portion registers 150°. Cover roast with foil, and let stand 15 minutes before slicing.

4. Meanwhile, cut apples into bite-size pieces; sprinkle with lemon juice.

5. Add cider and next 4 ingredients to skillet. Cook, over medium heat, stirring occasionally, 10 minutes or until slightly thickened. Add apples, and cook, stirring occasionally, 20 minutes or just until apples are tender and liquid is absorbed. Stir in butter until melted, and remove skillet from heat. Stir any accumulated pan juices from roast into compote. Serve compote immediately with pork.

test-kitchen secret

Trussing the roast promotes even cooking. If you prefer, ask your butcher to do it for you.

Pork Loin Roast with Carolina Apple Compote

Rosemary-Garlic Pork with Roasted
Vegetables & Caramelized Apples

Rosemary-Garlic Pork with Roasted Vegetables & Caramelized Apples

Makes 6 servings
Hands-On Time: 41 min. **Total Time:** 2 hr., 24 min., including Caramelized Apples

- 1 lb. carrots, peeled and cut into 2-inch pieces
- 1 lb. parsnips, peeled and cut into 2-inch pieces
- 2 medium-size sweet onions, quartered
- 3 tsp. salt, divided
- 1½ tsp. freshly ground pepper, divided
- ⅓ cup olive oil, divided
- 3 Tbsp. fresh rosemary leaves, divided
- 1 (4-lb.) boneless pork loin roast
- 2 Tbsp. Dijon mustard
- 4 garlic cloves, coarsely chopped
- 6 large garlic bulbs
- ¼ cup apple cider vinegar
- Caramelized Apples

1. Preheat oven to 425°. Combine first 3 ingredients in a large bowl; sprinkle with 1 tsp. salt and ½ tsp. pepper.
2. Sauté vegetables in 3 Tbsp. hot oil in a 7½-qt. roasting pan over medium-high heat 8 minutes or until caramelized. Remove from heat, and stir in 1 Tbsp. rosemary.
3. Tie pork with kitchen string, securing at 1-inch intervals. Sprinkle pork with remaining 2 tsp. salt and 1 tsp. pepper, and place on top of vegetables in pan. Stir together mustard, chopped garlic, 2 Tbsp. olive oil, and remaining 2 Tbsp. rosemary; spread over pork.
4. Cut off pointed ends of garlic bulbs. Drizzle with remaining 1 tsp. oil. Arrange garlic bulbs, cut sides down, around pork in pan.
5. Bake at 425° for 1 hour and 10 minutes or until a meat thermometer inserted into thickest portion of pork registers 160°. Let stand 10 minutes.
6. Transfer pork and roasted vegetables to a serving platter, reserving drippings in pan. Add apple cider vinegar to pan, and bring to a boil over medium-high heat; reduce heat to medium, and simmer, stirring often, 3 minutes or until thickened. Pour over vegetables. Slice pork, and serve with roasted vegetables, garlic bulbs, and Caramelized Apples.

Caramelized Apples

Makes 6 servings
Hands-On Time: 10 min. **Total Time:** 18 min.

- ¼ cup firmly packed dark brown sugar
- 4 Pink Lady apples, quartered
- 4 Granny Smith apples, quartered
- Salt and pepper
- 2 Tbsp. olive oil

1. Rub brown sugar on cut sides of apples; sprinkle with desired amount of salt and pepper.
2. Cook apples in hot oil in a 12-inch skillet over medium-high heat 8 minutes or until caramelized and crisp-tender.

make ahead

Spinach-and-Herb Stuffed Pork

Makes 10 servings
Hands-on Time: 30 min. **Total Time:** 2 hr.

- 1 (10-oz.) package frozen chopped spinach, thawed and drained
- 1 (3-oz.) package cream cheese, softened
- 4 green onions, chopped
- ¼ cup chopped fresh basil
- 2 to 3 garlic cloves, minced
- 1½ tsp. chopped fresh tarragon
- ¼ tsp. ground red pepper
- 1 (3- to 4-lb.) boneless pork loin roast
- ¼ tsp. salt
- ⅛ tsp. pepper

1. Stir together first 7 ingredients.
2. Cut roast lengthwise, cutting to but not through other side. Open cut piece to enlarge roast; pound to ½-inch thickness, making a large rectangle. Sprinkle with salt and pepper. Spoon spinach mixture evenly over pork. Beginning with long side, roll jelly-roll fashion, and tie securely with kitchen string at 2-inch intervals. Place roast on a lightly greased rack in a shallow roasting pan.
3. Bake at 325° for 1 hour and 15 minutes or until a meat thermometer inserted into thickest portion registers 160°. Increase temperature to 375°, and bake 10 more minutes or until browned. Remove from oven, and let stand 5 minutes. Remove string.

Holiday Pork Loin Roast

Makes 8 to 10 servings
Hands-on Time: 15 min. **Total Time:** 1 hr., 35 min.

- 1 (4-lb.) boneless pork loin roast
- ½ tsp. salt
- ½ tsp. pepper
- 6 shallots, peeled and thinly sliced
- ⅓ cup pepper relish

1. Preheat oven to 375°. Tie roast at 2-inch intervals with kitchen string; sprinkle with salt and pepper; place in an aluminum foil–lined jelly-roll pan. Bake at 375° for 1 hour or until a meat thermometer inserted into thickest portion registers 150°. Stir together shallots and pepper relish; spoon evenly over top of roast, and bake 10 to 15 more minutes or until shallots are tender. Let stand 10 minutes before slicing.

Holiday Pork Loin
Roast

Roast Pork Loin with Crumb Crust

Roast Pork Loin with Crumb Crust

Makes 6 servings
Hands-on Time: 30 min. **Total Time:** 1 hr., 55 min.

1 (4 ½-lb.) boneless pork loin, trimmed
2 tsp. salt
1 tsp. pepper
1 cup fine, dry breadcrumbs
¼ cup olive oil
2 Tbsp. finely chopped fresh parsley
2 Tbsp. chopped garlic
2 Tbsp. coarse-grained Dijon mustard

1. Sprinkle pork loin with salt and pepper. Place pork loin on an aluminum foil–lined broiler pan.
2. Stir together breadcrumbs and next 4 ingredients; press breadcrumb mixture onto top of pork loin.
3. Bake at 425° for 15 minutes; cover pork loosely with aluminum foil. Bake 1 hour to 1 hour and 15 minutes or until a meat thermometer inserted in thickest portion registers 155°. Let stand 10 minutes before slicing.

Cumin-Crusted Pork Cutlets

Makes 4 to 6 servings
Hands-on Time: 27 min. **Total Time:** 27 min.

- 3 whole wheat bread slices
- 2 Tbsp. self-rising yellow cornmeal mix
- ½ tsp. ground cumin
- 8 thinly sliced boneless pork loin chops (about 1¼ lb.)
- ½ tsp. salt
- ¼ tsp. pepper
- 1 large egg
- 2 Tbsp. whole grain mustard
- ¼ cup olive oil

1. Process bread in a food processor until finely crumbled. Combine breadcrumbs, cornmeal mix, and cumin in a shallow bowl.
2. Sprinkle pork chops with salt and pepper. Whisk together egg, mustard, and 2 Tbsp. water until blended. Dip pork in egg mixture; dredge in breadcrumb mixture, pressing to adhere.
3. Cook half of pork in 2 Tbsp. hot oil in a large nonstick skillet over medium heat 3 to 4 minutes on each side or until golden brown. Keep warm in a 200° oven. Repeat procedure with remaining pork and oil. Serve warm.

Cumin-Crusted
Pork Cutlets

Savory Herb Pork Chops

Makes 4 servings
Hands-on Time: 15 min. **Total Time:** 1 hr., 15 min.

- 1 cup apple juice, divided
- 3½ Tbsp. light brown sugar, divided
- 1 Tbsp. Dijon mustard
- 4 (¾-inch-thick) boneless pork loin chops
- 1 tsp. salt, divided
- 1 tsp. coarsely ground pepper, divided
- 2 Tbsp. vegetable oil
- ½ cup chopped onion
- 2 garlic cloves, minced
- 2 tsp. chopped fresh rosemary
- 2 Tbsp. balsamic vinegar, divided
- 1 Tbsp. all-purpose flour

Garnishes: thinly sliced apples, fresh rosemary sprigs

1. Stir together ¼ cup apple juice, 1 Tbsp. brown sugar, and mustard in a large zip-top plastic freezer bag; add pork. Seal bag, and shake well to coat. Chill 30 minutes, turning once. Remove pork from marinade, discarding marinade. Pat pork dry, and sprinkle with ½ tsp. salt and ½ tsp. pepper.
2. Cook pork in hot oil in large skillet over medium-high heat 3 minutes on each side. Remove chops from skillet.
3. Cook onion and garlic in hot drippings, 1 minute, stirring constantly. Add remaining ¾ cup apple juice to skillet, stirring to loosen particles from bottom of skillet. Stir in rosemary, 1 Tbsp. brown sugar, 1 Tbsp. balsamic vinegar, and remaining ½ tsp. salt and pepper.
4. Bring onion mixture to a boil. Reduce heat to medium low, and simmer 3 to 5 minutes or until mixture is reduced by half.
5. Add pork to onion mixture, turning to coat. Cover and cook 5 to 10 minutes or until a meat thermometer inserted in thickest portion registers 155°. Remove from heat, and place pork on a serving platter. Cover with aluminum foil. Let stand 5 minutes.
6. Meanwhile, whisk together ¼ cup water, 1 Tbsp. flour, remaining 1½ Tbsp. brown sugar, and remaining 1 Tbsp. balsamic vinegar in skillet until smooth. Bring to a boil over medium-low heat. Reduce heat to low, and simmer 1 to 2 minutes or until slightly thickened and bubbly. Drizzle sauce over pork, or serve alongside pork, if desired. Garnish, if desired.

Easy Pork Grillades Over Panko-Crusted Grits Patties

Easy Pork Grillades Over Panko-Crusted Grits Patties

Makes 6 servings
Hands-on Time: 55 min. **Total Time:** 4 hr., 15 min., including grits patties

Panko-Crusted Grits Patties
- 1¼ pounds boneless pork loin chops
- ¼ cup all-purpose flour
- 2 teaspoons Old Bay seasoning
- 4 tablespoons olive oil, divided
- 1 cup chopped celery
- ½ cup chopped green bell pepper
- ½ cup chopped red bell pepper
- 2 cups sliced baby portobello mushrooms
- 1 (14.5-oz.) can diced tomatoes with garlic and onion
- ½ cup low-sodium chicken broth
- 1½ teaspoons chopped fresh thyme, or ½ tsp. dried
- ¾ teaspoon chopped fresh oregano, or ¼ tsp. dried
- ¼ to ½ tsp. dried crushed red pepper
- ¼ teaspoon salt

1. Prepare Panko-Crusted Grits Patties; keep warm.
2. Trim fat from pork chops, and cut pork crosswise into thin strips. Combine flour and Old Bay seasoning; dredge pork in flour mixture.
3. Cook half of pork in 2 Tbsp. hot oil in a large skillet over medium-high heat 3 minutes on each side or until browned.
4. Repeat procedure with 1 Tbsp. oil and remaining pork. Remove pork from skillet.
5. Sauté celery and bell peppers in remaining 1 Tbsp. oil in skillet 30 seconds. Add mushrooms, and sauté 2 minutes. Add tomatoes and next 5 ingredients; cook over medium heat 5 minutes. Add pork; cover, reduce heat, and simmer 5 minutes. Serve over Panko-Crusted Grits Patties.

Panko-Crusted Grits Patties

Makes 6 servings
Hands-on Time: 20 min. **Total Time:** 3 hr., 20 min.

- 2 cups uncooked stone-ground grits
- 2 tsp. salt
- 1 cup freshly grated Parmesan cheese
- 1 large egg, lightly beaten
- 1½ cups Japanese breadcrumbs (panko)
- ¼ to ½ tsp. ground red pepper (optional)
- Vegetable cooking spray

1. Bring grits, salt, and 6 cups water to a boil in a large heavy saucepan over medium heat, stirring constantly. Reduce heat to low; simmer, stirring frequently, 20 to 25 minutes or until very thick. Remove from heat; stir in Parmesan cheese until melted.
2. Spoon grits into a 13- x 9-inch pan lined with heavy-duty plastic wrap; spread in an even layer. Cool 15 minutes. Place a dry paper towel over grits, and cover with plastic wrap. Chill 2 hours or until very firm.
3. Preheat oven to 425°. Turn chilled grits out onto a cutting board; remove plastic wrap and paper towel, and cut grits into 12 squares.
4. Whisk together 1 large egg and 2 Tbsp. water in a bowl. Combine panko and, if desired, ground red pepper in a shallow dish. Dip grits patties into egg wash, and dredge in panko mixture. Place grits patties on a baking sheet coated with cooking spray.
5. Bake at 425° for 25 minutes or until lightly browned.

Rosemary Rib Roast

Makes 8 servings
Hands-on Time: 10 min. **Total Time:** 2 hr., 30 min.

6   garlic cloves, pressed
2   tsp. salt
2   tsp. pepper
1   tsp. crushed rosemary
2   Tbsp. olive oil
1   (7-lb.) 4-rib prime rib roast, chine bone removed
1   cup sour cream
2   Tbsp. lemon juice
2   Tbsp. horseradish

1. Preheat oven to 450°. Combine first 5 ingredients in a small bowl; rub over roast. Let stand at room temperature 30 minutes.

2. Bake roast at 450° for 45 minutes on lower rack of oven. Reduce temperature to 350°, and bake rib roast 45 to 50 additional minutes or until a meat thermometer registers 145° (medium-rare) or 160° (medium). Let roast stand 20 minutes.

3. Combine sour cream, lemon juice, and horseradish; serve with roast.

test-kitchen secret

Prime rib is often on sale around the holidays, so it's a fairly economical choice. Have the butcher remove the chine bone and then tie it back on—this will give you the flavor from the bone but allow you to easily remove it for carving.

Rosemary Rib Roast

Perfect Prime Rib

Makes 6 servings
Hands-on Time: 5 min. **Total Time:** 2 hr., 5 min.,
including sauce

- 1½ tsp. kosher salt
- 1 tsp coarsely ground pepper
- 1 Tbsp. extra virgin olive oil
- 1 (6-lb.) prime rib roast (about 3 ribs)
- Fluffy Horseradish Sauce
- Garnish: rosemary sprigs

1. Preheat oven to 450°. Combine salt, pepper, and olive oil; rub evenly over roast. Place roast on a wire rack in an aluminum foil–lined roasting pan.
2. Bake at 450° for 45 minutes; reduce oven temperature to 350°, and bake 45 minutes or until a meat thermometer inserted in thickest portion registers 145° (medium-rare) or to desired degree of doneness. Remove from oven, cover loosely with aluminum foil, and let stand 20 minutes before slicing. Serve roast with Fluffy Horseradish Sauce. Garnish, if desired.

Fluffy Horseradish Sauce

With just 4 ingredients, this sauce is easy to whip up while the roast is standing.

Makes about 2 cups
Hands-on Time: 10 min. **Total Time:** 10 min.

- 1 cup whipping cream
- 4 tablespoons prepared horseradish
- 1 to 2 Tbsp. chopped fresh parsley
- ¼ teaspoon garlic salt

1. Beat 1 cup whipping cream at medium-high speed with a heavy-duty stand mixer 1 minute or until stiff peaks form.
2. Fold in remaining ingredients. Serve immediately, or cover and refrigerate up to 8 hours.

Marinated Beef Tenderloin

Makes 10 to 12 servings
Hands-on Time: 51 min. **Total Time:** 9 hr., 9 min.,
including sauce

- 2 (16-oz.) bottles zesty Italian dressing
- ⅓ cup soy sauce
- ⅓ cup Burgundy or other dry red wine
- 1 garlic clove, minced
- ½ tsp. lemon pepper
- 1 (5- to 6-lb.) beef tenderloin, trimmed
- Lettuce leaves
- Horseradish Sauce

1. Stir together first 5 ingredients, and pour into a large shallow dish or zip-top plastic bag; add tenderloin. Cover or seal, and chill 8 hours, turning meat occasionally.
2. Remove tenderloin from marinade, discarding marinade.
3. Grill tenderloin, covered with grill lid, over high heat (400° to 500°) 24 minutes, turning beef occasionally. Reduce temperature to medium-low heat (less than 300°); grill, covered with grill lid, 12 more minutes or until a meat thermometer inserted into thickest portion registers 145° (medium-rare) to 160° (medium). Let stand 15 minutes before slicing.
4. Place tenderloin on a tray lined with lettuce. Serve with Horseradish Sauce.

Note: Tenderloin may be placed on a rack in a shallow roasting pan and baked at 450° for 30 to 40 minutes or until a meat thermometer inserted into thickest portion registers 145° (medium-rare) to 160° (medium).

Horseradish Sauce

Makes 1 cup
Hands-on Time: 5 min. **Total Time:** 5 min.

- 1 cup mayonnaise
- 1½ Tbsp. prepared horseradish

1. Stir together mayonnaise and horseradish until blended. Cover and chill up to 2 days.

Beef Tenderloin

Beef Tenderloin

Makes 12 to 14 servings
Hands-on Time: 10 min. **Total Time:** 1 hr., 10 min.

1   cup dry sherry
1   cup lite soy sauce
5   green onions, finely chopped
1   (5- to 6-lb.) beef tenderloin, trimmed
2   Tbsp. olive oil
Garnish: rosemary sprigs

1. Preheat oven to 450°. Stir together first 3 ingredients.
2. Rub tenderloin with olive oil, and place on a wire rack in a roasting pan. Pour sherry mixture into roasting pan.
3. Bake at 450°, basting occasionally, 45 to 50 minutes or until a meat thermometer inserted into thickest portion registers 140° for medium-rare. Bake beef tenderloin longer until thermometer registers 160° for medium or 170° for medium-well.
4. Cover tenderloin loosely with aluminum foil; let stand 15 minutes before slicing. Garnish, if desired. Serve with pan drippings.

Holiday Roast with Gravy

(Pictured on page 102)

Makes 8 to 10 servings
Hands-on Time: 35 min. **Total Time:** 10 hr., 45 min.

1 (4½- to 5-lb.) eye-of-round roast
2 Tbsp. minced garlic
1 Tbsp. plus 1½ tsp. chopped fresh rosemary
2 tsp. pepper
2 tsp. dried oregano
3 Tbsp. vegetable oil, divided
1 (15-oz.) can tomato sauce
½ cup dry red wine
1 large onion, chopped
2 Tbsp. Greek seasoning
3 Tbsp. all-purpose flour
1 cup low-sodium beef broth

1. Cut 12 (1-inch-deep) slits in top and bottom of roast.
2. Stir together garlic, next 3 ingredients, and 1 Tbsp. vegetable oil to form a paste. Rub mixture into slits. Cover and chill at least 8 hours or up to 12 hours. Let roast stand at room temperature 30 minutes.
3. Preheat oven to 325°. Brown roast on all sides in remaining 2 Tbsp. hot oil in a heavy-duty roasting pan over medium-high heat 5 to 6 minutes.
4. Stir together tomato sauce and next 3 ingredients; pour over roast in roasting pan.
5. Bake, covered, at 325° for 1 hour and 35 minutes or until a meat thermometer inserted into thickest portion registers 135°. Remove roast, reserving sauce in roasting pan. Keep roast warm.
6. Whisk together flour and beef broth until smooth; whisk into sauce mixture in pan. Cook mixture, whisking frequently, over medium heat 15 to 20 minutes or until thickened. Serve gravy with roast.

Roasted Lamb

Makes 8 servings
Hands-on Time: 20 min. **Total Time:** 2 hr., 30 min.

1 (5-lb.) boneless leg of lamb
2 lemons, halved and divided
¼ cup chopped fresh oregano
2½ tsp. salt
2 tsp. pepper
1 garlic bulb, unpeeled
¼ cup olive oil
1 cup low-sodium chicken broth
Garnishes: roasted garlic cloves, baby carrots, radishes, lettuce leaves

1. Preheat oven to 350°. Unroll lamb, if necessary. Rub 1 lemon half on all sides of lamb, squeezing juice from lemon. Stir together oregano, salt, and pepper; rub on lamb. Roll up lamb, and tie with kitchen string.
2. Place lamb on a lightly greased rack in a roasting pan. Separate garlic cloves (do not peel), and place around roast. Drizzle olive oil over lamb and garlic cloves.
3. Squeeze juice from remaining 1½ lemons into a bowl. Stir together juice and chicken broth; pour into roasting pan.
4. Bake at 350° for 2 hours to 2 hours and 15 minutes or until a meat thermometer inserted into thickest portion registers 140° (medium) or to desired degree of doneness. Remove lamb from pan; cover with aluminum foil, and let stand 10 minutes before slicing. Garnish, if desired.

Roasted Boston Butt: Substitute 1 (5-lb.) bone-in pork shoulder roast (Boston butt) for lamb. Rub lemon and oregano mixture over roast as directed. (Do not tie up roast.) Proceed as directed, increasing bake time to 3 to 3½ hours or until fork-tender. Shred pork into large pieces using two forks, if desired. Hands-on time: 20 min. Total time: 3 hr., 30 min.

Savory Baked Chicken

If you don't have a food processor, place garlic cloves on a cutting board, and sprinkle with 1 tsp. salt. Rub ingredients on the board with the flat side of a chef's knife blade until garlic is smooth.

Makes 4 servings
Hands-on Time: 20 min. **Total Time:** 9 hr., 40 min.

- 10   garlic cloves
- 1½   tsp. salt, divided
- 1   cup plain low-fat yogurt
- 1   Tbsp. grated lime rind
- 1   (4½-lb.) whole chicken
- 3   fresh cilantro sprigs
- Vegetable cooking spray
- ½   tsp. coarsely ground pepper
- Garnishes: fresh cilantro sprigs, steamed green beans

1. Process garlic cloves and 1 tsp. salt in a food processor 2 seconds or until smooth, stopping to scrape down sides as needed. Remove and reserve 1 Tbsp. garlic mixture. Stir together remaining garlic mixture, yogurt, and lime rind.
2. If applicable, remove giblets from chicken, and reserve for another use. Rinse chicken, and pat dry. Loosen and lift skin from chicken with fingers (do not detach skin); spread reserved 1 Tbsp. garlic mixture evenly underneath the skin. Place cilantro sprigs underneath skin. Carefully replace skin, and secure with wooden picks. Spread yogurt mixture evenly over chicken and inside cavity. Cover and chill 8 hours.
3. Preheat oven to 375°. Wipe excess yogurt mixture from outside of chicken with a paper towel. Place chicken on a lightly greased wire rack in an aluminum foil–lined broiler or jelly-roll pan. Coat chicken with cooking spray, and sprinkle with pepper and remaining ½ tsp. salt.
4. Bake at 375° for 45 minutes; cover loosely, and bake 25 minutes more or until a meat thermometer inserted into thickest portion registers 165°. Let chicken stand 10 minutes before slicing. Garnish, if desired.

Savory Baked Chicken

1. Preheat oven to 325°. Sauté chopped onion in a lightly greased skillet over medium-high heat 5 to 6 minutes or until tender. Stir in next 6 ingredients. Remove from heat. Tear corn tortillas into bite-size pieces, and stir into chicken mixture. Stir in half of shredded Cheddar cheese.

2. Spread chicken mixture into 6 (2½-cup) buttered oven-safe bowls or ramekins, and top evenly with remaining cheese.

3. Bake, covered, at 325° for 45 minutes or until bubbly. Uncover and bake 15 more minutes or until golden brown.

Note: Chicken Sopa may be baked in a buttered 13- x 9-inch baking dish as directed. To make ahead, assemble, cover tightly, and freeze up to 1 month. Thaw in refrigerator overnight, let stand at room temperature 30 minutes, and bake as directed.

make ahead

Creamy Slow-cooker Chicken

Shred the cooked chicken, and toss with hot cooked pasta. Create a casserole or jump-start a filling for easy enchiladas or a fast pot pie. Or splurge and spoon this dish over freshly baked biscuits.

Makes 6 servings
Hands-on Time: 10 min. **Total Time:** 4 hr., 25 min.

  6   skinned and boned chicken breasts (about 2½ lb.)
  2   tsp. seasoned salt
  2   Tbsp. canola oil
  1   (10¾-oz.) can reduced-fat cream of mushroom soup
  1   (8-oz.) package ⅓-less-fat cream cheese
  ½   cup dry white wine
  1   (0.7-oz.) envelope Italian dressing mix
  1   (8-oz.) package sliced fresh mushrooms

1. Sprinkle chicken with seasoned salt. Cook chicken, in batches, in hot oil in a large skillet over medium-high heat 2 to 3 minutes on each side or just until browned. Transfer chicken to a 5-qt. slow cooker, reserving drippings in skillet.

2. Add soup, cream cheese, white wine, and Italian dressing mix to hot drippings in skillet. Cook over medium heat, stirring constantly, 2 to 3 minutes or until cheese is melted and mixture is smooth.

3. Arrange mushrooms over chicken in slow cooker. Spoon soup mixture over mushrooms. Cover and cook on LOW 4 hours. Stir well before serving.

Chicken Sopa

make ahead

Chicken Sopa

Makes 8 to 10 servings
Hands-on Time: 21 min. **Total Time:** 1 hr., 21 min.

  1   medium onion, chopped
  1   (10¾-oz.) can cream of mushroom soup
  1   (10¾-oz.) can cream of chicken soup
  1   (14-oz.) can chicken broth
  2   (4-oz.) cans roasted diced green chiles
  ¼   tsp. garlic powder
  4   cups chopped cooked chicken
  12   corn tortillas
  1   (8-oz.) block sharp Cheddar cheese, shredded and divided

Turkey Cutlets with Lemon-Caper Sauce

Makes 4 servings
Hands-on Time: 25 min. **Total Time:** 25 min.

- ⅓ cup all-purpose flour
- ½ tsp. salt
- ½ tsp. pepper
- 1 lb. turkey cutlets
- 3 Tbsp. butter, divided
- 1 Tbsp. olive oil
- ½ cup dry white wine
- 3 Tbsp. fresh lemon juice
- 2 garlic cloves, minced
- 2 Tbsp. chopped fresh flat-leaf parsley
- 2 Tbsp. capers
- Garnishes: lemon wedges, chopped fresh flat-leaf parsley

1. Combine flour, salt, and pepper; dredge turkey cutlets in dry mixture.
2. Melt 2 Tbsp. butter with olive oil in a large skillet over medium-high heat; add turkey cutlets, and cook, in batches, 1½ minutes on each side or until golden. Transfer cutlets to a serving dish, and keep warm.
3. Add white wine, lemon juice, and remaining 1 Tbsp. butter to skillet, stirring to loosen particles from bottom of skillet. Cook 2 minutes or just until thoroughly heated.
4. Stir in garlic, parsley, and capers; spoon over turkey. Garnish, if desired. Serve immediately.

Turkey Cutlets with Lemon-Caper Sauce

editor's favorite

Roasted Dry-Rub Turkey with Gravy

This recipe, with its Paprika-Brown Sugar Rub, yields a turkey with dark crusty skin. That's good—it will remind you of the crispy outside pieces of barbecued meats.

Makes 8 to 10 servings
Hands-on Time: 45 min. **Total Time:** 3 hr., 10 min., including rub

- ¼ cup butter, softened
- 3 garlic cloves, minced
- 1 Tbsp. chopped fresh thyme
- 1 (14-lb.) whole fresh turkey
- Paprika–Brown Sugar Rub
- 2 Granny Smith apples, quartered
- 1 (32-oz.) container low-sodium chicken broth
- 3 Tbsp. butter
- 5 Tbsp. all-purpose flour
- Garnishes: whole collard green leaves, green apples, lemon slices

1. Preheat oven to 350°. Combine first 3 ingredients.
2. Remove giblets and neck from turkey; pat turkey dry with paper towels. Loosen and lift skin from turkey breast using fingers without removing skin; rub butter mixture underneath skin. Carefully replace skin; secure skin at both ends using wooden picks to prevent skin from shrinking.
3. Sprinkle 2 Tbsp. Paprika–Brown Sugar Rub inside cavity. Place apples inside cavity. Tie ends of legs together with kitchen string; tuck wingtips under. Place turkey, breast side up, on a rack in a roasting pan. Rub 6 Tbsp. Paprika–Brown Sugar Rub over outside of turkey. Pour chicken broth into roasting pan.
4. Bake turkey at 350°, on lowest oven rack, 2 to 2½ hours or until skin is well browned and a meat thermometer

Roasted Dry-Rub Turkey with Gravy

inserted into thickest portion of thigh registers 170°. Shield with aluminum foil during last hour of cooking to prevent excessive browning, if necessary. (Do not baste.) Transfer turkey to a serving platter, reserving drippings in roasting pan. Let turkey stand 20 minutes before carving.

5. Meanwhile, pour pan drippings through a fine wire-mesh strainer into a 4-cup glass measuring cup. Let stand 10 minutes. Skim fat from surface of pan drippings. (Add chicken broth, if needed, to equal 3 cups.)

6. Melt 3 Tbsp. butter over medium heat in a medium saucepan. Whisk in flour, and cook, whisking constantly, 3 to 4 minutes or until golden. Whisk in 3 cups drippings, and bring to a boil over medium-high heat. Reduce heat to low, and simmer 5 minutes, whisking occasionally. Serve with turkey. Garnish, if desired.

Paprika–Brown Sugar Rub

Makes about 1 cup
Hands-on Time: 5 min. **Total Time:** 5 min.

½	cup firmly packed brown sugar
2	Tbsp. kosher salt
2	Tbsp. smoked paprika
2	tsp. dried crushed red pepper
2	tsp. onion powder
2	tsp. dry mustard
1	tsp. coarsely ground pepper

1. Combine all ingredients. Store in an airtight container up to 4 weeks.

simple SUPPERS

White Bean–and–Collard Soup

Makes 12 cups
Hands-on Time: 30 min. **Total Time:** 1 hr., 45 min.

2   thick hickory-smoked bacon slices
2   cups chopped smoked ham
1   medium onion, finely chopped
5   (16-oz.) cans navy beans
1   cup barbecue sauce
1   (6-oz.) can tomato paste
1   Tbsp. chicken bouillon granules
1   tsp. ground chipotle chile pepper
½   tsp. dried thyme
½   tsp. freshly ground pepper
3   cups shredded collard greens
Hot sauce

1. Cook bacon in a large Dutch oven over medium-high heat 4 to 5 minutes or until crisp; remove bacon, and drain on paper towels, reserving 2 Tbsp. drippings in Dutch oven. Crumble bacon.
2. Sauté ham and onion in hot drippings 10 minutes or until tender.
3. Add beans, next 6 ingredients, and 8 cups water to ham and onion. Bring to a boil over medium-high heat. Cover, reduce heat to medium-low, and simmer, stirring occasionally, 1 hour. Stir in collards; cook 10 minutes or until tender. Serve with crumbled bacon and hot sauce.

White Bean–and–Collard Soup

Pot-Likker Soup

Cooking the ham hocks the day before and chilling the broth overnight will allow you to skim the fat easily.

Makes 6 to 8 servings
Hands-on Time: 20 min. **Total Time:** 14 hr., 28 min., including croutons

 2   (1-lb.) smoked ham hocks
 1   medium onion, chopped
 1   medium carrot, diced
 1   Tbsp. vegetable oil
 1   garlic clove, chopped
 ½   cup dry white wine
 ½   tsp. salt
 ¼   tsp. dried crushed red pepper
 1   (14.5-oz.) can vegetable broth
 ½   (16-oz.) package fresh collard greens, washed
     and trimmed
 Cornbread Croutons

1. Bring ham hocks and 8 cups water to a boil in a Dutch oven over medium-high heat. Boil hocks 5 minutes; drain. Reserve hocks; wipe Dutch oven clean.
2. Sauté onion and carrot in hot oil in Dutch oven over medium heat 4 to 5 minutes or until tender; add garlic, and cook 1 minute. Add wine; cook, stirring occasionally, 2 minutes or until wine is reduced by half.
3. Add hocks, 8 cups water, salt, and crushed red pepper to onion mixture, and bring to a boil. Cover, reduce heat to low, and simmer 3 hours or until ham hocks are tender.
4. Remove hocks, and let cool 30 minutes. Remove meat from bones; discard bones. Transfer meat to an airtight container; cover and chill. Cover Dutch oven with lid, and chill soup 8 hours.
5. Skim and discard fat from soup in Dutch oven. Stir in meat and vegetable broth.
6. Bring mixture to a boil. Gradually stir in collards. Reduce heat, and simmer, stirring occasionally, 45 to 50 minutes or until collards are tender. Serve with Cornbread Croutons.

Kitchen-Express Pot-Likker Soup: Omit ham hocks and salt. Prepare recipe as directed in Step 2, sautéing ½ lb. smoked boneless pork loin, chopped, with onion and carrot. Stir in 2 Tbsp. jarred ham soup base, broth, 8 cups water, and red pepper. Bring to a boil. Gradually stir in collards; reduce heat, and simmer 45 minutes or until collards are tender. Hands-On Time: 20 min.; Total Time: 1 hr., 13 min.

Spanish Kale–and–White Bean Soup: Omit ham hocks, broth, salt, and red pepper. Sauté ½ lb. smoked chorizo, chopped, in Dutch oven over medium-high heat 6 to 8 minutes or until browned. Remove with a slotted spoon; wipe Dutch oven clean. Proceed with recipe as directed in Step 2, sautéing 1 medium potato, cubed, with onion and carrot. Stir in 1 (48-oz.) container chicken broth. Proceed with recipe as directed in Step 6, substituting ½ (16-oz.) package fresh kale, washed and trimmed, for collards, and stirring in browned chorizo with kale. Stir in 1 (15.5-oz.) can white beans, rinsed and drained, and, if desired, 1 (14-oz.) can chicken broth during last 5 minutes of cooking. Omit Cornbread Croutons. This hearty soup makes a great meal by itself, or serve it with crusty bread and cheese (we like Manchego). Hands-On Time: 20 min.; Total Time: 1 hr., 26 min.

Cornbread Croutons

Makes 6 to 8 servings
Hands-on Time: 10 min. **Total Time:** 1 hr., 55 min.

 2   Tbsp. bacon drippings or vegetable oil
 1   cup self-rising white cornmeal mix
 1   cup buttermilk
 1   large egg
 ½   tsp. salt, divided
 ½   tsp. pepper, divided

1. Preheat oven to 450°. Coat bottom and sides of an 8-inch square pan with bacon drippings; heat in oven 5 minutes.
2. Whisk together cornmeal, buttermilk, egg, ¼ tsp. salt, and ¼ tsp. pepper; pour batter into hot pan.
3. Bake at 450° for 15 to 17 minutes or until lightly browned. Turn out onto a wire rack; cool completely (about 30 minutes). Reduce oven temperature to 325°.
4. Cut cornbread into 1½-inch squares. Place on a baking sheet; sprinkle with remaining salt and pepper.
5. Bake at 325° for 30 to 35 minutes or until crisp and lightly browned. Remove to a wire rack; cool completely (about 30 minutes). Store in airtight container up to 1 day.

Butternut Squash Soup

Makes 8 servings
Hands-on Time: 25 min. **Total Time:** 1 hr., 15 min.

6   bacon slices
1   large onion, chopped
2   carrots, chopped
2   celery ribs, chopped
1   Granny Smith apple, peeled and finely chopped
2   garlic cloves, chopped
4   (12-oz.) packages frozen butternut squash, thawed
1   (32-oz.) container low-sodium, fat-free chicken broth
2   to 3 Tbsp. fresh lime juice
1½ Tbsp. honey
2   tsp. salt
1   tsp. ground black pepper
⅛   tsp. ground allspice
⅛   tsp. ground nutmeg
⅛   tsp. ground red pepper
¼   cup whipping cream
Garnishes: sour cream, fresh thyme sprigs

1. Cook bacon slices in a Dutch oven until crisp. Remove bacon, and drain on paper towels, reserving 2 Tbsp. bacon drippings in Dutch oven. Coarsely crumble bacon, and set aside.

2. Sauté onion and carrots in bacon drippings in Dutch oven over medium-high heat 5 minutes or until onion is tender. Add celery and apple, and sauté 5 minutes. Add garlic, and sauté 30 seconds. Add butternut squash and chicken broth. Bring to a boil; reduce heat, and simmer 20 minutes or until carrots are tender.

3. Process squash mixture, in batches, in a blender or food processor until smooth.

4. Return to Dutch oven. Add lime juice, honey, and next 6 ingredients. Simmer 10 to 15 minutes or until thickened. Garnish, if desired. Top each serving with bacon.

Cream of Potato–and–Onion Soup

Makes 12 cups
Hands-on Time: 1 hr. **Total Time:** 1 hr., 40 min.

- 2 Tbsp. butter
- 1 Tbsp. olive oil
- 4 large sweet onions, chopped (about 5 cups)
- 1 tsp. sugar
- 3 Tbsp. all-purpose flour
- 1 (32-oz.) container chicken broth
- 1 (32-oz.) package frozen Southern-style cubed hash browns
- ½ tsp. dried thyme
- 1 bay leaf
- 1 tsp. salt
- ½ tsp. pepper
- 1 cup grated Gruyère or Swiss cheese
- 1 cup half-and-half

Garnishes: chopped fresh chives, freshly ground pepper

1. Melt butter with oil in a large Dutch oven over medium heat. Add onions and sugar. Cook, stirring often, 45 to 50 minutes or until onions are caramel colored.
2. Sprinkle onions with flour, and stir to coat. Add chicken broth. Bring mixture to a boil over medium heat, and cook 20 minutes. Add hash browns and 2 cups water. Reduce heat to low, add thyme and next 3 ingredients, and simmer 30 minutes.
3. Stir in cheese and half-and-half; cook, stirring constantly, over medium heat 5 minutes or until cheese is melted. Remove bay leaf before serving. Garnish, if desired.

Zucchini-Potato Soup

Inspired by the classic potato-and-leek vichyssoise (vihsh-ee-SWAHZ), we added zucchini and gave this recipe a Southern twist with some crisp, crumbled bacon.

Makes 7 cups
Hands-on Time: 40 min. **Total Time:** 1 hr., 5 min.

- 1 medium leek
- 4 bacon slices
- ½ cup chopped celery
- 1 garlic clove, minced
- 4 cups low-sodium fat-free chicken broth
- 1 lb. zucchini, sliced (about 3 small squash)
- ½ lb. small new potatoes, quartered
- 1 cup half-and-half
- ⅓ cup chopped fresh parsley
- ¼ tsp. kosher salt
- ¼ tsp. pepper

1. Remove root, tough outer leaves, and tops from leek, leaving 2 inches of dark leaves. Thinly slice leek; rinse well, and drain.
2. Cook bacon in a large Dutch oven over medium-high heat 8 to 10 minutes or until crisp; remove bacon, and drain on paper towels, reserving 2 Tbsp. drippings in Dutch oven. Crumble bacon.
3. Sauté leek, celery, and garlic in hot bacon drippings 3 to 4 minutes or until tender. Add chicken broth, zucchini, and potatoes, and simmer 20 to 25 minutes. Stir in half-and-half, parsley, salt, and pepper. Remove from heat, and cool 5 minutes.
4. Process potato mixture, in batches, in a blender or food processor until smooth, stopping to scrape down sides as needed. Sprinkle with crumbled bacon, and serve immediately, or if desired, cover and chill 4 to 6 hours.

Cream of Potato–and–Onion Soup

Ham-and-Bean Soup

This is a great way to use leftover holiday ham. You'll need about 2 cups to replace the ham steak. Don't forget to toss in the bone for added flavor.

Makes 8 servings
Hands-on Time: 28 min. **Total Time:** 1 hr., 38 min.

- 1 (16-oz.) lean ham steak
- 2 Tbsp. olive oil
- 1 large onion, diced
- 1 bunch green onions, chopped
- 2 large carrots, diced
- 2 celery ribs, diced
- 1 Tbsp. jarred ham-flavored soup base
- ½ tsp. pepper
- 2 (15-oz.) cans navy beans, drained
- 2 (15-oz.) cans cannellini beans, drained
- 1 (15½-oz.) can black-eyed peas, drained
- 4 large Yukon gold potatoes, peeled and diced (about 2 lb.)

Garnish: Fall Potato Leaves

1. Trim fat from ham steak; coarsely chop ham. Reserve bone.
2. Cook ham in hot oil in a Dutch oven over medium-high heat, stirring often, 6 to 8 minutes or until browned. Add diced onion, and next 5 ingredients, and sauté 5 minutes or until onion is tender.
3. Stir in reserved ham bone, drained navy beans, and next 3 ingredients; add water to cover. Bring to a boil; cover, reduce heat to low, and cook, stirring occasionally, 45 minutes. Remove and discard bone before serving. Garnish, if desired.

Ham-and-Bean Soup with Fresh Spinach:
Prepare recipe as directed, stirring in 1 (5-oz.) package fresh baby spinach, thoroughly washed, just before serving.

Fall Potato Leaves

Makes about 20 leaves
Hands-on Time: 25 min. **Total Time:** 25 min.

- 1 large sweet potato (about 12 oz.)
- 1 large Yukon gold potato (about 8 oz.)
- ½ cup canola oil

Kosher salt to taste

1. Cut potatoes into ⅛-inch-thick slices, placing slices in a large bowl of ice water as you work to prevent discoloration.
2. Cut potato slices into leaves, using assorted 2- to 3-inch leaf-shaped cookie cutters. Return leaves to ice water until ready to use.
3. Drain potato leaves, and dry well with paper towels. Cook potato leaves, in batches, in hot oil in a large skillet over medium-high heat 1 minute on each side or until golden brown. Season with salt to taste.

Ham-and-Bean Soup

make-ahead tip

To make ahead, prepare recipe as directed; place cooked leaves in a single layer in a jelly-roll pan. Freeze on pan until firm, then transfer to a zip-top plastic freezer bag. To reheat, place leaves in a single layer on a lightly greased baking sheet. Preheat oven to 350°, and bake 8 to 10 minutes or until thoroughly heated.

Basil-Tomato Soup

Makes 15 cups
Hands-on Time: 45 min. **Total Time:** 1 hr., 10 min.

- 2 medium onions, chopped
- 4 Tbsp. olive oil, divided
- 3 (35-oz.) cans Italian-style whole peeled tomatoes with basil
- 1 (32-oz.) can chicken broth
- 1 cup loosely packed fresh basil leaves
- 3 garlic cloves
- 1 tsp. lemon zest
- 1 Tbsp. lemon juice
- 1 tsp. salt
- 1 tsp. sugar
- ½ tsp. pepper
- 1 (16-oz.) package frozen breaded cut okra

1. Sauté onions in 2 Tbsp. hot oil in a large Dutch oven over medium-high heat 9 to 10 minutes or until tender. Add tomatoes and chicken broth. Bring to a boil, reduce heat to medium-low, and simmer, stirring occasionally, 20 minutes. Process mixture with a hand-held blender until smooth.
2. Process basil, next 4 ingredients, ¼ cup water, and remaining 2 Tbsp. oil in a food processor until smooth, stopping to scrape down sides as needed. Stir basil mixture, sugar, and pepper into soup. Cook 10 minutes or until thoroughly heated.
3. Meanwhile, cook okra according to package directions. Serve with soup.

Basil-Tomato Soup; Grilled Pimiento-Cheese Sandwiches

---

make ahead

Grilled Pimiento-Cheese Sandwiches

Makes 11 sandwiches
Hands-on Time: 26 min. **Total Time:** 26 min.

- 1 cup mayonnaise
- 1 (4-oz.) jar diced pimiento, drained
- 1 tsp. Worcestershire sauce
- 1 tsp. finely grated onion
- 2 (8-oz.) blocks sharp Cheddar cheese, shredded
- White bread slices
- Mayonnaise

1. Stir together 1 cup mayonnaise, diced pimiento, Worcestershire sauce, and onion. Stir in shredded sharp Cheddar cheese. (Store in an airtight container in refrigerator up to 1 week, if desired.) Spread ¼ cup pimiento cheese mixture on 1 side of a white bread slice; top with another bread slice. Lightly spread both sides of sandwich with mayonnaise. Repeat with remaining pimiento cheese mixture for desired number of sandwiches. Cook, in batches, on a hot griddle or large nonstick skillet over medium heat 4 to 5 minutes on each side or until golden brown and cheese melts.

---

test-kitchen secret

Home-Cooked Convenience: Freeze family-size portions of soups, stews, and sauces in empty cereal boxes for space-saving stackable storage. Line a box with a large zip-top plastic freezer bag, folding the edges of the bag over the edges of the box (the way you would place a liner in a trash can), so that the box supports the bag. Fill  the bag, seal it, and freeze it vertically while still inside the box. Once the soup is frozen, remove the filled bag from the box, and stack horizontally. Downsize to smaller freezer bags and boxes for fewer servings.

Muffuletta Calzones

Muffuletta Calzones

Pizza dough from the grocery store bakery encases traditional muffuletta ingredients—salami, ham, cheese, and olives.

Makes 4 servings
Hands on Time: 20 min. **Total Time:** 40 min.

- 1 cup jarred mixed pickled vegetables, rinsed and finely chopped
- 1 (7-oz.) package shredded provolone-Italian cheese blend
- 8 thin slices Genoa salami, chopped (about ⅛ lb.)
- ½ cup diced cooked ham
- ¼ cup sliced pimiento-stuffed Spanish olives
- 2 Tbsp. olive oil, divided
- 1 lb. bakery pizza dough
- 2 Tbsp. grated Parmesan cheese

1. Preheat oven to 425°. Stir together pickled vegetables, next 4 ingredients, and 1 Tbsp. olive oil. Set aside.
2. Place dough on a lightly floured surface. Cut dough into 4 equal pieces. Roll each piece into a 7-inch circle.
3. Place 2 dough circles on a lightly greased baking sheet. Spoon vegetable mixture on top of dough circles, mounding mixture on dough and leaving a 1-inch border. Moisten edges of dough with water, and top with remaining 2 dough circles. Press and crimp edges to seal.
4. Cut small slits in tops of dough to allow steam to escape. Brush with remaining 1 Tbsp. olive oil, and sprinkle with Parmesan cheese.
5. Bake at 425° for 20 to 24 minutes or until dough turns golden brown.

Meatball Sandwiches

Kids and adults alike will love these hearty favorites.

Makes 16 servings
Hands-on Time: 10 min. **Total Time:** 35 min.

32	bite-size frozen meatballs
1	(9-oz.) jar mango chutney
1	cup chicken broth
16	fresh dinner rolls
1	(16-oz.) jar sweet-hot pickle sandwich relish

1. Stir together first 3 ingredients in a medium saucepan. Bring to a boil over medium-high heat; reduce heat to low, and simmer, stirring occasionally, 25 to 30 minutes.
2. Cut rolls vertically through top, cutting to but not through bottom. Place 2 meatballs in each roll. Top with desired amount of relish.

Note: We tested with Wickles Hoagie & Sub Sandwich Relish.

> *make-ahead tip*
> Prepare meatballs as directed through Step 1. Store in an airtight container in refrigerator 3 to 4 days.

Meatball Sandwiches

Turkey-Artichoke-Pecan Salad

Makes 4 servings
Hands-on Time: 10 min. **Total Time:** 10 min.

- 5   Tbsp. red wine vinegar
- 2   Tbsp. chopped fresh parsley
- 2   Tbsp. chopped fresh basil
- ½   tsp. salt
- ½   tsp. pepper
- ¼   cup olive oil
- 2½ cups chopped cooked turkey
- 1   (14-oz.) can artichoke hearts, coarsely chopped
- ¼   cup green onions, thinly sliced
- 1   cup chopped pecans, toasted
- 1   (4-oz.) container feta cheese

1. Whisk together vinegar, parsley, basil, salt, and pepper. Whisk in olive oil until blended. Toss with chopped turkey, chopped artichoke hearts, sliced green onions, chopped pecans, and feta cheese. Serve immediately.

test-kitchen secret

Toasting brings out the flavor of the nuts, but nuts can go from toasted to charred very quickly in an oven. Arrange nuts in a single layer on a baking sheet, and bake at 350° for about 5 to 8 minutes.

Turkey-Artichoke-Pecan Salad

Spicy Pork-and-Orange Chopped Salad

Combining romaine and coleslaw mix makes this dish crispy and crunchy. The soy sauce–flavored almonds are a new favorite in our Test Kitchen. Find them at your grocer's alongside cocktail peanuts.

Makes 4 servings
Hands-on Time: 28 min. **Total Time:** 33 min.

1	lb. pork tenderloin, cut into ½-inch pieces
2½	tsp. Szechwan seasoning blend
½	tsp. salt
1	Tbsp. olive oil
2	oranges
½	cup bottled low-fat sesame-ginger dressing
1	cup seeded and chopped cucumber
¼	cup chopped fresh cilantro
1	romaine lettuce heart, chopped
3	cups shredded coleslaw mix
½	cup wasabi–and–soy sauce–flavored almonds

Garnish: orange slices

1. Toss pork with Szechwan seasoning and salt to coat. Sauté pork in hot oil in a large nonstick skillet over medium-high heat 8 to 10 minutes or until done.
2. Peel oranges, and cut into ½-inch-thick slices. Cut slices into chunks.
3. Pour dressing into a salad bowl. Stir in oranges, cucumber, and cilantro. Let stand 5 minutes. Add romaine, coleslaw mix, and pork; toss gently. Sprinkle with almonds. Garnish, if desired. Serve immediately.

Note: We tested with McCormick Gourmet Collection Szechwan Seasoning and Blue Diamond Bold Wasabi & Soy Sauce Almonds.

Dianne's Southwestern Cornbread Salad

Makes 10 to 12 servings
Hands-on Time: 30 min. **Total Time:** 2 hr., 45 min.

1	(6-oz.) package Mexican cornbread mix
1	(1-oz.) envelope buttermilk Ranch salad dressing mix
1	small head romaine lettuce, shredded
2	large tomatoes, chopped
1	(15-oz.) can black beans, rinsed and drained
1	(15-oz.) can whole kernel corn with red and green peppers, drained
1	(8-oz.) package shredded Mexican four-cheese blend
6	bacon slices, cooked and crumbled
5	green onions, chopped

1. Prepare cornbread according to package directions; cool and crumble. Set aside.
2. Prepare salad dressing according to package directions.
3. Layer a large bowl with half each of cornbread, lettuce, and next 6 ingredients; spoon half of dressing over top. Repeat layers with remaining ingredients and dressing. Cover and chill at least 2 hours before serving.

Spicy Pork-and-Orange Chopped Salad

Roasted Tomato–and–Feta Shrimp

Makes 6 servings
Hands-on Time: 10 min. **Total Time:** 35 min.

- 2 pt. grape tomatoes
- 3 garlic cloves, sliced
- 3 Tbsp. olive oil
- 1 tsp. kosher salt
- ½ tsp. pepper
- 1½ lb. peeled and deveined, medium-size raw shrimp (31/40 count)
- ½ cup chopped jarred roasted red bell peppers
- ½ cup chopped fresh parsley
- 1 (4-oz.) package crumbled feta cheese
- 2 Tbsp. fresh lemon juice
- Crusty French bread, sliced

1. Preheat oven to 450°. Place grape tomatoes and next 4 ingredients in a 13- x 9-inch baking dish, tossing gently to coat. Bake 15 minutes. Stir in shrimp and peppers. Bake 10 to 15 minutes or just until shrimp turn pink. Toss with parsley, feta cheese, and lemon juice. Serve immediately with crusty French bread and 1 (5-oz.) package mixed salad greens and your favorite Greek dressing.

Tomato 'n' Beef Casserole with Polenta Crust

Makes 6 servings
Hands-on Time: 55 min. **Total Time:** 1 hr., 25 min.

- 1 tsp. salt
- 1 cup plain yellow cornmeal
- ½ tsp. Montreal steak seasoning
- 1 cup (4 oz.) shredded sharp Cheddar cheese, divided
- 1 lb. ground chuck
- 1 cup chopped onion
- 1 medium zucchini, cut in half lengthwise and sliced (about 2 cups)
- 1 Tbsp. olive oil
- 2 (14½-oz.) cans petite diced tomatoes, drained
- 1 (6-oz.) can tomato paste
- 2 Tbsp. chopped fresh flat-leaf parsley

1. Preheat oven to 350°. Bring 3 cups water and 1 tsp. salt to a boil in a 2-qt. saucepan over medium-high heat. Whisk in cornmeal; reduce heat to low, and simmer, whisking constantly, 3 minutes or until thickened. Remove from heat, and stir in steak seasoning and ¼ cup Cheddar cheese. Spread cornmeal mixture into a lightly greased 11- x 7-inch baking dish.

2. Brown ground chuck in a large nonstick skillet over medium-high heat, stirring often, 10 minutes or until meat crumbles and is no longer pink; drain and transfer to a bowl.

3. Sauté onion and zucchini in hot oil in skillet over medium heat 5 minutes or until crisp-tender. Stir in beef, tomatoes, and tomato paste; simmer, stirring often, 10 minutes. Pour beef mixture over cornmeal crust. Sprinkle with remaining ¾ cup cheese.

4. Bake at 350° for 30 minutes or until bubbly. Sprinkle casserole with parsley just before serving.

Italian Beef Casserole with Polenta Crust:
Substitute Italian sausage for ground chuck and Italian six-cheese blend for Cheddar cheese. Prepare recipe as directed, sautéing 1 medium-size green bell pepper, chopped, with onion in Step 3.

Vanessa's Make-Ahead
Beefy Lasagna

freezer friendly • make ahead

Vanessa's Make-Ahead Beefy Lasagna

Makes 8 servings
Hands-on Time: 25 min. **Total Time:** 1 hr., 35 min.

- 12 uncooked lasagna noodles
- 1 (24-oz.) container 4% small-curd smooth-and-creamy cottage cheese
- 1 (16-oz.) container ricotta cheese
- 2 large eggs, lightly beaten
- ½ cup refrigerated pesto
- 1 tsp. salt
- 2½ cups (10 oz.) shredded mozzarella cheese, divided
- 1 lb. lean ground beef
- ½ cup finely chopped onion
- 2 (24-oz.) jars tomato-and-basil pasta sauce

1. Preheat oven to 375°. Prepare noodles according to package directions.
2. Meanwhile, stir together cottage cheese, ricotta cheese, and next 3 ingredients. Stir in 1 cup mozzarella cheese.
3. Cook ground beef and chopped onion in a large skillet over medium-high heat, stirring often, 6 to 7 minutes or until meat crumbles and is no longer pink; drain. Stir in pasta sauce.
4. Layer 1 cup beef mixture, 3 noodles, and 2½ cups cottage cheese mixture in a lightly greased 13- x 9-inch baking dish. Top with 3 noodles, 2 cups beef mixture, and 3 more noodles. Top with remaining cottage cheese mixture, 3 noodles, and beef mixture. Sprinkle with remaining 1½ cups mozzarella cheese.
5. Bake, covered, at 375° for 40 to 45 minutes. Uncover and bake 20 more minutes or until cheese is browned. Let stand 10 to 15 minutes before serving.

Note: We tested with Classico Di Napoli Tomato & Basil Pasta Sauce and both LeGrand Garden Pesto and Buitoni Reduced Fat Pesto with Basil.

make-ahead tip

Freeze unbaked lasagna up to 3 months. To bake, thaw in refrigerator 24 hours. Let stand 30 minutes; bake as directed.

Crabmeat-and-Spinach Lasagna

Press drained spinach between paper towels to absorb additional liquid.

Makes 8 servings
Hands-on Time: 45 min. **Total Time:** 2 hr.

 9 uncooked lasagna noodles
 2 tablespoons butter or margarine
 ½ cup finely chopped celery
 ½ cup finely chopped onion
 1 red bell pepper, finely chopped
 3 garlic cloves, minced
 3 (8-oz.) cartons sour cream
 ¼ cup chopped fresh basil
 ¼ tsp. salt
 ⅛ tsp. ground white pepper
 ⅛ tsp. ground nutmeg
 2 (10-oz.) packages frozen chopped spinach, thawed and well drained
 1 lb. fresh lump crabmeat, drained
 4 cups (16 oz.) shredded mozzarella and provolone cheese, divided
 Garnish: fresh basil leaves

1. Cook noodles according to package directions; drain and set aside.
2. Melt butter in a large skillet over medium-high heat; add celery and next 3 ingredients. Sauté 4 to 5 minutes or until vegetables are tender.
3. Combine sour cream and next 4 ingredients in a bowl; stir in vegetable mixture and spinach. Add crabmeat; toss.
4. Arrange 3 lasagna noodles in bottom of a lightly greased 13- x 9-inch baking dish; top noodles with half of crab-meat mixture. Top with half of cheese. Repeat layers with 3 lasagna noodles and remaining crabmeat mixture. Top with remaining 3 lasagna noodles.
5. Cover and bake at 350° for 50 minutes or until lasagna is thoroughly heated. Uncover and top evenly with remaining 2 cups cheese. Bake, uncovered, 15 more minutes or until cheese is melted. Let stand 10 minutes before serving. Garnish, if desired.

Note: We tested with Sargento Chef Style Mozzarella & Provolone cheese blend.

Zesty King Ranch Chicken Casserole

For an even zestier version of this casserole, use original diced tomatoes and green chiles.

Makes 8 servings
Hands-on Time: 15 min. **Total Time:** 50 min.

 2 Tbsp. butter
 ½ (10-oz.) package frozen diced onion, red and green bell peppers, and celery
 2 (10 ¾-oz.) cans cream of chicken soup
 2 (10-oz.) cans mild diced tomatoes and green chiles
 1 tsp. Mexican-style chili powder*
 3 cups shredded deli-roasted chicken
 3 cups freshly grated sharp Cheddar cheese
 3 cups coarsely crumbled lime-flavored white corn tortilla chips
 Garnishes: fresh cilantro sprigs, lime wedges

1. Preheat oven to 400°. Melt butter in a large skillet over medium-high heat. Add frozen vegetables, and sauté 4 to 5 minutes or until tender. Transfer to a medium bowl; stir in soup, diced tomatoes, and chili powder.
2. Layer half of chicken in a lightly greased 13- x 9-inch baking dish. Top with half of soup mixture and 1 cup Cheddar cheese. Sprinkle with 1½ cups tortilla chips. Repeat layers once. Top with remaining 1 cup cheese.
3. Bake at 400° for 25 to 30 minutes or until bubbly. Let stand 10 minutes before serving. Garnish, if desired.

*1 teaspoon chili powder and ⅛ teaspoon ground red pepper may be substituted.

Sausage-and-Grits
Dressing

all the TRIMMINGS

Sausage-and-Grits Dressing

Makes 8 servings
Hands-on Time: 1 hr. **Total Time:** 4 hr., 10 min.

- 1 (32-oz.) container chicken broth
- 1¼ cups uncooked stone-ground white or yellow grits
- 1 cup (4 oz.) freshly shredded Parmesan cheese
- Cooking spray
- 1 lb. ground hot pork sausage
- ⅓ cup butter
- 5 celery ribs with leaves, finely chopped
- 4 garlic cloves, minced (about 1 Tbsp.)
- 1 large onion, chopped
- ½ cup chopped fresh parsley
- 1 large egg, lightly beaten

1. Combine broth and grits in a large, heavy saucepan over medium-high heat; bring to a boil, stirring constantly. Reduce heat, and simmer, uncovered, 20 to 25 minutes or until very thick, stirring often. Remove from heat, and add Parmesan cheese, stirring to melt cheese. Spoon grits mixture into a 13- x 9-inch baking pan lined with heavy-duty plastic wrap or coated with cooking spray. Cool completely (30 minutes). Cover and chill grits 2 hours or until very firm.
2. Preheat oven to 450°. Invert grits onto a large cutting board, and remove plastic wrap. Cut grits into ¾-inch cubes. Place in a single layer on a large baking sheet or jelly-roll pan coated with cooking spray. Bake at 450° for 20 minutes; turn grits cubes, and bake 12 more minutes or until crisp and browned. Reduce oven temperature to 350°.
3. Cook sausage in a large skillet, stirring to crumble, until sausage is no longer pink; remove sausage from skillet, reserving drippings in skillet. Add butter to drippings in skillet, and place over medium-high heat until butter melts. Add celery, garlic, and onion; sauté 10 minutes or until vegetables are tender. Combine onion mixture, sausage, grits cubes, and parsley, tossing gently. Drizzle egg over grits mixture, and toss gently; spoon into an 11- x 7-inch baking dish coated with cooking spray. Bake, uncovered, at 350° for 40 to 45 minutes or until browned.

Apple-Walnut Dressing

Makes 4 servings
Hands-on Time: 1 hr. **Total Time:** 1 hr.

- 1 (3.5-oz.) bag brown rice, uncooked
- 1 medium-size Granny Smith apple, peeled and chopped
- ¾ tsp. apple pie spice
- 2 Tbsp. lemon juice
- 4 ounces turkey sausage
- ¾ cup chopped onion
- ½ cup chopped celery
- ¼ cup chopped walnuts
- ¼ cup raisins
- ½ tsp. salt
- ½ tsp. pepper
- ⅛ tsp. rubbed sage
- ⅓ cup low-sodium chicken broth
- 2 to 4 Tbsp. honey
- Garnish: fresh parsley sprigs

1. Prepare rice according to package directions.
2. Stir together chopped apple, apple pie spice, and lemon juice.
3. Brown sausage in a lightly greased large nonstick skillet. Cook over medium heat, stirring occasionally, 5 to 7 minutes or until sausage crumbles and is no longer pink. Add onion and next 3 ingredients; cook, stirring occasionally, 5 to 7 minutes or until vegetables are crisp-tender. Add apple mixture, salt, pepper, and sage; cook 3 minutes, stirring constantly. Add rice, broth, and honey; cook, stirring constantly, 2 to 3 minutes or until thoroughly heated. Garnish, if desired.

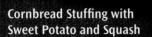

Cornbread Stuffing with Sweet Potato and Squash

make ahead

Cornbread Stuffing with Sweet Potato and Squash

Makes 10 servings
Hands-on Time: 47 min. **Total Time:** 1 hr., 57 min.

- 1 cup frozen diced onion, red and green bell peppers, and celery
- 2 small garlic cloves, pressed
- 1 Tbsp. canola oil
- 1½ lb. butternut squash, peeled, seeded, and cut into ¼-inch cubes
- 2 medium-size sweet potatoes, peeled and cut into ¼-inch cubes
- 1 Granny Smith apple, peeled and cut into ¼-inch cubes
- 3 Tbsp. melted butter
- 2 Tbsp. brown sugar
- 1 Tbsp. chopped fresh sage
- 2 tsp. Creole seasoning, divided
- 2 (14-oz.) cans low-sodium fat-free chicken broth, divided
- 1 (8-oz.) package cornbread stuffing mix
- 1 large egg, lightly beaten
- ⅓ cup chopped pecans
- Garnish: fresh or dried sage leaves

1. Preheat oven to 375°. Sauté frozen onion mixture and garlic in 1 Tbsp. hot oil in a large, deep skillet over medium-high heat 2 minutes or until vegetables are tender.
2. Stir in squash, next 5 ingredients, 1 tsp. Creole seasoning, and ¼ cup water. Cover, reduce heat to medium, and cook, stirring occasionally, 15 minutes or until butternut squash and sweet potatoes are tender. Stir in 1 can chicken broth.
3. Remove from heat; allow to cool 15 minutes. Stir together stuffing mix, egg, and remaining 1 can chicken broth and 1 tsp. Creole seasoning in a medium bowl. Fold into cooled squash mixture. Spoon stuffing mixture into a lightly greased 13- x 9-inch baking dish.
4. Bake stuffing, covered with aluminum foil, at 375° for 25 minutes. Uncover and sprinkle stuffing with pecans; bake 20 minutes or until dressing is thoroughly heated and pecans are toasted. Let stand 10 minutes before serving. Garnish, if desired.

test-kitchen secret

If you're taking a slow-cooker dish to grandmother's house, you may want to invest in a model that features a lock top and insulated carrying case. Or you can attach heavy-duty rubber bands around the handles and lid, and then wrap the slow cooker in towels or newspaper to keep contents warm.

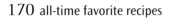

make ahead

Sage Cornbread Dressing

Use all 3 cups of broth if you like a really moist dressing.

Makes 8 to 10 servings
Hands-on Time: 47 min. **Total Time:** 2 hr., 2 min.

2	(6-oz.) packages buttermilk cornbread mix
⅓	cup butter
1	cup chopped celery
½	cup chopped onion
1	Tbsp. chopped fresh or 1½ tsp. dried sage
½	tsp. pepper
¼	tsp. salt
4	white bread slices, cut into ½-inch cubes (about 2 cups)
2½	to 3 cups chicken broth
2	large eggs, lightly beaten
	Garnish: fresh sage leaves

1. Prepare cornbread according to package directions for a double recipe. Let cool 30 minutes; crumble cornbread into a large bowl.
2. Melt ⅓ cup butter in a large skillet over medium heat; add chopped celery and onion, and sauté 10 to 12 minutes or until tender. Stir in sage, pepper, and salt. Stir celery mixture and bread cubes into crumbled cornbread in bowl, stirring gently until blended. Add chicken broth and eggs, and gently stir until moistened. Spoon mixture into a lightly greased 11- x 7-inch baking dish.
3. Bake at 350° for 45 to 50 minutes or until golden brown. Garnish, if desired.

Note: We tested with Martha White Cotton Country Cornbread Mix.

Sausage Dressing: Prepare recipe as directed through Step 1. Omit ⅓ cup butter. Cook 1 (16-oz.) package pork sausage in a large skillet over medium-high heat, stirring often, 10 to 12 minutes or until meat crumbles and is no longer pink. Remove cooked sausage from skillet using a slotted spoon, and drain, reserving 2 tsp. drippings in skillet. Add chopped celery and onion, and saute 10 to 12 minutes or until vegetables are tender; stir in sage, pepper, and salt. Stir in cooked sausage. Proceed with recipe as directed. Follow make-ahead directions, if desired.

Oyster Dressing: Prepare recipe as directed through Step 2, stirring 1 (12-oz.) container fresh oysters, drained, into cornbread mixture. Proceed with recipe as directed, increasing bake time to 50 to 55 minutes or until golden. Follow make-ahead directions, if desired.

Sage Cornbread Dressing

> *make-ahead tip*
>
> To make ahead, prepare recipe as directed through Step 2. Cover with plastic wrap; cover with heavy-duty aluminum foil or container lid. Freeze unbaked dressing up to 3 months, if desired. Thaw in refrigerator 24 hours. Let stand at room temperature 30 minutes. Bake, uncovered, at 350° for 1 hour and 10 minutes to 1 hour and 15 minutes or until golden.

Cornbread Dressing

Cornbread Dressing

Makes 12 to 16 servings
Hands-on Time: 20 min. **Total Time:** 4 hr., 20 min.

5   cups crumbled cornbread
1   (14-oz.) package herb stuffing
2   (10¾-oz.) cans cream of chicken soup
2   (14-oz.) cans chicken broth
1   large sweet onion, diced
1   cup diced celery
4   large eggs, lightly beaten
1   tablespoon rubbed sage
½   teaspoon pepper
2   tablespoons butter, cut up

1. Combine first 9 ingredients in a large bowl.
2. Pour cornbread mixture into a lightly greased 6-qt. slow cooker. Dot with butter. Cover dressing, and cook on LOW 4 to 6 hours or until set and thoroughly cooked.

Note: We tested with Pepperidge Farm Herb Seasoned Stuffing. Two (6-oz.) packages of Martha White Buttermilk Cornbread & Muffin Mix, prepared according to package directions, yields 5 cups crumbs.

Sausage-Apple Cornbread Dressing: Cook 1 (16-oz.) package ground pork sausage in a large skillet over medium-high heat, stirring often, 8 to 10 minutes or until meat crumbles and is no longer pink; drain. Stir sausage and 2 Granny Smith apples, peeled and diced, into cornbread mixture in Step 1.

make ahead

Grandma Erma's Spirited Cranberry Sauce

You'll need about 1 lb. of cranberries. Most are sold in 12-oz. bags, so pick up 2 and freeze the extra.

Makes about 3½ cups
Hands-on Time: 15 min. **Total Time:** 8 hr., 30 min.

- 2 cups sugar
- ½ cup port
- 4 cups fresh cranberries
- ¼ cup orange liqueur

1. Stir together sugar, port, and ¾ cup water in a heavy 3-qt. saucepan until blended. Add cranberries; bring to a boil, and cook over medium-high heat, stirring often, 8 to 10 minutes or until cranberry skins begin to split. Remove from heat, and let cool 15 minutes.
2. Pulse cranberry mixture in a food processor 3 to 4 times or until cranberries are almost pureed; stir in orange liqueur. Cover and chill 8 hours before serving. Store in refrigerator in an airtight container up to 2 weeks. Serve chilled or at room temperature.

Note: We tested with Grand Marnier orange liqueur.

Grandma Erma's Spirited Cranberry Sauce

make ahead

Cranberry Sauce

Vary the character of this tasty holiday sauce by adding in some toasted, chopped nuts.

Makes about 5½ cups
Hands-on Time: 20 min. **Total Time:** 12 hr., 20 min.

- 2 (12-oz.) packages fresh cranberries
- 1 cup granulated sugar
- 1 cup firmly packed light brown sugar
- 1 cup fresh orange juice
- 2 Tbsp. grated fresh ginger
- 1 cup sweetened dried cranberries
- 1 Tbsp. orange zest

1. Stir together first 5 ingredients and ½ cup water in a lightly greased 3½- to 4-qt. slow cooker.
2. Cover and cook on HIGH 3 to 3½ hours or until cranberries begin to pop.
3. Uncover and cook 30 minutes. Stir in dried cranberries and orange zest. Cool sauce completely, stirring often (about 1 hour; mixture will thicken as it cools). Cover and chill 8 hours. Store in refrigerator up to 2 weeks.

test-kitchen secret
Quickly grate fresh ginger and citrus zest using a microplane zester.

Roasted Grape Chutney

Cranberry Chutney

Store any leftover chutney in an airtight container in the refrigerator up to a week. Serve it with fried turkey, roasted pork tenderloin, or grilled pork chops.

Makes about 4½ cups
Hands-on Time: 30 min. **Total Time:** 30 min.

- ¾ cup sugar
- 3 cups (12 oz.) fresh cranberries
- 1 pink grapefruit, peeled, seeded, and chopped
- 1 orange, peeled, seeded, and chopped
- 1 Granny Smith apple, peeled and diced
- 1 Anjou pear, peeled and diced
- 1½ cups mixed dried fruit
- 1 tsp. ground cinnamon
- ½ tsp. ground nutmeg
- ¼ tsp. ground cloves
- ⅛ tsp. salt

1. Bring 1 cup water to a boil over medium heat; add sugar, stirring until dissolved. Reduce heat to medium-low; stir in cranberries and remaining ingredients, and simmer, stirring constantly, 10 minutes. Remove from heat, and let cool.

Roasted Grape Chutney

Makes 1⅓ cups
Hands-on Time: 10 min. **Total Time:** 1 hr.

- 1 cup seedless red grapes, halved
- 1 cup seedless green grapes, halved
- 1 Tbsp. olive oil
- 1 Tbsp. red wine vinegar
- 1 tsp. dried thyme
- ½ tsp. kosher salt
- ¼ tsp. pepper

1. Preheat oven to 425°. Stir together all ingredients. Spread grape mixture on an aluminum foil–lined baking sheet. Bake 20 minutes or until grapes begin to shrivel. Remove from oven, and let cool 30 minutes. Store in refrigerator up to 3 days.

Anytime Turkey Gravy

Makes about 2½ cups
Hands-on Time: 1 hr., 35 min. **Total Time:** 1 hr., 35 min.

- 2½ lb. dark meat turkey pieces (wings and necks)
- 2 Tbsp. vegetable oil
- 1 medium onion, chopped
- 2 celery ribs, chopped
- 1 (49.5-oz.) can chicken broth
- ½ cup chopped fresh parsley
- ⅓ cup butter
- ⅓ cup all-purpose flour
- ½ tsp. freshly ground pepper
- ½ tsp. poultry seasoning
- ¼ tsp. rubbed sage

1. Cook turkey pieces in hot oil in a Dutch oven over medium-high heat 6 to 8 minutes on each side or until lightly browned. Add onion and celery, and sauté 4 minutes. Gradually stir in chicken broth, stirring to loosen particles from bottom of skillet; stir in parsley. Bring to a boil; cover, reduce heat to medium-low, and simmer, stirring occasionally, 30 minutes. Pour mixture through a wire-mesh strainer into a large bowl, discarding solids.
2. Melt butter in Dutch oven over medium heat; whisk in flour, and cook, whisking constantly, 1 to 2 minutes or until mixture is golden and smooth. Gradually whisk in broth mixture; increase heat to medium-high, and bring to a boil. Reduce heat to medium, and simmer, stirring occasionally, 15 to 20 minutes or to desired thickness. Stir in remaining ingredients.

Roasted Turkey Gravy

Makes about 3 cups
Hands-on Time: 17 min. **Total Time:** 17 min.

- ¼ cup butter
- ¼ cup all-purpose flour
- 2½ cups chicken broth
- ½ cup pan drippings
- ¼ tsp. poultry seasoning
- ⅛ tsp. freshly ground pepper

1. Melt butter in a skillet over medium heat; whisk in flour, and cook, whisking constantly, 1 to 2 minutes or until golden and smooth. Gradually whisk in chicken broth and pan drippings; increase heat to medium-high, and bring to a boil. Reduce heat to medium, and simmer, stirring occasionally, 5 minutes or to desired thickness. Stir in remaining ingredients.

make ahead

Make-Ahead Turkey Gravy

To make ahead, cool gravy 45 minutes. Cover and chill up to 3 days. To serve, add a few tablespoons of broth, and reheat over medium heat.

Makes 4 cups
Hands-on Time: 37 min. **Total Time:** 1 hr., 52 min.

2¼	lb. turkey drumsticks
3	carrots, cut into pieces
1	large onion, quartered
6	fresh parsley sprigs
⅓	cup vegetable oil
½	cup all-purpose flour
6	cups low-sodium chicken broth
½	tsp. pepper
Salt to taste	

1. Preheat oven to 400°. Pat drumsticks dry. Cook drumsticks and next 3 ingredients in hot oil in a large roasting pan over medium-high heat. Cook drumsticks 3 minutes on each side; cook vegetables at the same time, stirring often.

2. Bake drumsticks and vegetables in roasting pan at 400° for 30 minutes or until a meat thermometer inserted into thickest portion of drumsticks registers 160°. Remove from oven. Remove and discard vegetables and parsley using a slotted spoon, leaving drippings in pan. Reserve drumsticks for another use.

3. Whisk flour into hot drippings in pan, and cook over medium heat, whisking constantly, 1 minute. Gradually whisk in chicken broth until smooth. Whisk in pepper.

4. Bring to a boil over medium-high heat, whisking occasionally. Reduce heat to medium, and gently boil, whisking occasionally, 45 minutes or until thick enough to coat the back of a spoon. Season with salt to taste.

Make-Ahead Turkey Gravy

step-by-step

1. Brown drumsticks and veggies.

2. Reserve flavorful pan drippings.

3. Whisk in chicken broth, and stir until smooth.

4. Cook gravy to thicken and develop flavor.

SUPERB SIDE
kicks

Tee's Corn Pudding

Tee's Corn Pudding

This classic recipe has a rich, soufflé-like texture without the hassle. The result is an impressive holiday side dish the entire family will love.

Makes 8 servings
Hands-on Time: 25 min. **Total Time:** 1 hr., 10 min.

12	to 13 ears fresh corn, husks removed
¼	cup sugar
3	Tbsp. all-purpose flour
2	tsp. baking powder
1½	tsp. salt
6	large eggs
2	cups whipping cream
½	cup butter, melted

1. Preheat oven to 350°. Cut kernels from cobs into a large bowl (about 6 cups). Scrape milk and remaining pulp from cobs; discard cobs.
2. Combine sugar and next 3 ingredients. Whisk together eggs, whipping cream, and sugar mixture, whisking until smooth; stir in corn. Pour mixture into a lightly greased 13- x 9-inch baking dish.
3. Bake at 350° for 40 to 45 minutes or until set. Let stand 5 minutes.

Parmesan Corn Pudding

Makes: 8 servings
Hands-on Time: 15 min. **Total Time:** 55 min.

- 2 (12-oz.) packages frozen white shoepeg corn, thawed and divided
- ⅓ cup sugar
- ¼ cup all-purpose flour
- 2 Tbsp. plain yellow cornmeal
- ½ tsp. salt
- 6 Tbsp. butter, melted
- 1½ cups milk
- 4 large eggs
- 2 Tbsp. chopped fresh chives
- ½ cup (2 oz.) shredded Parmesan cheese

Garnish: chopped fresh chives

1. Preheat oven to 350°. Place 1 package of corn and next 7 ingredients (in order listed) in a large food processor. Process corn mixture until smooth, stopping to scrape down sides as needed.

2. Transfer mixture to a large bowl; stir in chives and remaining corn. Pour mixture into a lightly greased 2-qt. baking dish; sprinkle with cheese.

3. Bake at 350° for 40 to 45 minutes or until set. Garnish, if desired.

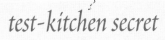

test-kitchen secret

Purée half of the frozen corn in the food processor to create a creamier texture and fresh, off-the-cob flavor.

Parmesan Corn Pudding

Orange-Ginger-Glazed Carrots

Ground ginger is more potent than fresh, so if you opt for the substitution, 1 tsp. will be plenty.

Makes 6 servings
Hands-on Time: 45 min. **Total Time:** 45 min.

- 1 (1-lb.) package baby carrots, thoroughly washed
- 1 tsp. grated orange rind
- ¼ cup fresh orange juice
- 2 tsp. butter
- 2 tsp. honey
- 1 to 3 tsp. freshly grated ginger*
- ¼ tsp. salt
- ⅛ tsp. pepper

1. Stir together all ingredients and 1 cup water in a medium saucepan over medium heat, and bring to a boil. Reduce heat, and simmer, stirring occasionally, 30 to 35 minutes or until liquid evaporates and carrots are glazed.

*1 tsp. ground ginger may be substituted.

Green Bean Casserole

Makes 10 servings
Hands-on Time: 15 min. **Total Time:** 4 hr., 45 min.

- 2 (16-oz.) packages frozen French-cut green beans, thawed
- 1 (10-oz.) container refrigerated Alfredo sauce
- 1 (8-oz.) can diced water chestnuts, drained
- 1 (6-oz.) jar sliced mushrooms, drained
- 1 cup (4 oz.) shredded Parmesan cheese
- ½ tsp. freshly ground pepper
- 1 (6-oz.) can French fried onions, divided
- ½ cup chopped pecans

1. Stir together first 6 ingredients and half of French fried onions; spoon green bean mixture into a lightly greased 4-qt. slow cooker.
2. Cover and cook on LOW 4½ hours or until bubbly.
3. Heat pecans and remaining half of French fried onions in a small nonstick skillet over medium-low heat, stirring often, 1 to 2 minutes or until toasted and fragrant; sprinkle over casserole just before serving.

Basic Green Bean Casserole

We found mixing Japanese breadcrumbs (panko) and French fried onions made for a crisp, less greasy topping. You can find panko with other breadcrumbs on the baking aisle or on the ethnic foods aisle. This dish is delightful with any simple grilled or roasted meat, poultry, or pork.

Makes 6 to 8 servings
Hands-on Time: 10 min. **Total Time:** 1 hr., 4 min., including sauce and green beans

Buttermilk White Sauce
Simple Blanched Green Beans (recipe on page 181)
- 1 cup French fried onions, crushed
- ½ cup Japanese breadcrumbs (panko)

1. Preheat oven to 350°. Stir together white sauce and green beans. Place mixture in a lightly greased 13- x 9-inch or 3-qt. baking dish.
2. Combine French fried onions and breadcrumbs. Sprinkle over green bean mixture. Bake at 350° for 25 to 30 minutes or until golden brown and bubbly. Serve immediately.

Note: We tested with French's French Fried Onions.

Green Bean Casserole

make ahead

Buttermilk White Sauce

Measure the flour as you would for baking by lightly spooning it into a measuring cup and leveling with the back of a knife. This will help you avoid a thick, paste-like sauce. Don't try to add both milk and buttermilk at one time—the sauce will curdle.

Makes about 2 cups
Hands-on Time: 15 min. **Total Time:** 15 min.

- 2 Tbsp. butter
- ¼ cup all-purpose flour
- 1½ cups milk
- ½ cup buttermilk
- 1 Tbsp. Ranch dressing mix
- ¼ tsp. salt
- ¼ tsp. pepper

1. Melt butter in a medium-size heavy saucepan over medium heat; whisk in flour until smooth. Cook 1 minute, whisking constantly. Gradually whisk in 1½ cups milk; cook over medium heat, whisking constantly, 3 to 4 minutes or until mixture is thickened and bubbly. Remove from heat, and whisk in buttermilk and remaining ingredients.

Note: Sauce can be made up to 2 days ahead. Prepare recipe as directed; cover and chill in an airtight container. Whisk in 2 Tbsp. milk, and microwave at HIGH 1 minute, stirring at 30-second intervals.

make ahead

Simple Blanched Green Beans

Makes 6 to 8 servings
Hands-on Time: 14 min. **Total Time:** 14 min.

1. Cook 1½ lb. fresh green beans, trimmed, in boiling salted water to cover 4 to 6 minutes or to desired degree of doneness; drain. Use immediately, or plunge into ice water to stop the cooking process; drain and pat dry. Store in a zip-top plastic bag in refrigerator up to 2 days.

Cheddar-Pecan Green Bean Casserole

We suggest you shred the Cheddar cheese yourself for smooth and even melting.

Makes 6 to 8 servings
Hands-on Time: 10 min. **Total Time:** 1 hr., 4 min., including sauce and green beans

    Buttermilk White Sauce
  1 cup finely chopped jarred roasted red bell peppers
  1 cup (4 oz.) freshly shredded sharp Cheddar cheese, divided
    Simple Blanched Green Beans
  1 cup French fried onions, crushed
  ½ cup Japanese breadcrumbs (panko)
  ½ cup chopped pecans

1. Preheat oven to 350°. Combine Buttermilk White Sauce, peppers, and ½ cup cheese in a large bowl; add green beans, tossing gently to combine. Place mixture in a lightly greased 13- x 9-inch or 3-qt. baking dish.

Cheddar-Pecan Green Bean Casserole

2. Combine French fried onions, Japanese breadcrumbs, chopped pecans, and remaining ½ cup cheese, and sprinkle over green bean mixture.
3. Bake at 350° for 25 to 30 minutes or until golden brown and bubbly. Serve immediately.

Simple Pecan–Green Bean Casserole: Omit shredded sharp Cheddar cheese. Preheat oven to 350°. Place French fried onions, Japanese breadcrumbs, and chopped pecans in an even layer in a 15- x 10-inch jelly-roll pan. Bake 8 to 10 minutes or until toasted, stirring after 5 minutes. Prepare Buttermilk White Sauce and Simple Blanched Green Beans as directed. (Do not plunge beans into ice water.) Gently toss together green beans and roasted red bell peppers, and spoon onto a serving platter. Top with Buttermilk White Sauce, and sprinkle with toasted pecan mixture. Makes 6 to 8 servings. Hands-on Time: 10 min.; Total Time: 49 min., including sauce and green beans.

Green Beans with
Mushrooms and Bacon

Green Beans with Mushrooms and Bacon

Makes 8 servings
Hands-on Time: 40 min. **Total Time:** 40 min.

2	lb. fresh haricots verts (tiny green beans)*
8	bacon slices
3	cups sliced shiitake mushrooms (about 7 oz.)
¼	cup chopped shallots
⅛	to ¼ tsp. dried crushed red pepper
½	tsp. freshly ground black pepper
¼	tsp. salt

1. Cook beans in boiling salted water to cover in a Dutch oven over medium-high heat 3 minutes or until crisp-tender; drain. Plunge into ice water to stop the cooking process; drain.
2. Cook bacon in a large skillet over medium-low heat 8 to 10 minutes or until crisp; remove bacon, and drain on paper towels, reserving 1½ Tbsp. drippings in skillet. Crumble bacon.

3. Sauté mushrooms and shallots in hot drippings over medium-high heat 5 minutes or until shallots are tender. Add green beans and crushed red pepper; sauté 1 to 2 minutes or until thoroughly heated. Stir in crumbled bacon, black pepper, and salt.

*Snap (or string) beans may be substituted. Increase cook time in Step 1 to 4 to 5 minutes.

Asparagus with Mushrooms and Bacon:
Substitute 2 lb. fresh asparagus for haricots verts. Snap off and discard tough ends of asparagus. Cut asparagus into 1½ -inch pieces. Proceed with recipe as directed, cooking asparagus pieces 2 to 4 minutes in Step 1.

Sugar Snaps with Mushrooms and Bacon:
Substitute 1½ lb. sugar snap peas, trimmed, for haricots verts. Proceed with recipe as directed, cooking sugar snaps 4 minutes in Step 1.

Roasted Haricots Verts with Creole Mustard Sauce

Makes 8 servings
Hands-on Time: 23 min. **Total Time:** 37 min.

  4 (8-oz.) packages trimmed haricots verts
  2 Tbsp. olive oil
  ¼ tsp. fresh ground pepper
  3 garlic cloves, thinly sliced
  4 bacon slices
  ⅔ cup chopped onion
  2 garlic cloves, minced
1½ Tbsp. chopped fresh thyme
1½ cups chicken broth
  2 Tbsp. Creole mustard
  1 Tbsp. sherry vinegar

1. Preheat oven to 475°. Toss together first 4 ingredients in a bowl until beans are coated. Spread beans in a single layer in 2 large rimmed baking sheets. Bake at 475° for 14 minutes or until browned. Meanwhile, cook bacon in a skillet over medium heat 7 to 8 minutes or until crisp; remove bacon, and drain on paper towels, reserving drippings in skillet. Crumble bacon.
2. Sauté onion and garlic in hot drippings 4 minutes or until onion is tender; stir in thyme and broth. Bring to a boil over medium-high heat; boil 5 minutes or until liquid is reduced to 1 cup. Stir in mustard and vinegar; cook 4 minutes or until liquid almost evaporates.
3. Place beans in a large bowl. Pour the sauce over the beans, tossing to coat. Sprinkle with bacon. Serve hot.

Sweet Onion Pudding

Makes 10 servings
Hands-on Time: 55 min. **Total Time:** 4 hr., 55 min.

  ½ cup butter
  6 medium-size sweet onions, thinly sliced
  6 large eggs, lightly beaten
  2 cups whipping cream
  1 cup (4 oz.) shredded Parmesan cheese
  3 Tbsp. all-purpose flour
  2 Tbsp. sugar
  2 tsp. baking powder
  1 tsp. salt
  2 cups soft, fresh breadcrumbs

1. Melt butter in a large skillet over medium heat; add onions. Cook, stirring often, 30 to 40 minutes or until caramel colored; remove from heat.
2. Whisk together eggs, cream, and Parmesan cheese in a large bowl. In a separate bowl, combine flour and next 3 ingredients; gradually whisk into egg mixture until blended. Stir onions and breadcrumbs into egg mixture; spoon into a lightly greased 6-qt. slow cooker.
3. Cover and cook on LOW 4 to 5 hours or until center is set and edges are golden brown.

Note: Onions can be cooked up to 2 days ahead. Cover and chill until ready to assemble pudding.

Maple–Sweet Potato Cups

Swing by the freezer section for one of our favorite convenience items—frozen sweet potatoes. If you want to skip the meringue in Step 2, top with miniature marshmallows instead. (Pictured on page 102)

Makes 8 servings
Hands-on Time: 15 min. **Total Time:** 25 min.

  2 (24-oz.) packages frozen steam-and-mash sweet potatoes
  ⅓ cup butter, cut up
  ⅓ cup firmly packed light brown sugar
  ⅓ cup pure maple syrup
  3 tsp. orange zest
  1 tsp. salt
  4 egg whites
  ½ cup granulated sugar

1. Preheat oven to 400°. Steam potatoes according to package directions. Mash together sweet potatoes and next 5 ingredients. Spoon mixture into 8 (6-oz.) custard cups. Place on a baking sheet.
2. Beat egg whites at high speed with an electric mixer until foamy. Add sugar, 1 Tbsp. at a time, beating until stiff peaks form and sugar is dissolved. Spread meringue over sweet potato mixture.
3. Bake at 400° for 10 minutes or until golden brown.

Note: We tested with Ore-Ida Steam n' Mash Cut Sweet Potatoes.

Classic Sweet Potato Casserole

Classic Sweet Potato Casserole

This mouthwatering casserole will satisfy lovers of crunchy pecans and cornflakes as well as marshmallows.

Makes 6 to 8 servings
Hands-on Time: 20 min. **Total Time:** 2 hr., 40 min.

4½   lb. sweet potatoes
1   cup granulated sugar
½   cup butter, softened
¼   cup milk
2   large eggs
1   tsp. vanilla extract
¼   tsp. salt
1¼   cups cornflakes cereal, crushed
¼   cup chopped pecans
1   Tbsp. brown sugar
1   Tbsp. butter, melted
1½   cups miniature marshmallows

1. Preheat oven to 400°. Bake sweet potatoes for 1 hour or until tender. Let stand until cool to touch (about 20 minutes); peel and mash sweet potatoes. Reduce oven temperature to 350°.
2. Beat mashed sweet potatoes, granulated sugar, and next 5 ingredients at medium speed with an electric mixer until smooth. Spoon potato mixture into a greased 11- x 7-inch baking dish.
3. Combine cornflakes cereal and next 3 ingredients in a small bowl. Sprinkle over casserole in diagonal rows 2 inches apart.
4. Bake at 350° for 30 minutes. Remove from oven; let stand 10 minutes. Sprinkle marshmallows in alternate rows between cornflake mixture; bake 10 more minutes. Let stand 10 minutes before serving.

Apple-Pecan-Stuffed Sweet Potatoes

Makes 8 servings
Hands-on Time: 32 min. **Total Time:** 2 hr., 2 min.

4   medium-size sweet potatoes (3½ lb.)
¾   cup coarsely chopped pecans
¼   cup butter
1   large Rome Beauty apple, chopped
¼   cup golden raisins
½   cup firmly packed brown sugar
½   tsp. ground cinnamon
¼   tsp. ground nutmeg

1. Preheat oven to 425°. Place potatoes on an aluminum foil–lined baking sheet. Bake 1 hour and 15 minutes or until tender.
2. Heat nuts in a nonstick skillet over medium-low heat, stirring often, 5 to 7 minutes or until toasted. Remove nuts from skillet.
3. Melt butter in skillet over medium-high heat. Add apple and raisins; sauté 2 to 3 minutes or until apple is tender. Stir in brown sugar, cinnamon, and nutmeg. Remove from heat.
4. Cut potatoes in half lengthwise; scoop pulp into a large bowl, leaving shells intact. Add apple mixture to pulp in bowl; stir until blended. Spoon mixture into shells. Place on baking sheet.
5. Bake at 350° for 15 to 20 minutes or until thoroughly heated. Top with nuts.

Perfect Mashed Potatoes

Yukon gold potatoes yield a texture that's just right for holding a pool of flavorful gravy or melted butter.

Makes about 6 cups
Hands-on Time: 22 min. **Total Time:** 39 min.

3   lb. Yukon gold potatoes
2   tsp. salt, divided
⅓   cup butter
⅓   cup half-and-half
4   ounces cream cheese, softened
¾   tsp. coarsely ground pepper

1. Peel potatoes, and cut into 1-inch pieces. Bring potatoes, 1 tsp. salt, and cold water to cover to a boil in a medium-size Dutch oven over medium-high heat. Reduce heat to medium-low, and cook 16 to 20 minutes or until fork-tender; drain.
2. Return potatoes to Dutch oven. Cook until water evaporates and potatoes look dry. Mound potatoes on 1 side; add butter, next 3 ingredients, and remaining 1 tsp. salt to opposite side of Dutch oven. Cook 1 to 2 minutes or until butter is melted and mixture boils.
3. Remove from heat; beat potatoes at medium speed with a hand-held electric mixer 30 seconds to 1 minute or to desired degree of smoothness. (Do not over-beat.) Serve potatoes immediately.

Golden Potato and Leek Gratin

To test gratin for doneness, pierce potatoes with a long wooden pick. The gratin is ready when the pick slides easily through the potatoes.

Makes 6 to 8 servings
Hands-on Time: 35 min. **Total Time:** 1 hr., 10 min.

- 2   medium leeks
- 1   Tbsp. extra virgin olive oil
- 3   lb. Yukon gold potatoes, peeled and thinly sliced
- 1   (14-oz.) can vegetable broth
- 1   garlic clove, pressed
- ½   tsp. freshly ground pepper
- 1   (15-oz.) jar Creamy Alfredo Sauce
- ½   tsp. salt
- 1   cup (4 oz.) shredded Italian six-cheese blend

1. Preheat oven to 375°. Remove and discard root ends and dark green tops of leeks. Cut leeks into thin slices; rinse well, and drain.
2. Cook leeks in hot oil in a large skillet over medium heat, stirring often, 5 minutes or until lightly golden. Stir in potatoes and next 3 ingredients; cover and cook, stirring occasionally, 20 minutes or until potatoes are slightly tender. Drain potato mixture. Add Alfredo sauce and salt, gently stirring just until coated.
3. Spoon potato mixture into a lightly greased 11- x 7-inch baking dish; top with cheese.
4. Bake, covered, at 375° for 20 minutes; uncover and bake 15 more minutes or until potatoes are tender and cheese is lightly browned.

Potato Gratin with Rosemary Crust

This gratin pairs well with prime rib or beef tenderloin. Rosemary is a bossy herb that can take over a dish; use it sparingly. We call for only 1 Tbsp. to season the entire dish.

Makes: 10 servings
Hands-on Time: 45 min. **Total Time:** 2 hr., 20 min.

- 1   (14.1-oz.) package refrigerated piecrusts
- 1   Tbsp. chopped fresh rosemary
- ¼   tsp. freshly ground pepper
- 2   cups (8 oz.) shredded Gruyère cheese, divided
- 1½   lb. Yukon gold potatoes
- 1½   lb. sweet potatoes
- 1   tsp. kosher salt
- ⅔   cup heavy cream
- 1   garlic clove, minced
- Garnish: fresh rosemary sprigs

1. Preheat oven to 450°. Unroll piecrusts on a lightly floured surface. Sprinkle rosemary, pepper, and ½ cup cheese over 1 piecrust; top with remaining piecrust. Roll into a 13-inch circle. Press on bottom and up sides of a 9-inch springform pan; fold edges under. Chill.
2. While crust chills, peel and thinly slice Yukon gold and sweet potatoes.
3. Layer one-third each of Yukon gold potatoes, sweet potatoes, and salt in prepared crust. Sprinkle with ¼ cup cheese. Repeat layers twice, pressing layers down slightly to fit crust.
4. Microwave cream and garlic in a 1-cup microwave-safe measuring cup at HIGH 45 seconds; pour over potato layers in pan. Sprinkle with remaining ¾ cup cheese. Cover pan with heavy-duty aluminum foil. Place on a baking sheet.
5. Bake at 450° for 1 hour. Uncover and bake 25 more minutes or until potatoes are done and crust is richly browned. Let stand 10 to 15 minutes. Carefully transfer to a serving plate, and remove sides of pan. If desired, carefully slide gratin off bottom of pan using a long knife or narrow spatula. Garnish, if desired.

Potato Gratin with Rosemary Crust

1. Sandwich in the seasoning: Layer 2 refrigerated piecrusts with finely chopped rosemary, Gruyère, and a sprinkling of freshly ground pepper.

2. Take it to the top: Fit the crust into a springform pan, gently pressing and shaping dough over bottom and up sides. Tuck edges under, and chill.

3. Keep it slow and steady: Gradually add cream mixture, drizzling over sliced potato filling. Top with cheese, cover with foil, and slide into oven.

Two-Cheese Squash Casserole

Two-Cheese Squash Casserole

For a tasty and colorful twist, substitute sliced zucchini for half of the yellow squash.

Makes 10 to 12 servings
Hands-on Time: 25 min. **Total Time:** 1 hr., 8 min.

- 4 lb. yellow squash, sliced
- 1 large sweet onion, finely chopped
- 1 cup (4 oz.) shredded Cheddar cheese
- ½ cup chopped fresh chives
- 1 (8-oz.) container sour cream
- 1 tsp. garlic salt
- 1 tsp. freshly ground pepper
- 2 large eggs, lightly beaten
- 2½ cups soft, fresh breadcrumbs, divided
- 1¼ cups (5 oz.) freshly shredded Parmesan cheese, divided
- 2 Tbsp. butter, melted

1. Preheat oven to 350°. Cook yellow squash and onion in boiling water to cover in a Dutch oven 8 minutes or just until tender; drain squash mixture well.
2. Combine squash mixture, Cheddar cheese, next 5 ingredients, 1 cup breadcrumbs, and ¾ cup Parmesan cheese. Spoon into a lightly greased 13- x 9-inch baking dish.
3. Stir together melted butter and remaining 1½ cups breadcrumbs and ½ cup Parmesan cheese. Sprinkle breadcrumb mixture over top of casserole.
4. Bake at 350° for 35 to 40 minutes or until set.

Glazed Butternut Squash

Makes 4 servings
Hands-on Time: 45 min. **Total Time:** 45 min.

- 3 lb. butternut squash, peeled*
- ½ cup apple cider*
- ¼ cup water
- 2 Tbsp. butter
- 1 Tbsp. sugar
- 1 tsp. salt
- ½ tsp. pepper
- ¼ cup chopped toasted pecans
- 1 Tbsp. chopped fresh or 1 tsp. dried sage

1. Cut squash in half lengthwise; remove and discard seeds. Cut each half into 4 wedges; cut wedges into 2-inch pieces.
2. Stir together 3 lb. squash, ½ cup apple cider, and next 5 ingredients in a 12-inch, deep-sided, nonstick skillet over medium-high heat; bring to a boil. Cover, reduce heat, and simmer, gently stirring occasionally, 25 minutes. Uncover and cook 5 minutes or until liquid thickens and squash is tender. Gently stir in pecans and sage until well combined.

*3 lb. sweet potatoes may be substituted for butternut squash and ½ cup apple juice may be substituted for apple cider.

Creamed Turnip Greens

Don't miss this Southern spin on a steakhouse favorite.

Makes 4 servings
Hands-on Time: 25 min. **Total Time:** 25 min.

- 1 Tbsp. butter
- ½ sweet onion, chopped
- 2 garlic cloves, minced
- 1 (16-oz.) bag frozen turnip greens, thawed
- ½ cup chicken broth
- ½ tsp. dried crushed red pepper (optional)
- 2 Tbsp. all-purpose flour
- 1 cup milk
- 5 oz. cream cheese, cut into pieces
- Salt to taste
- Garnish: freshly shaved Parmesan cheese

1. Melt butter in a large nonstick skillet over medium-high heat. Stir in onion and garlic, and sauté 3 minutes or until tender. Stir in turnip greens, chicken broth, and, if desired, red pepper; cook 4 to 5 minutes or until liquid evaporates.
2. Sprinkle turnip green mixture with flour, and sauté mixture 2 minutes. Gradually stir in milk, and cook, stirring occasionally, 3 minutes. Add cream cheese, stirring until melted. Season with salt to taste. Garnish, if desired.

Lightened Creamed Turnip Greens: Substitute 2% milk and ⅓-less-fat cream cheese for milk and cream cheese. Proceed with recipe as directed.

Balsamic Root Vegetables

For a delicious twist, top with a sprinkling of cooked and crumbled bacon just before serving.

Makes 6 to 8 servings
Hands-on Time: 25 min. **Total Time:** 4 hr., 25 min.

1½ lb. sweet potatoes
1 lb. parsnips
1 lb. carrots
2 large red onions, coarsely chopped
¾ cup sweetened dried cranberries
1 Tbsp. light brown sugar
3 Tbsp. olive oil
2 Tbsp. balsamic vinegar
1 tsp. salt
½ tsp. freshly ground pepper
⅓ cup chopped fresh flat-leaf parsley

1. Peel first 3 ingredients, and cut into 1½-inch pieces. Combine parsnips, carrots, onions, and dried cranberries in a lightly greased 6-qt. slow cooker; layer sweet potatoes over top.
2. Whisk together sugar and next 4 ingredients in a small bowl; pour over vegetable mixture. (Do not stir.)
3. Cover and cook on HIGH 4 to 5 hours or until vegetables are tender. Toss with parsley just before serving.

party pointer

White plates and serving pieces are great for holiday entertaining. Add some holiday color with greenery, berries, and ornaments.

Balsamic Root Vegetables

Classic Baked Macaroni and Cheese

Classic Baked Macaroni and Cheese

Whisk warm milk into the flour mixture to ensure a lump-free sauce. We also recommend shredding your own cheese for a creamier texture.

Makes 6 to 8 servings
Hands-on Time: 22 min. **Total Time:** 42 min.

- 2   cups milk
- 2   Tbsp. butter
- 2   Tbsp. all-purpose flour
- ½   tsp. salt
- ¼   tsp. freshly ground black pepper
- 1   (10-oz.) block extra sharp Cheddar cheese, shredded and divided
- ¼   tsp. ground red pepper (optional)
- ½   (16-oz.) package elbow macaroni, cooked

1. Preheat oven to 400°. Microwave milk at HIGH for 1½ minutes. Melt butter in a large skillet or Dutch oven over medium-low heat; whisk in flour until smooth. Cook, whisking constantly, 1 minute.
2. Gradually whisk in warm milk, and cook, whisking constantly, 5 minutes or until thickened.
3. Whisk in salt, black pepper, 1 cup shredded cheese, and, if desired, red pepper until smooth; stir in pasta. Spoon pasta mixture into a lightly greased 2-qt. baking dish; top with remaining cheese. Bake at 400° for 20 minutes or until golden and bubbly.

Wild Rice Pilaf

Makes 8 to 10 servings
Hands-on Time: 15 min. **Total Time:** 4 hr.

- 1   cup uncooked brown rice
- 1   cup uncooked wild rice
- 2   Tbsp. butter, melted
- 1   (32-oz.) container chicken broth
- 1   cup diced sweet onion
- ¾   tsp. freshly ground pepper
- 1   (5.5-oz.) package dried cherries, coarsely chopped (about 1 cup)
- 1   cup coarsely chopped pecans

1. Stir together first 3 ingredients in a lightly greased 3-qt. slow cooker, stirring until rice is coated. Stir in chicken broth, onion, and pepper.
2. Cover and cook on HIGH 3½ to 4 hours or until rice is tender. Stir in cherries with a fork; turn off heat, cover, and let stand 15 minutes.
3. Meanwhile, heat pecans in a small nonstick skillet over medium-low heat, stirring often, 3 to 4 minutes or until toasted and fragrant. Stir into rice just before serving.

Fresh Fruit with Lemon-Mint Sauce

Makes 5 servings
Hands-on Time: 20 min. **Total Time:** 2 hr., 20 min.

- 3   large oranges, peeled and sectioned
- 2   large red grapefruits, peeled and sectioned
- 2   cups seedless red grapes, halved
- 2   Tbsp. chopped fresh mint
- 1   (6-oz.) container low-fat vanilla yogurt
- 1   tsp. grated lemon rind
- 2   Tbsp. fresh lemon juice
- 1   tsp. honey
- Garnish: fresh mint sprigs

1. Place first 4 ingredients in a medium bowl, gently tossing to combine. Cover and chill 2 hours.
2. Stir together yogurt and next 3 ingredients just before serving, and serve with fruit mixture. Garnish, if desired.

Kitchen-Express Fresh Fruit with Lemon-Mint Sauce: Substitute 2 (24-oz.) jars refrigerated orange-and-grapefruit salad mix, drained, for oranges and grapefruits.

Citrus-Walnut Salad

Citrus-Walnut Salad

Makes 8 servings
Hands-on Time: 15 min. **Total Time:** 31 min., including vinaigrette

- ½ cup walnut pieces
- 8 heads Belgian endive (about 2¼ lb.)
- ½ cup firmly packed fresh parsley leaves
- Cumin-Dijon Vinaigrette
- 2 red grapefruits, peeled and sectioned

1. Preheat oven to 350°. Bake walnuts in a single layer in a shallow pan 6 to 8 minutes or until toasted and fragrant, stirring halfway through.
2. Remove and discard outer leaves of endive heads. Rinse endive with cold water, and pat dry. Cut each endive head diagonally into ¼-inch-thick slices, and place in a serving bowl. Add walnuts, parsley leaves, and desired amount of dressing; gently toss to coat. Top with grapefruit. Serve with any remaining dressing.

Cumin-Dijon Vinaigrette

Makes ¾ cup
Hands-on Time: 10 min. **Total Time:** 10 min.

- ½ cup extra virgin olive oil
- 3 Tbsp. white wine vinegar
- 2 Tbsp. Dijon mustard
- ¼ tsp. ground cumin
- ¼ tsp. salt
- ¼ tsp. sugar

1. Whisk together all ingredients.

Spinach-Apple Salad with Maple-Cider Vinaigrette

test-kitchen secrets

What to do with all those citrus rinds?
- Put some down the disposal for a fresh scent.
- Freshen the air. Simmer in water with cloves and cinnamon.
- Use orange cups to serve mashed sweet potatoes or sorbet.
- Make citrus sugar. Combine 1½ tsp. coarsely grated citrus peel and ½ cup granulated sugar. Press peel with a spoon to release oils. Store in a container up to 1 month.

Spinach-Apple Salad with Maple-Cider Vinaigrette

This make-ahead salad is great for casual or fancy parties and is easy to tote to a neighborhood get-together.

Makes 8 servings
Hands-on Time: 20 min. **Total Time:** 50 min.

Sugared-Curried Pecans
- 1 (6-oz.) package pecan halves
- 2 Tbsp. butter, melted
- 3 Tbsp. sugar
- ¼ tsp. ground ginger
- ⅛ tsp. curry powder
- ⅛ tsp. kosher salt
- ⅛ tsp. ground red pepper

Maple-Cider Vinaigrette
- ⅓ cup cider vinegar
- 2 Tbsp. pure maple syrup
- 1 Tbsp. Dijon mustard
- ¼ tsp. kosher salt
- ¼ tsp. pepper
- ⅔ cup olive oil

Spinach-Apple Salad
- 1 (10-oz.) package fresh baby spinach, thoroughly washed
- 1 Gala apple, thinly sliced
- 1 small red onion, thinly sliced
- 1 (4-oz.) package crumbled goat cheese

1. Prepare pecans: Preheat oven to 350°. Toss pecans in butter. Stir together sugar and next 4 ingredients in a bowl; add pecans, tossing to coat. Spread in a single layer in a nonstick aluminum foil–lined pan. Bake 10 to 13 minutes or until lightly browned and toasted. Cool in pan on a wire rack 20 minutes; separate pecans with a fork.
2. Prepare vinaigrette: Whisk together cider vinegar and next 4 ingredients. Gradually whisk in oil until well blended.
3. Prepare salad: Combine spinach and next 3 ingredients in a bowl. Drizzle with desired amount of Maple-Cider Vinaigrette; toss to coat. Sprinkle with Sugared-Curried Pecans. Serve salad with any remaining vinaigrette.

Note: Pecans may be made up to 1 week ahead. Store in an airtight container. Vinaigrette may be made up to 3 days ahead. Cover and chill until ready to serve.

Green Salad with Orange Vinaigrette

Makes 4 servings
Hands-on Time: 10 min. **Total Time:** 15 min., including vinaigrette

- 1 head Bibb lettuce, torn
- 2 cups torn green leaf lettuce
- 2 green onions, chopped
- ¼ cup thinly sliced red onion
- Orange Vinaigrette

1. Combine first 4 ingredients in a large bowl. Drizzle with Orange Vinaigrette, and toss to coat.

Orange Vinaigrette

Makes about ½ cup
Hands-on Time: 5 min. **Total Time:** 5 min.

- 1 tsp. orange zest
- ¼ cup fresh orange juice
- 2 Tbsp. lemon juice
- 1 tsp. Dijon mustard
- ½ tsp. salt
- ¼ tsp. freshly ground pepper
- 6 Tbsp. olive oil

1. Whisk together first 6 ingredients. Gradually whisk in olive oil until well blended.

Grapefruit Vinaigrette: Omit orange zest and lemon juice. Substitute grapefruit juice for orange juice. Proceed as directed, whisking in 1 Tbsp. honey with grapefruit juice. Serve over green salad, grilled fish, baked chicken, or steamed green beans.

Winter Fruit Salad

Makes 8 servings
Hands-on Time: 30 min. **Total Time:** 1 hr., 30 min.

½   cup mayonnaise
2   Tbsp. honey
1   tsp. lemon zest
1½ Tbsp. fresh lemon juice
¼   tsp. ground ginger
Pinch of salt
1   large Braeburn apple, chopped
1   large Granny Smith apple, chopped
1   large pear, chopped
1½ (6-oz.) packages fresh baby spinach
4   thick-cut bacon slices, cooked and crumbled
⅓   cup honey-roasted flavored sliced almonds
⅓   cup sweetened dried cranberries

1. Whisk together first 6 ingredients in a medium bowl; reserve ¼ cup. Stir apples and pear into remaining mayonnaise mixture. Cover and chill 1 hour.
2. Place spinach on a serving platter or 8 individual serving plates. Spoon apple mixture over spinach; sprinkle with bacon, almonds, and dried cranberries. Serve immediately with reserved dressing.

Waldorf Salad with Savory Blue Cheesecakes

Makes 12 servings
Hands-on Time: 20 min. **Total Time:** 6 hr., 2 min., including cheesecakes

½   cup chopped walnuts
1   large Gala apple, diced
1   large Granny Smith apple, diced
2   Tbsp. fresh lemon juice
2   celery ribs, finely chopped
½   cup golden raisins
1   (11.5-oz.) bottle refrigerated blue cheese vinaigrette, divided
2   (5-oz.) packages spring mix
Savory Blue Cheesecakes

1. Preheat oven to 350°. Bake walnuts in a single layer in a shallow pan 5 to 7 minutes or until nuts are lightly toasted and fragrant.

2. Toss diced apples with lemon juice in a medium bowl; add walnuts, celery, raisins, and ½ cup vinaigrette, stirring to coat.
3. Divide greens among 12 salad plates; place 1 Savory Blue Cheesecake over greens on each plate. Spoon about ½ cup apple mixture over each cheesecake. Serve with remaining vinaigrette.

Note: We tested with Marie's Blue Cheese Vinaigrette.

Savory Blue Cheesecakes

Makes 12 servings
Hands-on Time: 10 min. **Total Time:** 5 hr., 35 min.

12 paper baking cups
Vegetable cooking spray
2   (8-oz.) packages cream cheese, softened
½   cup sour cream
1   (4-oz.) package crumbled blue cheese
1   Tbsp. all-purpose flour
½   tsp. dried parsley flakes
½   tsp. dried marjoram
¼   tsp. granulated garlic
2   large eggs

1. Preheat oven to 325°. Place 12 paper baking cups in a muffin pan, and coat with cooking spray.
2. Beat cream cheese and next 6 ingredients at medium speed with an electric mixer until well blended. Add eggs, 1 at a time, beating just until yellow disappears after each addition. Spoon cream cheese mixture into prepared baking cups, filling completely full.
3. Bake at 325° for 40 minutes or until set. Let cool in pan on a wire rack 15 minutes. Remove from pan to wire rack, and let cool completely (about 15 minutes). Cover and chill 4 hours. Freeze 15 to 30 minutes or until cheesecakes can be easily removed from baking cups. Remove and discard baking cups.

Waldorf Salad with Savory Blue Cheesecakes

Roasted Root Vegetable Salad

1. Preheat oven to 400°. Peel sweet potatoes, and cut into ¾-inch cubes. Peel parsnips, and cut into ½-inch slices. Peel beets, and cut into ½-inch-thick wedges.
2. Toss sweet potatoes and parsnips with 2 Tbsp. olive oil in a large bowl; place in a single layer in a lightly greased 15- x 10-inch jelly-roll pan. Sprinkle with 1¼ tsp. salt and ½ tsp. pepper.
3. Toss beets with remaining 1 Tbsp. olive oil; arrange coated beets in a single layer on a separate aluminum foil–lined 15- x 10-inch jelly-roll pan. Sprinkle with remaining ½ tsp. salt and ½ tsp. pepper.
4. Bake at 400° for 40 to 45 minutes or just until tender. Let cool completely (about 20 minutes).
5. Meanwhile, whisk together bottled dressing and next 3 ingredients. Place vegetables in a large bowl, and drizzle with desired amount of dressing; toss gently to coat. Serve at room temperature or chilled over arugula with any remaining dressing.

Roasted Root Vegetable Salad

Makes 6 servings
Hands-on Time: 30 min. **Total Time:** 1 hr., 30 min.

  2 large sweet potatoes (about 1 ½ lb.)
  4 large parsnips (about 1 lb.)
  6 medium beets (about 1½ lb.)
  3 Tbsp. olive oil, divided
1¾ tsp. salt, divided
  1 tsp. pepper, divided
  ½ cup bottled olive oil–and–vinegar dressing
  1 Tbsp. chopped fresh parsley
  1 Tbsp. horseradish
  1 tsp. Dijon mustard
     Fresh arugula

Roasted Sweet Potato Salad with Citrus Vinaigrette

Makes 4 servings
Hands-on Time: 20 min. **Total Time:** 1 hr., 10 min., including vinaigrette

  1 lb. medium-size sweet potatoes, peeled and cut into wedges
  1 medium-size sweet onion, cut into wedges
  1 Tbsp. olive oil
  1 garlic clove
  ¾ tsp. salt
  ½ tsp. freshly cracked pepper
  1 (5-oz.) package fresh mâche
     Citrus Vinaigrette

1. Preheat oven to 400°. Heat a 17- x 10-inch cast-iron pan or 12-inch cast-iron skillet in oven 10 minutes. Toss together sweet potato wedges and next 5 ingredients in a large bowl. Place sweet potato mixture in hot pan.
2. Bake at 400° for 25 minutes. Stir potatoes once, and bake 15 more minutes or until potatoes are tender and begin to caramelize.
3. Spoon potato mixture over fresh mâche; drizzle with Citrus Vinaigrette.

**Roasted Sweet Potato
Salad with Citrus Vinaigrette**

Citrus Vinaigrette

Makes about ½ cup
Hands-on Time: 10 min. **Total Time:** 10 min.

1 (½-inch) piece fresh ginger, peeled
2 Tbsp. red wine vinegar
1 Tbsp. chopped sweet onion
1 Tbsp. honey
1 tsp. orange zest
¼ tsp. dry mustard
¼ tsp. salt
¼ cup olive oil

1. Pulse first 7 ingredients in a blender or food processor until blended. With blender running, add olive oil in a slow, steady stream, processing until smooth. Pour through a fine wire-mesh strainer into a bowl; discard solids.

Green Salad with White Wine Vinaigrette

Makes: 6 to 8 servings
Hands-on Time: 15 min. **Total Time:** 20 min.

1 (8-oz.) package haricots verts (tiny green beans)
½ cup olive oil
¼ cup white wine vinegar
1 Tbsp. country-style Dijon mustard
½ tsp. salt
¼ tsp. pepper
½ (5-oz.) package fresh baby spinach
½ (5-oz.) package fresh arugula
2 cups torn Bibb lettuce
1 avocado, peeled and chopped
½ cup chopped fresh parsley
¼ cup chopped fresh tarragon
Garnishes: shaved Parmesan cheese, croutons

1. Cook green beans in boiling salted water to cover 4 to 5 minutes or until crisp-tender; drain. Plunge into ice water to stop the cooking process; drain.
2. Whisk together olive oil and next 4 ingredients.
3. Toss together spinach, next 5 ingredients, and green beans in a large bowl. Drizzle with olive oil mixture; toss gently to coat. Garnish, if desired. Serve immediately.

Lucky Black-eyed Pea Salad

Chubba Bubba's Broccoli Salad

Makes: 6 to 8 servings
Hands-on Time: 25 min. **Total Time:** 1 hr., 25 min.

½ (16-oz.) package bacon
1 (12-oz.) package broccoli florets, chopped
1 (10-oz.) package cauliflower florets, chopped
1 cup (4 oz.) shredded Cheddar cheese
½ cup finely chopped carrot
¼ cup finely chopped red onion
½ cup mayonnaise
1 Tbsp. sugar
2 Tbsp. red wine vinegar

1. Cook bacon in a large skillet over medium-high heat 10 to 12 minutes or until crisp; remove bacon, and drain on paper towels. Crumble bacon.
2. Cook broccoli and cauliflower in boiling salted water to cover 2 minutes or until crisp-tender; drain. Plunge into ice water to stop the cooking process; drain well. Place cauliflower and broccoli in a large bowl. Add cheese, carrot, and onion.
3. Stir together mayonnaise, sugar, and vinegar. Pour over cauliflower mixture; toss to coat. Top with bacon. Cover and chill 1 to 8 hours.

Panzanella Salad with Cornbread Croutons

Lucky Black-eyed Pea Salad

Makes: 6 servings
Hands-on Time: 20 min. **Total Time:** 10 hr., 5 min.

1 (16-oz.) package frozen black-eyed peas
¼ cup chopped fresh cilantro
¼ cup red pepper jelly
¼ cup red wine vinegar
2 Tbsp. olive oil
1 jalapeño pepper, seeded and minced
¾ tsp. salt
¼ tsp. freshly ground pepper
1 cup diced red bell pepper
⅓ cup diced red onion
2 large fresh peaches, peeled and diced
2 cups torn watercress

1. Prepare peas according to package directions, simmering only until al dente; drain and let cool 1 hour.
2. Whisk together cilantro and next 6 ingredients in a large bowl. Add cooked black-eyed peas, bell pepper, and onion, tossing to coat; cover and chill 8 hours. Stir peaches and watercress into pea mixture just before serving.

Panzanella Salad with Cornbread Croutons

Think cornbread salad with an Italian accent. A light, lemony vinaigrette replaces the traditional sour cream–and–mayo dressing.

Makes: 6 to 8 servings
Hands-on Time: 25 min. **Total Time:** 1 hr., 15 min., including cornbread

  Skillet Cornbread, cooled completely
  1 yellow bell pepper, diced
  1 small red onion, diced
  ½ cup olive oil, divided
  2 tsp. lemon zest
  ¼ cup fresh lemon juice
  ½ tsp. honey
  Salt and freshly ground pepper to taste
  1 pt. grape tomatoes, halved
  ½ English cucumber, quartered and sliced
  ½ cup pitted kalamata olives, halved
  ½ cup torn fresh basil leaves

1. Preheat oven to 400°. Cut cornbread into 1-inch cubes. Bake cubes in a single layer on a lightly greased jelly-roll pan 15 minutes or until edges are golden, stirring once.
2. Meanwhile, sauté bell pepper and onion in 1 Tbsp. hot olive oil in a small skillet over medium-high heat 5 minutes or until crisp-tender.
3. Whisk together lemon zest, lemon juice, honey, remaining 7 Tbsp. olive oil, and salt and pepper to taste in a large bowl; stir in onion mixture, tomatoes, and next 3 ingredients. Add toasted cornbread cubes, and toss to coat. Serve immediately.

Skillet Cornbread

This cornbread is a dead ringer for the cast-iron classic—minus the traditional skilletful of bacon drippings.

Makes: 8 servings
Hands-on Time: 10 min. **Total Time:** 35 min.

  2   tsp. canola oil
  1¾ cups self-rising white cornmeal mix
  2   cups nonfat buttermilk
  ¼   cup all-purpose flour
  2   Tbsp. butter, melted
  1   Tbsp. sugar

1. Preheat oven to 425°. Coat bottom and sides of a 10-inch cast-iron skillet with canola oil; heat skillet in oven 5 minutes. Meanwhile, whisk together next 5 ingredients. Pour batter into hot skillet. Bake 25 to 30 minutes until golden.

Roasted Baby Beet Salad

Trim the tops, but leave part of the stems to ensure the colorful pigment remains inside the beet during roasting.

Makes 6 servings
Hands-on Time: 20 min. **Total Time:** 1 hr., 35 min., including vinaigrette

  2   lb. assorted baby beets with tops
  1   Tbsp. olive oil
  Brown Sugar Vinaigrette
  5   cups loosely packed baby lettuces
  1   cup crumbled Gorgonzola cheese
  1   cup lightly salted roasted pecan halves

1. Preheat oven to 400°. Trim beet tops to ½ inch; gently wash beets. Place beets in a single layer in a shallow baking pan; drizzle with oil, tossing gently to coat. Cover pan tightly with aluminum foil.
2. Bake at 400° for 40 minutes or until tender. Transfer to a wire rack, and let cook 30 minutes.
3. Peel beets, and cut in half. Gently toss with ⅓ cup Brown Sugar Vinaigrette. Arrange lettuces on a serving platter. Top with beet mixture, Gorgonzola cheese, and pecans; serve with remaining Brown Sugar Vinaigrette.

Brown Sugar Vinaigrette

Makes ⅔ cup
Hands-on Time: 5 min. **Total Time:** 5 min.

  ⅓ cup white balsamic vinegar
  1 large shallot, minced
  2 Tbsp. light brown sugar
  ½ tsp. freshly ground pepper
  ½ tsp. vanilla extract
  ¼ tsp. salt
  ⅓ cup olive oil

1. Whisk together first 6 ingredients in a small bowl. Add olive oil in a slow, steady stream, whisking constantly until smooth.

Easy Orange Rolls

bountiful BREADS

editor's favorite

Easy Orange Rolls

Your family will definitely want to rise, shine, and dine when they smell these baking in the oven.

Makes 11 rolls
Hands-on Time: 15 min. **Total Time:** 40 min.

½ (8-oz.) package cream cheese, softened
¼ cup firmly packed light brown sugar
1½ tsp. orange zest
1 (11-oz.) can refrigerated French bread dough
2 Tbsp. granulated sugar
1 Tbsp. butter, melted
½ cup powdered sugar
1 Tbsp. orange juice

1. Preheat oven to 375°. Beat cream cheese, light brown sugar, and orange zest at medium speed with an electric mixer until smooth. Unroll French bread dough onto a lightly floured surface. Spread cream-cheese mixture over dough, leaving a ¼-inch border. Sprinkle with granulated sugar. Gently roll up dough, starting at 1 long side. Cut into 11 (1¼-inch) slices. Place slices, cut sides down, in a lightly greased 8-inch round cake pan. Brush top of dough with melted butter.
2. Bake at 375° for 25 to 30 minutes or until golden. Stir together powdered sugar and orange juice in a small bowl until smooth. Drizzle glaze over hot rolls. Serve immediately.

editor's favorite

Cinnamon Breakfast Rolls

Makes 32 rolls
Hands-on Time: 20 min. **Total Time:** 10 hr., 10 min.

1 (18.25-oz.) package French vanilla cake mix
5¼ cups all-purpose flour
2 (¼-oz.) envelopes active dry yeast
1 tsp. salt
2½ cups warm water (105° to 115°)
½ cup sugar
2 tsp. ground cinnamon
½ cup butter or margarine, divided and melted
½ cup raisins, divided
¾ cup chopped pecans, divided
1 cup powdered sugar
3 Tbsp. milk
½ tsp. vanilla extract

1. Stir together first 5 ingredients in a large bowl; cover dough, and let rise in a warm place (85°), free from drafts, 1 hour.
2. Combine ½ cup sugar and cinnamon. Set aside.
3. Turn dough out onto a well-floured surface; divide in half. Roll 1 portion into an 18- x 12-inch rectangle. Brush dough with half of butter; sprinkle with half of sugar mixture, half of raisins, and ¼ cup pecans.
4. Roll up dough starting at 1 long end; cut crosswise into 16 (1-inch-thick) slices. Place rolls, cut sides down, into a lightly greased 13- x 9-inch pan. Repeat procedure with remaining rectangle. Cover and chill 8 hours.
5. Remove from refrigerator, and let stand 30 minutes.
6. Preheat oven to 350°. Bake 20 to 25 minutes or until golden; cool slightly. Stir together powdered sugar, milk, and vanilla; drizzle over rolls. Sprinkle with remaining pecans. Serve immediately.

Cinnamon-Pecan Rolls

editor's favorite

Cinnamon-Pecan Rolls

Makes 12 rolls
Hands-on Time: 20 min. **Total Time:** 1 hr., 25 min.

- 1 cup chopped pecans
- 1 (16-oz.) package hot-roll mix
- ½ cup butter, softened
- 1 cup firmly packed light brown sugar
- 2 tsp. ground cinnamon
- 1 cup powdered sugar
- 2 Tbsp. milk
- 1 tsp. vanilla extract

1. Preheat oven to 350°. Bake pecans in a single layer in a shallow pan 5 to 7 minutes or until toasted and fragrant, stirring halfway through.

2. Prepare hot-roll dough as directed on back of package; let dough stand 5 minutes. Roll dough into a 15- x 10-inch rectangle; spread with softened butter. Stir together brown sugar and cinnamon; sprinkle over butter. Sprinkle pecans over brown sugar mixture. Roll up tightly, starting at 1 long end; cut into 12 slices. Place rolls, cut sides down, in a lightly greased 12-inch cast-iron skillet or 13- x 9-inch pan. Cover loosely with plastic wrap and a cloth towel; let rise in a warm place (85°), free from drafts, 30 minutes or until doubled in bulk.

3. Preheat oven to 375°. Uncover rolls, and bake for 20 to 25 minutes or until center rolls are golden brown and done. Let cool in pan on a wire rack 10 minutes. Stir together powdered sugar, milk, and vanilla; drizzle over rolls. Serve immediately.

make ahead • freezer friendly

Hurry-Up Homemade Crescent Rolls

Makes 1 dozen
Hands-on Time: 25 min. **Total Time:** 1 hr., 40 min.

- 1 (¼-oz.) envelope active dry yeast
- ¾ cup warm water (105° to 115°)
- 3 to 3½ cups all-purpose baking mix, divided
- 2 Tbsp. sugar
- All-purpose flour

1. Combine yeast and warm water in a 1-cup measuring cup; let stand 5 minutes. Combine 3 cups baking mix and sugar in a large bowl; gradually stir in yeast mixture.

2. Turn dough out onto a flat, floured surface, and knead, adding additional baking mix (up to ½ cup) as needed, until dough is smooth and elastic (about 10 minutes).

3. Roll dough into a 12-inch circle; cut flattened circle into 12 wedges. Roll up wedges, starting at wide end, to form a crescent shape; place, point sides down, on a lightly greased baking sheet. Cover and let rise in a warm place (85°), free from drafts, 1 hour or until doubled in bulk.

4. Preheat oven to 425°. Bake 10 to 12 minutes or until crescent rolls are golden.

Note: To make rolls in a heavy-duty electric stand mixer, prepare as directed in Step 1. Beat dough at medium speed, using dough hook attachment, about 5 minutes, beating in ½ cup additional baking mix, if needed, until dough leaves the sides of the bowl and pulls together, becoming soft and smooth. Proceed with recipe as directed in Step 3. We tested with Bisquick All-Purpose Baking Mix.

> *make-ahead tip*
>
> Rolls may be frozen up to 2 months. Bake at 425° for 5 minutes; cool completely (about 30 minutes). Wrap in aluminum foil, and freeze in an airtight container. Thaw at room temperature on a lightly greased baking sheet; bake at 425° for 7 to 8 minutes or until golden.

Refrigerator Yeast Rolls

Makes about 7 dozen
Hands-on Time: 45 min. **Total Time:** 9 hr., 48 min., including
Orange Butter

- 1 (¼-oz.) envelope active dry yeast
- 2 cups warm water (105° to 115°)
- 6 cups bread flour
- ½ cup sugar
- ½ tsp. salt
- ½ cup shortening
- 2 large eggs
- ½ cup butter, melted
- Orange Butter

1. Stir together yeast and warm water in a medium bowl;
let mixture stand 5 minutes.
2. Stir together flour, sugar, and salt in a large bowl. Cut
shortening into flour mixture with a pastry blender until
crumbly; stir in yeast mixture and eggs just until blended.
(Do not over-mix.) Cover and chill 8 hours.
3. Roll dough to ¼-inch thickness on a well-floured surface
(dough will be soft); cut with a 1½-inch round cutter, re-
rolling dough scraps as needed.
4. Brush rounds with melted butter. Make a crease across
each round with a knife, and fold rounds in half, gently
pressing edges together to seal. Place in a 15- x 10-inch
jelly-roll pan and a 9-inch round cake pan. (Edges of dough
should touch.) Cover and let rise in a warm place (85°), free
from drafts, 45 minutes or until doubled in bulk.
5. Preheat oven to 400°. Bake rolls 8 to 10 minutes or
until golden. Serve with Orange Butter.

Orange Butter

Feel free to shape your butter using butter molds. We used
3½-inch Christmas tree–shape molds. One recipe will make
four trees.

Makes ¾ cup
Hands-on Time: 5 min. **Total Time:** 5 min.

- ½ cup butter, softened
- ¼ cup orange marmalade

1. Stir together butter and marmalade until blended. Serve
immediately, or cover and chill until ready to serve. Store in
an airtight container in refrigerator up to 1 week.

**Hurry-Up Homemade
Crescent Rolls**

Refrigerator Yeast Rolls

**Easy Three-Seed
Pan Rolls**

Easy Three-Seed Pan Rolls

Makes 9 rolls
Hands-on Time: 10 min. **Total Time:** 3 hr., 25 min.

- 4   tsp. fennel seeds
- 4   tsp. poppy seeds
- 4   tsp. sesame seeds
- 9   frozen bread dough rolls
- 1   egg white, beaten
- Melted butter

1. Combine fennel, poppy, and sesame seeds in a small bowl. Dip dough rolls, 1 at a time, in egg white; roll in seed mixture. Arrange rolls, 1 inch apart, in a lightly greased 8-inch pan. Cover with lightly greased plastic wrap, and let rise in a warm place (85°), free from drafts, 3 to 4 hours or until doubled in bulk.

2. Preheat oven to 350°. Uncover rolls, and bake at 350° for 15 minutes or until golden. Brush with melted butter.

Note: We tested with Rhodes White Dinner Rolls for frozen bread dough rolls.

Three-Seed French Bread: Substitute 1 (11-oz.) can refrigerated French bread dough for frozen bread dough rolls. Combine seeds in a shallow dish. Brush dough loaf with egg white. Roll top and sides of dough loaf in seeds. Place, seam side down, on a baking sheet. Cut and bake dough loaf according to package directions.

test-kitchen secret

Worth the Splurge: The initial cost for these rolls is money well spent. You can make three scrumptious batches from the ingredients.

Jordan Rolls

This recipe comes from Christy Jordan's cookbook *Southern Plate*. Christy says the rolls are especially good with leftover ham because they make the best little sandwiches.

Makes 1½ dozen
Hands-on Time: 25 min. **Total Time:** 1 hr., 35 min.

- ½ cup sugar
- 2 (¼-oz.) envelopes rapid-rise yeast
- 1½ tsp. salt
- 5 cups all-purpose flour, divided
- ½ cup shortening
- 2 large eggs, lightly beaten
- 1½ cups warm water (110° to 120°)
- ¾ cup butter, melted and divided

1. Combine first 3 ingredients and 2 cups flour in a large bowl. Cut in shortening with a fork or pastry blender until crumbly. Stir in eggs. (Mixture will be lumpy and dry.) Stir in warm water, ½ cup melted butter, and remaining 3 cups flour until well blended. (Mixture will remain lumpy.) Cover dough with a kitchen towel, and let rise in a warm place (85°), free from drafts, 20 minutes. (Dough will rise only slightly.)

2. Turn dough out onto a floured surface. Sprinkle lightly with flour; knead 3 to 4 times. Pat or roll dough into a 13- x 9-inch rectangle (about ¾-inch thick). Cut dough into 18 rectangles using a pizza cutter. Place in a lightly greased 13- x 9-inch pan, and cover with towel. Let rise in a warm place (85°), free from drafts, 20 minutes.

3. Preheat oven to 350°. Bake rolls 25 minutes. Brush with remaining ¼ cup melted butter, and bake 5 more minutes or until golden.

Apple-Cheddar Muffins

The tart flavor of a Granny Smith apple mixes well with the extra-sharp Cheddar cheese for a melt-in-your mouth treat that's perfect for Christmas breakfasts, gift-giving, or an anytime snack.

Makes 12 servings
Hands-On Time: 16 min. **Total Time:** 45 min.

- 1 tbsp. butter
- 1 medium-size Granny Smith apple, peeled and chopped
- ½ cup chopped sweet onion
- 1 Tbsp. sugar
- 2⅓ cups all-purpose baking mix
- 1½ cups (6 oz.) shredded extra-sharp Cheddar cheese
- ¼ cup plain yellow cornmeal
- ¼ tsp. salt
- ¾ cup milk
- 2 large eggs
- ⅓ cup chopped pecans

1. Preheat oven to 425°. Melt butter in a small skillet over medium heat. Add chopped apple and next 2 ingredients; sauté 6 minutes or until onion is tender.

2. Combine baking mix and next 3 ingredients in a large bowl; make a well in center of mixture.

3. Whisk together milk and eggs; add to dry ingredients, stirring just until moistened. Stir apple mixture into batter. Spoon batter into 1 greased (12-cup) muffin pan, filling muffin cups two-thirds full. Sprinkle batter with ⅓ cup chopped pecans.

4. Bake at 425° for 14 minutes or until golden and a wooden pick inserted in center comes out with a few moist crumbs. Let cool in pan on a wire rack 5 minutes. Gently run a knife around edges of muffins to loosen. Remove muffins from pan to wire rack, and let cool 10 minutes. Serve warm.

Morning Glory Muffins

Makes about 1½ dozen
Hands-on Time: 20 min. **Total Time:** 43 min.

- ¼ cup milk
- ¼ cup vegetable oil
- 2 large eggs
- 1 (15.2-oz.) package cinnamon streusel muffin mix
- ½ tsp. ground cinnamon
- 1 (8-oz.) can crushed pineapple in juice
- ¾ cup grated peeled Granny Smith apple (about 1 small apple)
- ¾ cup shredded carrots
- ¾ cup chopped toasted pecans
- ½ cup raisins
- Paper baking cups
- Vegetable cooking spray
- 1 cup powdered sugar (optional)
- ½ tsp. grated lemon rind (optional)
- 1 to 2 Tbsp. fresh lemon juice (optional)

1. Whisk together first 3 ingredients until blended.
2. Remove and reserve streusel packet from muffin-mix package. Stir together contents of muffin-mix packet and cinnamon in a large bowl. Make a well in center of mixture. Add egg mixture, pineapple, and next 4 ingredients, stirring just until moistened.
3. Place baking cups in muffin pans. Spray with cooking spray. Spoon batter into baking cups, filling two-thirds full. Sprinkle evenly with reserved streusel packet.
4. Bake at 425° for 18 to 23 minutes or until golden. Cool in pans on wire racks 5 minutes. Remove from pans, and cool on wire racks.
5. Stir together powdered sugar, lemon rind, and lemon juice until smooth, and drizzle glaze over tops of muffins, if desired.

Morning Glory Muffins

Sweet Potato Biscuits

Makes 3 dozen
Hands-On Time: 20 min. **Total Time:** 32 min.

Baking the sweet potato in a hot oven for about 1 hour for these fluffy biscuits creates a sweet, caramelized flavor you won't get if you microwave it.

- ¾ cup cooked mashed sweet potato (about 1 medium)
- ½ cup butter, melted
- 3 Tbsp. light brown sugar
- ¼ tsp. ground cinnamon
- 2 cups all-purpose flour
- 2 tsp. baking powder
- 1 tsp. salt
- ½ tsp. baking soda
- ¾ cup buttermilk

1. Preheat oven to 400°. Combine sweet potato, butter, brown sugar, and cinnamon; beat at medium speed with an electric mixer until blended.
2. Combine flour, baking powder, and salt; stir well. Stir soda into buttermilk. Combine sweet potato mixture, flour mixture, and buttermilk mixture in a large bowl, stirring just until dry ingredients are moistened. Turn dough out onto a lightly floured surface, and knead gently 4 to 6 times.
3. Roll dough to ½-inch thickness; cut with a 1½-inch biscuit cutter. Place on ungreased baking sheets; bake at 400° for 12 to 15 minutes or until golden brown.

Best-Ever Scones

Makes: 8 servings
Hands-on Time: 15 min. **Total Time:** 33 min.

- 2 cups all-purpose flour
- ⅓ cup sugar
- 1 Tbsp. baking powder
- ½ tsp. salt
- ½ cup cold butter, cut into ½-inch cubes
- 1 cup whipping cream, divided
- Wax paper

1. Preheat oven to 450°. Stir together first 4 ingredients in a large bowl. Cut butter into flour mixture with a pastry blender until crumbly and mixture resembles small peas. Freeze 5 minutes. Add ¾ cup plus 2 Tbsp. cream, stirring just until dry ingredients are moistened.
2. Turn dough out onto wax paper; gently press or pat dough into a 7-inch round (dough will be crumbly). Cut round into 8 wedges. Place wedges 2 inches apart on a lightly greased baking sheet. Brush tops of wedges with remaining 2 Tbsp. cream just until moistened.
3. Bake at 450° for 13 to 15 minutes or until golden.

Chocolate-Cherry Scones: Stir in ¼ cup dried cherries, coarsely chopped, and 2 oz. coarsely chopped semisweet chocolate with the cream.

Apricot-Ginger Scones: Stir in ½ cup finely chopped dried apricots and 2 Tbsp. finely chopped crystallized ginger with the cream.

Cranberry-Pistachio Scones: Stir in ¼ cup sweetened dried cranberries and ¼ cup coarsely chopped roasted salted pistachios with the cream.

Brown Sugar-Pecan Scones: Substitute brown sugar for granulated sugar. Stir in ½ cup chopped toasted pecans with the cream.

Bacon, Cheddar, and Chive Scones: Omit sugar. Stir in ¾ cup (3 oz.) shredded sharp Cheddar cheese, ¼ cup finely chopped cooked bacon, 2 Tbsp. chopped fresh chives, and ½ tsp. freshly ground pepper with cream.

Ham-and-Swiss Scones: Omit sugar. Stir in ¾ cup (3 oz.) shredded Swiss cheese and ¾ cup finely chopped baked ham with cream.

Chocolate-Cherry Scones

Apricot-Ginger Scones

Cranberry-Pistachio Scones

Brown Sugar-Pecan Scones

test-kitchen secret

Scones are made with cream or milk and butter. Work quickly using cold butter, and keep the amount of mixing to a minimum for a flaky product.

Cream Cheese–Banana–Nut Bread

To get perfect slices, let the bread cool 30 minutes, and then cut with a serrated or electric knife. If desired, you can make a glaze by stirring together ½ cup powdered sugar, ½ tsp. orange zest, and 2 tbsp. fresh orange juice to drizzle over warm bread.

Makes 2 loaves
Hands-on Time: 15 min. **Total Time:** 2 hr., 7 min.

1¼	cups chopped pecans, divided
¼	cup butter, softened
1	(8-oz.) package ⅓-less-fat cream cheese, softened
1	cup sugar
2	large eggs
1½	cups whole wheat flour
1½	cups all-purpose flour
½	tsp. baking powder
½	tsp. baking soda
½	tsp. salt
1	cup buttermilk
1½	cups mashed very ripe bananas (1¼ lb. unpeeled bananas, about 4 medium)
½	tsp. vanilla extract

1. Preheat oven to 350°. Place ¾ cup chopped pecans in a single layer on a baking sheet, and bake 12 to 15 minutes or until toasted and fragrant, stirring after 6 minutes.
2. Beat butter and cream cheese at medium speed with an electric mixer until creamy. Gradually add sugar, beating until light and fluffy. Add eggs, 1 at a time, beating just until blended after each addition.
3. Combine whole wheat flour and next 4 ingredients; gradually add to butter mixture alternately with buttermilk, beginning and ending with flour mixture. Beat at low speed just until blended after each addition. Stir in bananas, ¾ cup toasted pecans, and vanilla. Spoon batter into 2 greased and floured 8- x 4-inch loaf pans. Sprinkle with remaining ½ cup pecans.
4. Bake at 350° for 1 hour or until a long wooden pick inserted in center comes out clean and sides of bread pull away from pan, shielding with aluminum foil during last 15 minutes to prevent excessive browning, if necessary. Cool bread in pans on wire racks 10 minutes. Remove from pans to wire racks. Let cool 30 minutes.

Cream Cheese–Banana–Nut Bread

make-ahead tip
To make ahead, proceed with recipe as directed through Step 4. Cool loaves completely, and tightly wrap with plastic wrap. Wrap again with aluminum foil. Freeze up to 1 month.

Praline-Apple Bread

Sour cream is the secret to the rich, moist texture of this bread. There's no butter or oil in the velvety batter—only in the glaze.

Makes 1 loaf
Hands-on Time: 25 min. **Total Time:** 2 hr., 41 min.

1½	cups chopped pecans, divided
1	(8-oz.) container sour cream
1	cup granulated sugar
2	large eggs
1	Tbsp. vanilla extract
2	cups all-purpose flour
2	tsp. baking powder
½	tsp. baking soda
½	tsp. salt
1½	cups finely chopped, peeled Granny Smith apples (about ¾ lb.)
½	cup butter
½	cup firmly packed light brown sugar

1. Preheat oven to 350°. Bake ½ cup pecans in a single layer in a shallow pan 6 to 8 minutes or until toasted and fragrant, stirring after 4 minutes.
2. Beat sour cream and next 3 ingredients at low speed with an electric mixer 2 minutes or until blended.
3. Stir together flour and next 3 ingredients. Add to sour cream mixture, beating just until blended. Stir in apples and ½ cup toasted pecans. Spoon batter into a greased and floured 9- x 5-inch loaf pan. Sprinkle with remaining 1 cup chopped pecans; lightly press pecans into batter.
4. Bake at 350° for 1 hour to 1 hour and 5 minutes or until a wooden pick inserted into center comes out clean, shielding with aluminum foil after 50 minutes to prevent excessive browning. Cool in pan on a wire rack 10 minutes; remove from pan to wire rack.
5. Bring butter and brown sugar to a boil in a 1-qt. heavy saucepan over medium heat, stirring constantly; boil 1 minute. Remove from heat, and spoon over top of bread; let cool completely (about 1 hour).

Note: To freeze, cool bread completely, and wrap in plastic wrap and aluminum foil. Freeze up to 3 months. Thaw at room temperature.

Praline-Apple Bread

Pam's Country Crust Bread

This top-rated bread has a tender crumb and soft crust.

Makes 2 loaves
Hands-on Time: 25 min. **Total Time:** 3 hr., 50 min.

2	(¼-oz.) envelopes active dry yeast
2	cups warm water (105° to 115°)
½	cup sugar, divided
2	large eggs
¼	cup vegetable oil
1	Tbsp. salt
1	Tbsp. lemon juice
6	to 6½ cups bread flour, divided
1	Tbsp. vegetable oil
1½	Tbsp. butter, melted

1. Combine yeast, warm water, and 2 tsp. sugar in bowl of a heavy-duty electric stand mixer; let stand 5 minutes. Stir in eggs, next 3 ingredients, 3 cups flour, and remaining sugar. Beat dough at medium speed, using paddle attachment, until smooth. Gradually beat in remaining 3 to 3½ cups flour until a soft dough forms.

2. Turn dough out onto a well-floured, flat surface, and knead until smooth and elastic (about 8 to 10 minutes), sprinkling surface with flour as needed. Place dough in a lightly greased large bowl, turning to grease top. Cover and let rise in a warm place (85°), free from drafts, about 1 hour or until doubled in bulk.

3. Punch dough down; turn out onto a lightly floured, flat surface. Divide dough in half. Roll each dough half into an 18- x 9-inch rectangle. Starting at 1 short end, tightly roll up each rectangle, jelly-roll fashion, pressing to seal edges as you roll. Pinch ends of dough to seal, and tuck ends under dough. Place each dough roll, seam side down, in a lightly greased 9- x 5-inch loaf pan. Brush tops with oil. Cover and let rise in a warm place (85º), free from drafts, 1 hour or until doubled in bulk.

4. Preheat oven to 375°. Bake 25 to 30 minutes or until loaves are deep golden brown and sound hollow when tapped. Remove from pans to a wire rack, and brush loaves with melted butter. Let cool completely (about 1 hour).

Country Crust Wheat Bread: Substitute 3 cups wheat flour for 3 cups bread flour.

Country Crust Cheese Bread: Sprinkle 1 cup (4 oz.) freshly shredded sharp Cheddar cheese onto each dough rectangle before rolling up.

Southern Soda Bread

Makes 2 loaves
Hands-on Time: 15 min. **Total Time:** 2 hr., 40 min.

4½	cups all-purpose flour
⅔	cup sugar
4½	tsp. baking powder
1½	tsp. baking soda
1½	tsp. salt
3	cups buttermilk
3	large eggs, lightly beaten
4½	Tbsp. butter, melted

1. Preheat oven to 350°. Whisk together first 5 ingredients in a large bowl. Make a well in center of dry mixture. Add buttermilk, eggs, and butter, whisking just until thoroughly blended. (Batter should be almost smooth.) Pour batter into 2 lightly greased 8½- x 4½-inch loaf pans.
2. Bake at 350° for 45 minutes. Rotate pans in oven, and shield with aluminum foil. Bake 30 to 35 minutes more or until a long wooden pick inserted in center comes out clean. Cool in pans on a wire rack 10 minutes. Carefully run a knife along edges of bread to loosen from pans. Remove from pans to wire rack, and cool completely (about 1 hour).

Southern Soda Bread

Watts Grocery Spoon Bread

Makes 8 servings
Hands-on Time: 25 min. **Total Time:** 1 hr., 15 min.

1	Tbsp. butter, softened
1¼	cups plus 2 Tbsp. plain white cornmeal
¾	cup all-purpose flour
2	Tbsp. sugar
2	tsp. salt
2	Tbsp. butter
4	large eggs
1	cup buttermilk
1	cup whipping cream
2	tsp. baking soda
1	tsp. chopped fresh thyme
⅛	to ¼ tsp. ground red pepper

1. Preheat oven to 375°. Grease a 2½-qt. soufflé dish with 1 Tbsp. butter. Dust with cornmeal. (Tap dish lightly to remove excess cornmeal.)
2. Combine 1¼ cups cornmeal and next 3 ingredients in a large bowl; make a well in center of mixture.
3. Bring 3 cups water to a boil in a saucepan over medium-high heat. Remove from heat, and whisk into cornmeal mixture, whisking until smooth. Add butter, whisking until butter is melted. Cool 5 minutes.
4. Whisk together eggs and next 5 ingredients; whisk into cornmeal mixture. Pour cornmeal mixture into prepared baking dish.
5. Bake at 375° for 45 to 50 minutes or until golden brown and center is almost set. Serve immediately.

party pointer

Spoon bread is perfect for holiday entertaining because it's surprisingly easy to make; just be sure to start with plain cornmeal, not a mix, which may contain baking soda. This soufflé-like dish invites a host of accompaniments—our favorite being any braised meat smothered in gravy, especially when flavored with smoked bacon drippings. The bread's great for breakfast, lunch, or dinner.

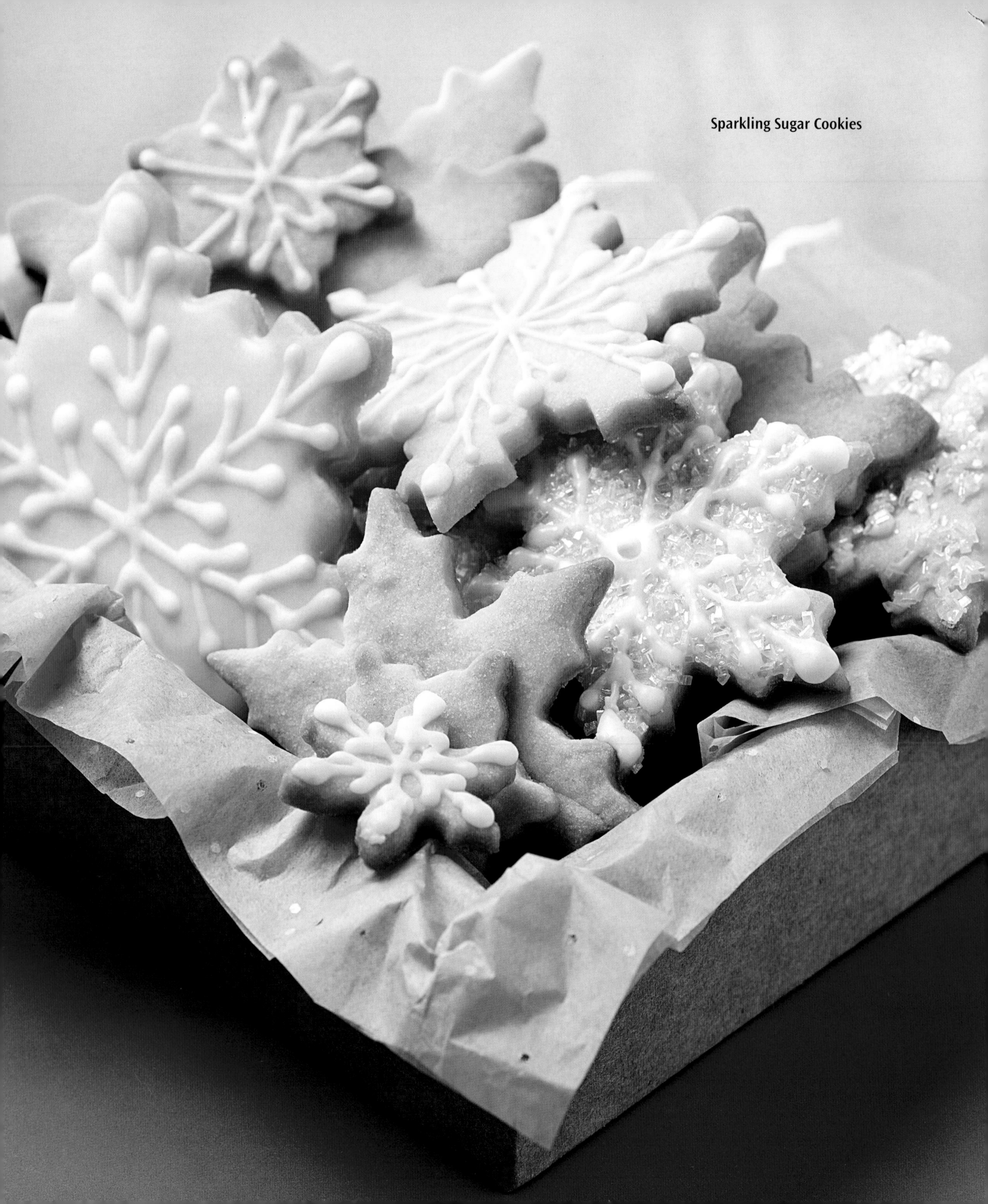

Sparkling Sugar Cookies

SUGAR *and spice*

Sparkling Sugar Cookies

Your yield will vary greatly depending on the size cookies you make. We tested a range of 1½ to 4¾ inches. The bake time remained the same for all sizes.

Makes 2 to 18 dozen
Hands-On Time: 1 hr. **Total Time:** 2 hr., 33 min., including glaze and icing

- 1   cup butter, softened
- 1   cup granulated sugar
- 1   large egg
- 1   tsp. vanilla extract
- 3   cups all-purpose flour
- ⅛   tsp. salt
- Parchment paper
- Sparkling sugar, white sprinkles or candies
- Simple Glaze
- Royal Icing

1. Beat butter at medium speed with an electric mixer until creamy; gradually add sugar, beating well. Add egg and vanilla, beating until blended.
2. Combine flour and salt; gradually add to butter mixture, beating until blended. Cover and chill 1 hour or until dough is firm.
3. Preheat oven to 350°. Divide cookie dough in half; roll each portion to ⅛-inch thickness on a lightly floured surface. Cut dough into assorted shapes with floured 1½- to 4¾-inch cutters; place on parchment paper-lined baking sheets.
4. Bake at 350° for 12 to 14 minutes or until cookies are lightly browned. Cool on baking sheets 1 minute; transfer to wire racks, and cool completely (about 20 minutes).
5. Decorate cookies as desired using sparkling sugar, white sprinkles or candies, Simple Glaze, and Royal Icing. Place on parchment paper, and let stand until glaze is set.

Simple Glaze

Makes about 1 cup
Hands-on Tme: 5 min. **Total Time:** 5 min.

- 1   (16-oz.) package powdered sugar
- 4   to 6 Tbsp. hot water
- Optional: food coloring paste

1. Stir together powdered sugar and hot water until smooth. Stir in food coloring paste, if desired.

Royal Icing

Makes about 1¾ cups
Hands-on Time: 5 min. **Total Time:** 5 min.

- 3   cups powdered sugar
- 2   Tbsp. meringue powder
- ¼   cup cold water

1. Beat all ingredients at high speed with a heavy-duty electric stand mixer, using a whisk attachment, until glossy, stiff peaks form. Place a damp cloth directly on surface of icing (to prevent a crust from forming) while icing cookies.

Note: Purchase meringue powder at cake-supply and crafts stores or supercenters.

Reindeer Gingersnaps

Reindeer Gingersnaps

Makes 16 cookies
Hands-on Time: 45 min. **Total Time:** 25 hr., 23 min., including drying time

1 (14.5-oz.) package gingerbread mix
Parchment paper
1 tsp. meringue powder
½ tsp. hot water
1 (12-oz.) container ready-to-spread fluffy white frosting
Decorations: 32 miniature candy canes, 32 licorice candies, 16 sour cherry candies

1. Preheat oven to 375°. Prepare gingerbread dough according to package instructions for gingersnap cookies.
2. Roll dough out on a lightly floured surface, and cut into 3½-inch ovals, using an egg-shaped or oval cookie cutter. Place 2 inches apart on parchment paper–lined baking sheets.

3. Bake at 375° for 8 to 10 minutes or until edges are lightly browned. Remove to wire racks, and let cool 30 minutes.
4. Stir together meringue powder and hot water until combined; stir in frosting. Spoon frosting mixture into a zip-top plastic freezer bag; snip off 1 corner of bag to make a small hole. Pipe 1 dot of frosting mixture at top of 1 cookie; press straight ends of 2 candy canes into piped dot to form antlers (prop up candy canes as needed). Pipe 2 large frosting ovals in center of cookie; press 1 licorice candy in each oval to form eyes. Pipe 1 dot of frosting at bottom of cookie; press 1 cherry candy in dot to form a nose. Repeat procedure with remaining cookies, frosting mixture, and candies. Let stand 24 hours to dry, if desired.

Note: We tested with Betty Crocker Gingerbread Cake & Cookie Mix and Betty Crocker Whipped Fluffy White Frosting.

Gingerbread Men

Easy Royal Icing dries rapidly. Work quickly, keeping extra icing covered tightly at all times.

Makes about 6½ dozen
Hands-on Time: 1 hr., 20 min. **Total Time:** 3 hr., 46 min., including icing

- 1 cup butter, softened
- 1 cup sugar
- 1½ tsp. baking soda
- 1 cup molasses
- 5 cups all-purpose flour
- 1½ Tbsp. ground ginger
- 1½ tsp. ground cinnamon
- ½ tsp. ground allspice
- ¼ tsp. salt
- Parchment paper
- Easy Royal Icing
- Red cinnamon candies

1. Beat butter and sugar at medium speed with an electric mixer until fluffy.
2. Stir together 1½ tsp. baking soda and ¼ cup water until dissolved; stir in molasses.
3. Combine flour and next 4 ingredients. Add to butter mixture alternately with molasses mixture, beginning and ending with flour mixture. Shape mixture into a ball; cover dough, and chill 1 hour.
4. Preheat oven to 350°. Roll dough to ¼-inch thickness on a lightly floured surface. Cut with a 2½-inch gingerbread man-shaped cutter. Place 2 inches apart on parchment paper–lined baking sheets.
5. Bake at 350° for 8 to 10 minutes or until edges are lightly browned. Let cool on baking sheets 5 minutes; transfer to wire racks, and let cool completely (about 20 minutes).
6. Spoon desired amount of Easy Royal Icing into a small zip-top plastic freezer bag. Snip 1 corner of bag to make a small hole. Pipe eyes, mouth, and buttons onto cookies. Top buttons with cinnamon candies.

Easy Royal Icing

Makes about 3 cups
Hands-on Time: 5 min. **Total Time:** 5 min.

- 1 (16-oz.) package powdered sugar
- 3 Tbsp. meringue powder
- 6 to 8 Tbsp. warm water

1. Beat powdered sugar, meringue powder, and 6 Tbsp. water at low speed with an electric mixer until blended. Beat at high speed 4 minutes or until stiff peaks form. Add remaining 2 Tbsp. water, ¼ tsp. at a time, to reach desired consistency.

Note: Purchase meringue powder at cake-supply and crafts stores or supercenters.

editor's favorite

Snowflake Shortbread

Makes about 7½ dozen
Hands-on Time: 25 min. **Total Time**: 1 hr., 42 min., including icing

- 1 cup butter, softened
- 1 cup powdered sugar
- 2 cups all-purpose flour
- ¼ tsp. salt
- Parchment paper
- Royal Icing (recipe on page 213)
- Sparkling sugar

1. Preheat oven to 325°. Beat butter at medium speed with a heavy-duty electric stand mixer until creamy. Gradually add powdered sugar, beating well.
2. Combine flour and salt; gradually add to butter mixture, beating until blended.
3. Roll dough to ⅛-inch thickness on a lightly floured surface. Cut with a 2-inch snowflake-shaped cutter, and place 1 inch apart on parchment paper-lined baking sheets.
4. Bake at 325° for 11 to 13 minutes or until edges are lightly browned. Cool on baking sheets 5 minutes. Transfer to wire racks, and cool completely (about 40 minutes). Decorate with Royal Icing, and sprinkle with sparkling sugar.

Snickerdoodles

Makes 4½ dozen
Hands-on Time: 20 min. **Total Time:** 1 hr., 28 min.

  1 cup butter, softened
  2 cups sugar
  2 large eggs
  ¼ cup milk
  1 tsp. vanilla extract
3¾ cups all-purpose flour
  1 tsp. baking powder
  2 tsp. ground cinnamon
  3 Tbsp. sugar
1½ Tbsp. ground cinnamon

1. Preheat oven to 375°. Beat butter at medium speed with an electric mixer until creamy. Gradually add 2 cups sugar, beating well. Add eggs, milk, and vanilla, beating well.
2. Combine flour, baking powder, and 2 tsp. cinnamon; gradually add to butter mixture, beating at low speed just until blended. (If desired, store dough in an airtight container in refrigerator up to 1 week.)
3. Combine 3 Tbsp. sugar and 1½ Tbsp. cinnamon in a small bowl. Roll cookie dough into 1¼-inch balls, and roll in sugar mixture. Place on ungreased baking sheets, and flatten slightly.
4. Bake at 375° for 11 to 13 minutes or until cookies are lightly browned. Cool on baking sheets 5 minutes. Transfer to wire racks, and cool completely (about 30 minutes).

test-kitchen secret

When baking many batches of cookies, spoon the dough onto sheets of parchment paper, assembly-line fashion. Then slide each batch onto a baking sheet when ready to bake. Using parchment paper eliminates the need to grease the baking sheets.

Blackberry Thumbprints

Makes about 5 dozen
Hands-on Time: 30 min. **Total Time:** 1 hr., 40 min.

  ½ cup slivered almonds
  1 cup butter, softened
  1 cup powdered sugar
  2 cups all-purpose flour
  ¼ tsp. salt
  ¼ tsp. ground cloves
  ¼ tsp. ground cinnamon
Parchment paper
  ½ cup seedless blackberry preserves

1. Preheat oven to 350°. Bake almonds in a single layer in a shallow pan 6 minutes or until toasted and fragrant, stirring halfway through. Cool almonds completely (about 20 minutes). Reduce oven temperature to 325°.
2. Process almonds in a food processor 30 seconds or until finely ground.
3. Beat butter at medium speed with a heavy-duty electric stand mixer until creamy. Gradually add 1 cup powdered sugar, beating well.
4. Combine flour, next 3 ingredients, and almonds; gradually add to butter mixture, beating until blended.
5. Shape dough into ¾-inch balls, and place 2 inches apart on parchment paper-lined baking sheets. Press thumb into each ball, forming an indentation.
6. Bake at 325° for 12 to 15 minutes or until cookie edges are lightly browned. Cool on baking sheets 2 minutes. Transfer to wire racks, and cool 30 minutes.
7. Place blackberry preserves in a zip-top plastic freezer bag; snip 1 corner of bag to make a small hole. Pipe preserves into indentations.

Almond Snowballs: Omit cloves, cinnamon, and preserves. Increase flour to 2½ cups. Prepare recipe as directed through Step 4, beating in 1 tsp. vanilla extract with butter and sugar. (Dough will be crumbly.) Shape and bake dough as directed, without making indentations. Cool on baking sheets 2 minutes. Transfer cookies to wire racks, and cool 10 minutes. Roll cookies in ½ cup powdered sugar. Makes about 5 dozen. Hands-on Time: 25 min.; Total Time: 1 hr., 30 min.

Peppermint-Pinwheel Cookies

These cookies are delicious eaten at room temperature, or chill them 30 minutes for a firm, cool filling.

Makes 4 dozen
Hands-On Time: 1 hr. **Total Time:** 6 hr., 33 min., including frosting

- ½ cup butter, softened
- 1 cup sugar
- 1 large egg
- ½ tsp. vanilla extract
- 1¾ cups all-purpose flour
- ½ tsp. baking soda
- ¼ tsp. salt
- ¾ tsp. red food coloring paste
- Parchment paper
- Peppermint Frosting

1. Beat butter at medium speed with a heavy-duty electric stand mixer until creamy; gradually add sugar, beating until light and fluffy. Add egg and vanilla, beating until blended, scraping bowl as needed.
2. Combine flour, baking soda, and salt; gradually add flour mixture to butter mixture, beating ingredients at low speed until blended.
3. Divide dough into 2 equal portions. Roll 1 portion of dough into a 12- x 8-inch rectangle on a piece of lightly floured plastic wrap.
4. Knead food coloring paste into remaining portion of dough while wearing rubber gloves. Roll tinted dough into a rectangle as directed in Step 3. Invert untinted dough onto tinted dough; peel off top piece of plastic wrap. Cut dough in half lengthwise, forming 2 (12- x 4-inch) rectangles. Roll up each rectangle, jelly roll-fashion, starting at 1 long side and using bottom piece of plastic wrap as a guide. Wrap in plastic wrap, and freeze 4 hours or up to 1 month. Preheat oven to 350°. Cut ends off each dough log, and discard. Cut dough into ¼-inch-thick pieces, and place on parchment paper-lined baking sheets.
5. Bake at 350° for 6 to 7 minutes or until puffed and set; cool cookies on baking sheets 5 minutes. Remove to wire racks, and cool completely (about 30 minutes).
6. Place Peppermint Frosting in a zip-top plastic freezer bag. Snip 1 corner of bag to make a small hole. Pipe about 2 tsp. frosting onto half of cookies; top with remaining cookies, gently pressing to form a sandwich.

Peppermint Frosting

Makes 1¾ cups
Hands-On Time: 10 min. **Total Time:** 10 min.

- ¼ cup butter, softened
- 1 (3-oz.) package cream cheese, softened
- 2 cups powdered sugar
- 1 Tbsp. milk
- ⅛ tsp. peppermint extract

1. Beat butter and cream cheese at medium speed with an electric mixer until creamy. Gradually add powdered sugar, beating at low speed until blended. Increase speed to medium, and gradually add milk and peppermint extract, beating until smooth.

test-kitchen secret

Avoid using tub butter products labeled spread, reduced-calorie, liquid, or soft-style. They contain less fat than regular butter and do not make satisfactory substitutes.

Peppermint-Pinwheel Cookies

Chocolate-Orange
Swirls

Pecan Crescents

Chocolate-Orange Swirls

Freshly grated rind accentuates the orange flavor in these memorable cookies.

Makes 2½ dozen
Hands-on Time: 25 min. **Total Time:** 2 hr., 45 min.

- 1 cup butter, softened
- 1 cup sugar
- 1 large egg
- 1 tsp. vanilla extract
- 3 cups all-purpose flour
- 1½ tsp. baking powder
- ¼ tsp. salt
- 1 tsp. orange zest
- 1½ tsp. orange extract
- 2 (1-oz.) semisweet chocolate baking squares, melted and cooled

1. Beat softened butter at medium speed with an electric mixer until creamy; gradually add sugar, beating well. Add egg and vanilla; beat well.
2. Combine flour, baking powder, and salt. Gradually add flour mixture to butter mixture, beating dough at low speed until blended.
3. Remove half of dough from bowl. Add orange zest and orange extract to dough in bowl, and beat well. Remove flavored dough from mixing bowl, and set aside. Return plain dough to mixing bowl; add melted chocolate, beating well. Cover and chill both portions of dough 1 hour.
4. Roll each half of dough to a 15- x 8-inch rectangle on floured wax paper. Invert orange dough onto top of chocolate dough; peel off top wax paper. Tightly roll dough, jelly-roll fashion, starting at short side and peeling wax paper from dough while rolling. Cover and chill 1 hour.
5. Preheat oven to 350°. Slice dough into ¼-inch-thick slices; place on ungreased baking sheets.
6. Bake at 350° for 10 to 12 minutes. Remove to wire racks to cool.

test-kitchen secret

To prevent flat-sided cookies, turn dough roll halfway through the second chilling time. Dental floss makes cutting the dough easier.

Pecan Crescents

These nutty cookies are much like traditional wedding cookies. Let your kids help roll the dough into logs and bend them into shape.

Makes about 5 dozen
Hands-on Time: 40 min. **Total Time:** 2 hr., 40 min.

    1   cup pecan halves, toasted
    1   cup butter, softened
    ¾   cup powdered sugar
    2   tsp. vanilla extract
    2½ cups sifted all-purpose flour
    2   cups powdered sugar

1. Pulse pecans in a food processor until coarse like sand.
2. Beat butter and ¾ cup powdered sugar at medium speed with an electric mixer until creamy. Stir in vanilla extract and ground pecans. Gradually add flour, beating until a soft dough forms. Cover and chill 1 hour.
3. Preheat oven to 350°. Divide dough into 5 portions; divide each portion into 12 pieces. Roll dough pieces into 2-inch logs, curving ends to form crescents. Place on ungreased baking sheets.
4. Bake at 350° for 10 to 12 minutes or until crescents are lightly browned. Cool on baking sheets 5 minutes. Roll warm cookies in 2 cups powdered sugar. Cool completely on wire racks, and roll cookies in remaining powdered sugar again after cooled.

test-kitchen secrets

· When rolling cookies, roll the dough between sheets of heavy-duty plastic wrap to prevent sticking or tearing.
· Place the rolling pin in the center of the dough, and roll outward with soft strokes.
· Coat hands with cooking spray before handling the dough to prevent it from sticking.
· Use a ruler or measuring spoon for the first few cookies to help you determine the right size; then you can judge the rest by eye.

Toasted Coconut Cookies

Take care to scoop equal amounts of dough each time so cookies will be about the same size. Allow 1 to 2 inches between balls of dough on the baking sheet so they won't run together as they bake.

Makes 4 dozen
Hands-on Time: 10 min. **Total Time:** 1 hr., 6 min.

    ¼   cup butter, softened
    ¼   cup shortening
    1   cup sugar
    1   large egg
    ½   tsp. coconut extract
    1½ cups all-purpose flour
    1   tsp. baking powder
    ½   tsp. baking soda
    ½   tsp. salt
    1   cup sweetened flaked coconut
    ½   cup crispy rice cereal
    ½   cup uncooked regular oats

1. Preheat oven to 325°. Beat butter and shortening at medium speed with an electric mixer until fluffy; gradually add sugar, beating until blended. Add egg and coconut extract, beating well.
2. Combine flour, baking powder, baking soda, and salt; gradually add to butter mixture, beating well after each addition. Stir in coconut, cereal, and oats.
3. Drop cookie dough by heaping teaspoonfuls onto lightly greased baking sheets.
4. Bake at 325° for 12 to 14 minutes or until golden. Let cookies cool slightly on baking sheets; remove to wire racks to cool completely.

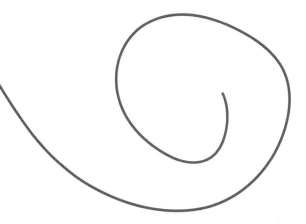

Chai Tea–Eggnog Cookies

Makes 2 dozen
Hands-on Time: 20 min. **Total Time:** 46 min.

Chai Tea–Eggnog
Cookies

 1   chai tea bag
 1   (17.5-oz.) package sugar cookie mix
 ½   cup melted butter
 1   large egg
 4   Tbsp. eggnog, divided
Parchment paper
Cinnamon sugar
 1   cup powdered sugar
 ½   tsp. freshly grated nutmeg

1. Preheat oven to 350°. Remove tea leaves from tea bag; discard bag.
2. Stir together tea leaves, cookie mix, butter, egg, and 2 Tbsp. eggnog until well blended.
3. Drop dough by tablespoonfuls onto parchment paper–lined baking sheets. Flatten dough slightly with bottom of a glass dipped in cinnamon sugar.
4. Bake at 350° for 8 to 10 minutes or until cookies are lightly browned. Remove from baking sheet to a wire rack, and cool completely (about 10 minutes).
5. Whisk together powdered sugar, nutmeg, and remaining 2 Tbsp. eggnog until smooth. Spoon over cooled cookies.

test-kitchen secret

Use shiny, heavy, aluminum baking sheets. Dark sheets may absorb heat, causing cookies to brown too much on the bottom; nonstick baking sheets work well if they are not too dark. Insulated baking sheets require a slightly longer baking time.

Almond Cookies

Makes about 4 dozen
Hands-on Time: 20 min. **Total Time:** 1 hr., 40 min.

 3   cups slivered almonds, toasted
 4   egg whites
1½   cups granulated sugar
 1   tsp. powdered sugar
 1   tsp. almond liqueur*
Parchment paper
Granulated sugar

1. Preheat oven to 300°. Process slivered almonds in a food processor until finely ground. (Do not over-process to a powder.)
2. Beat egg whites at high speed with an electric mixer until stiff peaks form. Fold in ground almonds, 1½ cups granulated sugar, powdered sugar, and liqueur.
3. Drop by rounded teaspoonfuls onto parchment paper–lined baking sheets; sprinkle with granulated sugar.
4. Bake at 300° for 20 minutes or until golden; remove to wire racks to cool.

*½ teaspoon almond extract may be substituted.

test-kitchen secret

To toast almonds, bake them in a shallow pan at 350°, stirring occasionally, 5 minutes or until toasted.

All-Time Favorite Chocolate Chip Cookies

Bake 10 minutes for a soft and chewy cookie, or bake up to 14 minutes for a crisp cookie.

Makes about 5 dozen
Hands-on Time: 30 min. **Total Time:** 1 hr., 35 min.

- ¾ cup butter, softened
- ¾ cup granulated sugar
- ¾ cup firmly packed dark brown sugar
- 2 large eggs
- 1½ tsp. vanilla extract
- 2¼ cups plus 2 Tbsp. all-purpose flour
- 1 tsp. baking soda
- ¾ tsp. salt
- 1½ (12-oz.) packages semisweet chocolate morsels
- Parchment paper

1. Preheat oven to 350°. Beat butter and sugars at medium speed with a heavy-duty electric stand mixer until butter mixture is creamy. Add eggs and 1½ tsp. vanilla, beating until blended.

2. Combine flour, baking soda, and salt in a small bowl; gradually add dry mixture to butter mixture, beating just until blended. Beat in chocolate morsels just until combined with dough.

3. Drop by tablespoonfuls onto parchment paper–lined baking sheets.

4. Bake at 350° for 10 to 14 minutes or until desired degree of doneness. Remove to wire racks, and cool completely (about 15 minutes).

All-Time Favorite Chocolate Chip Cookies

Mississippi Mud Cookies

Makes about 3 dozen
Hands-on Time: 25 min. **Total Time:** 55 min.

1	cup semisweet chocolate morsels
½	cup butter, softened
1	cup sugar
2	large eggs
1	tsp. vanilla extract
1½	cups all-purpose flour
1	tsp. baking powder
½	tsp. salt
1	cup chopped pecans
½	cup milk chocolate morsels
	Parchment paper
1	cup plus 2 Tbsp. miniature marshmallows

1. Preheat oven to 350°. Microwave semisweet chocolate morsels in a small microwave-safe glass bowl at HIGH 1 minute or until smooth, stirring every 30 seconds.

2. Beat butter and sugar at medium speed with an electric mixer until creamy; add eggs, 1 at a time, beating until blended after each addition. Beat in vanilla extract and melted chocolate.

3. Combine flour, baking powder, and salt; gradually add to chocolate mixture, beating until well blended. Stir in chopped pecans and ½ cup milk chocolate morsels.

4. Drop dough by heaping tablespoonfuls onto parchment paper–lined baking sheets. Press 3 marshmallows into top of each cookie.

5. Bake at 350° for 10 to 12 minutes or until set. Remove to wire racks.

So Good
Brownies

So Good Brownies

Makes 16 servings
Hands-on Time: 12 min. **Total Time:** 1 hr., 52 min.

- 4 (1-oz.) unsweetened chocolate baking squares
- ¾ cup butter
- 1½ cups granulated sugar
- ½ cup firmly packed brown sugar
- 3 large eggs
- 1 cup all-purpose flour
- 1 tsp. vanilla extract
- ⅛ tsp. salt

1. Preheat oven to 350°. Line bottom and all sides of an 8-inch pan with aluminum foil, allowing 2 to 3 inches to extend over sides; lightly grease foil.
2. Microwave 4 chocolate squares and butter in a large microwave-safe bowl at HIGH 1½ to 2 minutes or until melted and smooth, stirring at 30-second intervals. Whisk in granulated and brown sugars. Add eggs, 1 at a time, whisking just until blended after each addition. Whisk in flour, vanilla, and salt.
3. Pour mixture into prepared pan.
4. Bake at 350° for 40 to 44 minutes or until a wooden pick inserted in center of brownies comes out with a few moist crumbs. Cool completely on a wire rack (about 1 hour). Lift brownies from pan, using foil sides as handles. Gently remove foil, and cut brownies into 16 squares.

Peanut Butter–Streusel Brownies: Stir together ½ cup all-purpose flour, 2 Tbsp. light brown sugar, 2 Tbsp. granulated sugar, ⅓ cup chunky peanut butter, 2 Tbsp. melted butter, and ⅛ tsp. salt until blended and crumbly. Sprinkle peanut butter mixture over batter. Increase bake time to 50 to 54 minutes.

Flourless Peanut Butter–Chocolate Chip Cookies

Makes 2 dozen
Hands-on Time: 30 min. **Total Time:** 1 hr., 14 min.

- 1 cup creamy peanut butter
- ¾ cup sugar
- 1 large egg
- ½ tsp. baking soda
- ¼ tsp. salt
- 1 cup semisweet chocolate morsels
- Parchment paper

1. Preheat oven to 350°. Stir together peanut butter and next 4 ingredients in a medium bowl until well blended. Stir in chocolate morsels.
2. Drop dough by rounded tablespoonfuls 2 inches apart onto parchment paper–lined baking sheets.
3. Bake at 350° for 12 to 14 minutes or until puffed and lightly browned. Cool on baking sheets on a wire rack 5 minutes. Transfer to wire rack, and let cool 15 minutes.

test-kitchen secret

When portioning dough for Flourless Peanut Butter–Chocolate Chip Cookies, spray your tablespoon measure with cooking spray for easy release onto baking sheets.

test-kitchen secret

For indulgent and family-friendly, double-decker brownies, prepare So Good Brownies as directed through Step 3. Add a topping layer, and adjust the baking times slightly.

Pecan Pie Brownies

Salted Caramel-Pecan Bars

Makes 4 dozen
Hands-on Time: 15 min. **Total Time:** 1 hr., 5 min.

    1   cup chopped pecans
    12   whole graham crackers
    1   cup firmly packed brown sugar
    ¾   cup butter
    2   Tbsp. whipping cream
    1   tsp. vanilla extract
    ¼   tsp. kosher salt

1. Preheat oven to 350°. Bake pecans in a single layer in a shallow pan 10 to 12 minutes or until toasted and fragrant, stirring halfway through.
2. Line a 15- x 10-inch jelly-roll pan with aluminum foil; lightly grease foil. Arrange graham crackers in a single layer in prepared pan, slightly overlapping edges.
3. Combine brown sugar, butter, and cream in a medium-size heavy saucepan; bring to a boil over medium heat, stirring occasionally. Remove from heat; stir in vanilla and pecans. Pour butter mixture over crackers, spreading to coat.
4. Bake at 350° for 10 to 11 minutes or until lightly browned and bubbly.
5. Immediately sprinkle with salt, and slide foil from pan onto a wire rack. Cool completely (about 30 minutes). Break into bars.

Pecan Pie Brownies

Take the frozen pie out of the freezer 2 hours before you need to prepare this recipe so that it has time to thaw.

Makes 40 brownies
Hands-on Time: 25 min. **Total Time:** 1 hr., 15 min.

    1   (2-lb.) frozen pecan pie, thawed
    ½   cup butter
    1¾   cups (11.5-ounce package) semisweet chocolate
         chunks
    1   cup sugar
    2   large eggs
    1   cup milk
    1½   cups all-purpose flour
    1   tsp. baking powder
         Vegetable cooking spray

1. Cut pie into cubes. Set aside.
2. Preheat oven to 350°. Microwave butter and chocolate chunks in a glass bowl at HIGH 1 minute. Stir and microwave 1 more minute. Stir until mixture is smooth.
3. Beat chocolate mixture, sugar, eggs, milk, and half of pecan pie cubes at low speed with a heavy-duty stand mixer until blended.
4. Add flour and baking powder, stirring with a wooden spoon until blended. Stir remaining half of pie cubes into batter. (Batter will be thick.) Spoon brownie batter into a 13- x 9-inch pan coated with cooking spray.
5. Bake at 350° for 50 minutes. Cool brownies completely on a wire rack. Cut into triangles or squares.

Note: We tested Mrs. Edward's Frozen Pecan Pie.

Easy Cheesecake Bars

Makes 1 dozen
Hands-on Time: 15 min. **Total Time:** 5 hr., 53 min.

    1   cup all-purpose flour
    ⅓   cup firmly packed light brown sugar
    ¼   cup butter, softened
    3   (8-oz.) packages cream cheese, softened
    ¾   cup granulated sugar
    3   large eggs
    ⅓   cup sour cream
    ½   tsp. vanilla extract
         Garnish: fresh raspberries

1. Preheat oven to 350°. Beat flour, sugar, and butter at medium-low speed with an electric mixer until combined. Increase speed to medium, and beat until well blended and crumbly. Pat mixture into a lightly greased 13- x 9-inch pan. Bake 13 to 15 minutes or until lightly browned.
2. Beat cream cheese at medium speed with an electric mixer until creamy. Gradually add granulated sugar, beating until well blended. Add eggs, 1 at a time, beating at low speed just until blended after each addition. Add sour cream and vanilla, beating just until blended. Pour over baked crust.
3. Bake at 350° for 25 minutes or until set. Place on a wire rack until completely cooled (about 1 hour). Garnish, if desired. Cover and chill 4 to 24 hours; cut into bars.

Chocolate-Mint Brownie Pops

Makes 31 pops
Hands-on Time: 1 hr., 21 min. **Total Time:** 3 hr., 23 min.

½   cup butter
2   (1-oz.) squares unsweetened chocolate
1   (10-oz.) package crème de menthe baking morsels
1   cup sugar
2   large eggs, lightly beaten
1   tsp. vanilla extract
¾   cup all-purpose flour
¼   tsp. salt
    Parchment paper
2   Tbsp. shortening
5   (2-oz.) chocolate candy coating squares
31   (4-inch) white craft sticks
4   (2-oz.) vanilla candy coating squares
    Crushed peppermint candies

1. Preheat oven to 350°. Combine butter, unsweetened chocolate, and 1 cup crème de menthe baking morsels in a medium saucepan. Cook over low heat, stirring constantly until melted. Remove from heat; add 1 cup sugar, 2 eggs, and 1 tsp. vanilla, beating until smooth.
2. Combine flour and salt; stir into chocolate mixture until blended. Stir in remaining baking morsels.
3. Pour batter into a lightly greased 8-inch square pan. Bake at 350° for 32 minutes. Cool brownies completely in pan on a wire rack.
4. Using a 2-Tbsp. scoop, scoop out balls from cooked brownie in pan. Gently reshape into smooth balls; place on a large parchment paper–lined baking sheet. Chill brownie balls 30 minutes.
5. Place shortening and chocolate candy coating in a 2-cup glass measuring cup. Microwave at HIGH 1 minute or until melted. Stir until smooth. Insert a white craft stick into each brownie ball. Dip each ball into melted chocolate mixture, reheating as necessary to keep mixture liquid. Place dipped balls on a large parchment paper–lined baking sheet. Let stand until firm.
6. Place vanilla candy coating in a bowl. Microwave at HIGH 40 seconds or until melted. Spoon into a large zip-top plastic freezer bag; seal bag. Snip a small hole (about ⅛ inch in diameter) in 1 corner of bag. Squeeze stream of white chocolate onto dipped brownie balls to decorate as desired; sprinkle with crushed peppermint.

Red Velvet Brownies

Makes: 16 servings
Hands-on Time: 15 min. **Total Time:** 3 hr., 9 min., including cream cheese frosting

1   (4-oz.) bittersweet chocolate baking bar, chopped
¾   cup butter
2   cups sugar
4   large eggs
1½   cups all-purpose flour
1   (1-oz.) bottle red liquid food coloring
1½   tsp. baking powder
1   tsp. vanilla extract
⅛   tsp. salt
    Small-Batch Cream Cheese Frosting
    Garnish: white chocolate curls (directions on page 228)

1. Preheat oven to 350°. Line bottom and sides of a 9-inch square pan with aluminum foil, allowing 2 to 3 inches to extend over sides; lightly grease foil.
2. Microwave chocolate and butter in a large microwave-safe bowl at HIGH 1½ to 2 minutes or until melted and smooth, stirring at 30-second intervals. Whisk in sugar. Add eggs, 1 at a time, whisking just until blended after each addition. Gently stir in flour and next 4 ingredients. Pour mixture into prepared pan.
3. Bake at 350° for 44 to 48 minutes or until a wooden pick inserted in center comes out with a few moist crumbs. Cool completely on a wire rack (about 2 hours).
4. Lift brownies from pan, using foil sides as handles; gently remove foil. Spread Small-Batch Cream Cheese Frosting on top of brownies, and cut into 16 squares. Garnish, if desired.

Small-Batch Cream Cheese Frosting

Makes about 1⅔ cups
Hands-on Time: 10 min. **Total Time:** 10 min.

1   (8-oz.) package cream cheese, softened
3   Tbsp. butter, softened
1½   cups powdered sugar
⅛   tsp. salt
1   tsp. vanilla extract

1. Beat cream cheese and butter at medium speed with an electric mixer until creamy. Gradually add powdered sugar and salt, beating until blended. Stir in vanilla.

Raspberry–Red Velvet Petits Fours

Makes 24 servings
Hands-on Time: 25 min. **Total Time:** 2 hr.

1   (18.25-oz.) package red velvet cake mix
½   cup seedless raspberry jam
1   (16-oz.) container cream cheese frosting (optional)
White chocolate curls (optional; see box below)

1. Preheat oven to 350°. Prepare cake batter as directed. Pour batter into a greased and floured 13- x 9-inch pan.
2. Bake at 350° for 28 to 30 minutes or until a wooden pick inserted in center comes out clean. Cool in a pan on a wire rack for 10 minutes. Remove from pan to wire rack, and cool completely (about 1 hour).
3. Invert cake onto a cutting board. Cut off rounded top of cake. Trim and discard edges of cake.
4. Cut cake in half crosswise. Cut each half piece in half horizontally. Carefully lift top piece off each half of cake.
5. Stir jam in a small bowl until smooth and spreadable. Spread jam over bottom halves of cakes. Replace 2 halves of cakes. Cut each cake half into 12 squares. Transfer petits fours to a serving platter or cake pedestal.
6 For piping, if desired, remove lid and foil from frosting. Microwave frosting at HIGH for 20 seconds, stirring after 10 seconds. Stir until smooth and spreadable. Transfer frosting to a zip-top plastic freezer bag. Snip 1 corner of bag. Pipe frosting onto tops of petits fours, allowing to drip down sides. Or, add chocolate curls, if desired.

test-kitchen secret

How To Make Chocolate Curls

Pull a vegetable peeler along the sides of about a 4-oz. white chocolate bar, allowing curls to fall onto wax paper. If the chocolate is too firm, microwave chocolate bar on a microwave-safe plate at MEDIUM at 5-second intervals until you are able to make curls.

Fudge has good keeping quality, so you can make a lot of it and store it easily in an airtight container.

make ahead

Five Pounds of Chocolate Fudge

Purchase a candy thermometer in the utensils section of a grocery or discount store.

Makes 96 pieces
Hands-on Time: 25 min. **Total Time:** 25 min.

2   (12-oz.) packages semisweet chocolate morsels
1   cup butter or margarine
1   (7-oz.) jar marshmallow cream
4½   cups sugar
1   (12-oz.) can evaporated milk
Butter
2   Tbsp. vanilla extract
1½   cups chopped pecans, toasted

1. Combine chocolate morsels and next 2 ingredients in a large mixing bowl; set aside.
2. Combine 4½ cups sugar and evaporated milk in a buttered Dutch oven.
3. Cook mixture over medium heat, stirring constantly, until mixture reaches soft ball stage or candy thermometer registers 234°; pour over chocolate mixture. Beat at high speed with an electric mixer or with a wooden spoon until mixture thickens and begins to lose its gloss. Stir in vanilla extract and chopped pecans.
4. Spread into a buttered 15- x 10-inch jelly-roll pan. Cover and chill until firm. Cut into 1-inch squares. Store fudge in an airtight container at room temperature.

Easy Swirled Fudge

4. Microwave white chocolate bar and whipping cream in a small microwave-safe glass bowl at HIGH until white chocolate is melted (about 30 seconds to 1 minute), stirring at 30-second intervals. Stir until mixture is smooth. Let stand 1 to 3 minutes or until slightly thickened. Spoon mixture over fudge in pan, swirling with a paring knife. Cover and chill until firm (about 2 hours).

Note: We tested in an 1,100-watt and a 1,250-watt microwave oven. Cook times will vary depending on your microwave wattage; be sure to follow the descriptions in the recipe for best results.

Easy Chocolate-Chip-Cookie Fudge

This simple fudge requires little work on your part but yields spectacular results.

Makes 2¼ lb.
Hands-on Time: 15 min. **Total Time:** 4 hr., 25 min.

- 1   cup chopped pecans
- 1   (12-oz.) package semisweet chocolate morsels
- 1   (11.5-oz.) package milk chocolate morsels
- ½   cup evaporated milk
- 1½   tsp. vanilla extract
- ¼   tsp. salt
- 12   chocolate chip cookies, coarsely chopped (about 1¾ cups)

1. Preheat oven to 350°. Bake pecans in a single layer in a shallow pan 10 to 12 minutes or until toasted and fragrant, stirring halfway through.
2. Line bottom and sides of an 8-inch square baking dish with aluminum foil, allowing 2 to 3 inches to extend over sides; lightly grease foil.
3. Combine semisweet morsels and next 2 ingredients in a 3-qt. saucepan; cook over medium-low heat, stirring constantly, 5 minutes or until chocolate melts and mixture is smooth. Remove from heat; stir in pecans, vanilla, and salt. Stir in cookies. Spread chocolate mixture into prepared baking dish. Let stand 4 hours or until firm.
4. Lift fudge from dish using foil sides as handles. Remove and discard foil; cut fudge into squares.

editor's favorite

Easy Swirled Fudge

A very thin crust forms over the surface of the fudge while you microwave the white chocolate mixture. Don't worry— once you swirl the two together, the top will become smooth again.

Makes about 1¾ lb.
Hands-on Time: 15 min. **Total Time:** 2 hr., 18 min.

- Parchment paper
- ½   cup butter
- 1   (16-oz.) package powdered sugar, sifted
- ½   cup unsweetened cocoa
- ¼   cup milk
- ¼   tsp. salt
- 1   Tbsp. vanilla extract
- 1   (4-oz.) white chocolate baking bar, chopped
- 2   Tbsp. whipping cream

1. Line bottom and all sides of an 8-inch square pan with parchment paper, allowing 2 to 3 inches to extend over sides.
2. Microwave butter in a large microwave-safe glass bowl at HIGH for 30-second intervals until melted. Gently stir in powdered sugar and next 3 ingredients. (Mixture will be lumpy.)
3. Microwave 30 seconds; add vanilla. Beat powdered-sugar mixture at medium-low speed with an electric mixer until well blended and smooth. Pour fudge into prepared pan, spreading to edges of pan.

Milk Chocolate–Peppermint Bark

The bark makes great party favors and teacher gifts. (Pictured on page 135)

Makes 2¾ lb.
Hands-on Time: 25 min. **Total Time:** 6 hr., 25 min.

Parchment paper
1 tsp. butter
3 (11.5-oz.) packages milk chocolate morsels
12 cream-and-mint-filled chocolate sandwich cookies, broken into pieces
1 cup small pretzel sticks
1¼ cup soft peppermint candies, coarsely chopped and divided

1. Line a 15- x 10-inch jelly-roll pan with parchment paper; grease with butter.
2. Microwave milk chocolate morsels in a large bowl at HIGH 1 to 2 minutes or until melted and smooth, stirring at 45-second intervals. Gently stir in broken cookie pieces, pretzel sticks, and ¾ cup coarsely chopped soft peppermint candies. Spread in prepared pan. Sprinkle with remaining ½ cup chopped candies.
3. Let stand until firm (about 6 hours). Break or cut into pieces. Store in a cool place up to 3 days.

Note: We tested with Oreo Double Delight Mint 'N Creme Cookies. Do not freeze bark. Freezing will cause a powdery white coating called bloom.

test-kitchen secret

Make sure to just microwave the chocolate until melted and not overcook it for best results. The setting time of the bark can vary according to the temperature in your home.

Salty Chocolate-Pecan Candy

Once it's removed from the refrigerator, this candy will soften slightly at room temperature.

Makes 1¾ lb.
Hands-on Time: 10 min. **Total Time:** 1 hr., 25 min.

1 cup pecans, coarsely chopped
Parchment paper
3 (4-oz.) bittersweet chocolate baking bars
3 (4-oz.) white chocolate baking bars
1 tsp. coarse sea salt*

1. Preheat oven to 350°. Place pecans in a single layer on a baking sheet. Bake 8 to 10 minutes or until toasted, stirring halfway through. Reduce temperature to 225°.
2. Line a 17- x 12-inch jelly-roll pan with parchment paper. Break each chocolate bar into 8 equal pieces. (You will have 48 pieces total.) Arrange in a checkerboard pattern in jelly-roll pan, alternating dark and white chocolate. (Chocolate pieces will touch.)
3. Bake at 225° for 5 minutes or just until chocolate pieces are melted. Remove pan to a wire rack. Swirl chocolates into a marble pattern, using a wooden pick. Sprinkle evenly with pecans and salt.
4. Chill 1 hour or until firm. Break into pieces. Store in an airtight container in refrigerator up to 1 month.

*¾ tsp. kosher salt may be substituted.

Note: We tested with Ghirardelli 60% Cocoa Bittersweet Chocolate Baking Bars and Ghirardelli White Chocolate Baking Bars.

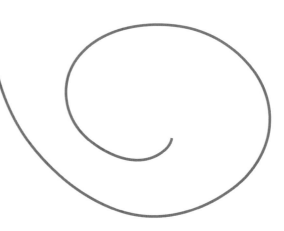

make ahead

Cappuccino-Walnut Toffee

Some brands of butter have slightly higher water content than others. We prefer Land O'Lakes butter for this recipe.

Makes about 2 lb.
Hands-on Time: 35 min. **Total Time:** 2 hr., 8 min.

- 2 cups chopped walnuts
- 1¼ cups butter
- 1 cup granulated sugar
- ⅓ cup firmly packed light brown sugar
- 1 Tbsp. dark unsulphured molasses
- 2 tsp. instant espresso
- ½ tsp. ground cinnamon
- ¼ tsp. salt
- 1 cup milk chocolate morsels
- 1 cup white chocolate morsels

1. Preheat oven to 350°. Butter a 15- x 10-inch jelly-roll pan. Bake walnuts in a single layer in a shallow pan 8 to 10 minutes or until toasted and fragrant, stirring halfway through. Let cool 30 minutes.

2. Melt butter in a 3½-qt. heavy saucepan over medium heat; stir in granulated sugar, next 5 ingredients, and ⅓ cup water. Cook, stirring constantly, until a candy thermometer registers 290° (soft crack stage), about 20 minutes.

3. Remove pan from heat, and stir in walnuts. Quickly pour mixture into prepared pan, and spread into an even layer. Immediately sprinkle milk chocolate and white chocolate morsels over top; let stand 5 minutes. Swirl chocolate using an off-set spatula.

4. Cover and chill until firm (about 1 hour). Break toffee into pieces. Store in an airtight container in refrigerator up to 7 days. Serve cold or at room temperature.

Salty Chocolate-Pecan Candy

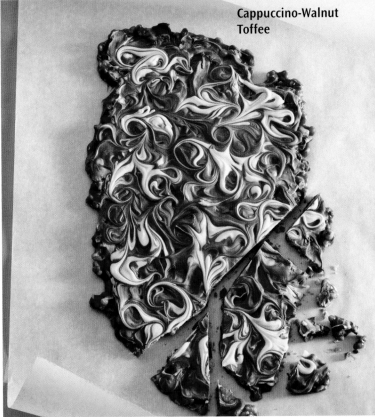

Cappuccino-Walnut Toffee

and everything NICE

editor's favorite

Chocolate-Citrus Cake with Candied Oranges

Makes 16 servings
Hands-on Time: 1 hr. **Total Time:** 6 hr., 38 min., including filling, frosting, and oranges

Parchment paper
2 (4-oz.) bittersweet chocolate baking bars, chopped
½ cup butter, softened
1⅔ cups granulated sugar
⅓ cup firmly packed light brown sugar
3 large eggs
2 cups all-purpose flour
1 tsp. baking soda
½ tsp. salt
1 (8-oz.) container sour cream
1 tsp. vanilla extract
1 cup hot brewed coffee
Whipped Ganache Filling
Seven-Minute Frosting
Candied Oranges
Garnishes: fresh citrus leaves, cranberries

1. Preheat oven to 350°. Grease and flour 2 (9-inch) round pans. Line bottoms of pans with parchment paper. Lightly grease parchment paper.
2. Melt chocolate bars in a microwave-safe bowl at HIGH 1½ minutes or until smooth, stirring at 30-second intervals.
3. Beat butter and sugars at medium speed with a heavy-duty electric stand mixer until well blended (about 3 minutes). Add eggs, 1 at a time, beating just until blended after each addition. Add melted chocolate, beating just until blended.

4. Sift together flour, baking soda, and salt. Gradually add to chocolate mixture alternately with sour cream, beginning and ending with flour mixture. Beat at low speed just until blended after each addition. (Mixture will be thick.) Stir vanilla into hot coffee. Gradually add coffee mixture to batter in a slow, steady stream, beating at low speed just until blended. Pour batter into prepared pans.
5. Bake at 350° for 38 to 42 minutes or until a wooden pick inserted in center comes out clean. Cool in pans on a wire rack 10 minutes. Remove from pans to wire rack, and let cool completely (about 1 hour).
6. Spread Whipped Ganache Filling between layers, spreading to edges of cake and leveling with an offset spatula. Gently press top cake layer down, pressing out a small amount of Ganache Filling from between layers, and spread filling around sides of cake, filling in any gaps between layers. Spread Seven-Minute Frosting over top and sides of cake. Swirl frosting using back of a spoon, if desired. Top with Candied Oranges. Garnish, if desired.

Whipped Ganache Filling

Makes about 3 cups
Hands-on Time: 10 min. **Total Time:** 2 hr., 10 min.

1 (12-oz.) package semisweet chocolate morsels
1½ cups whipping cream
1 Tbsp. orange liqueur

1. Microwave chocolate morsels and whipping cream in a 3-qt. microwave-safe glass bowl at HIGH 2½ minutes or until melted and smooth, stirring at 30-second intervals. Whisk in liqueur until smooth. Cover and chill 2 hours or until mixture is thickened.
2. Beat ganache at medium speed with an electric mixer 20 to 30 seconds or until soft peaks form and ganache lightens in color. (Do not over-mix.) Use immediately.

Chocolate-Citrus Cake
with Candied Oranges

Seven-Minute Frosting

Cover bowl with a damp paper towel or cloth to keep
frosting from drying out while you are frosting the cake.

Makes about 4 cups
Hands-on Time: 10 min. **Total Time:** 10 min.

  2   egg whites
1¼   cups sugar
  1   Tbsp. corn syrup
  1   tsp. orange liqueur

1. Pour water to depth of 1½ inches into a 2- to 2½-qt.
saucepan; bring to a boil over medium-high heat. Reduce
heat to medium, and simmer.
2. Combine egg whites, sugar, corn syrup, orange liqueur,
and ¼ cup water in a 2½-qt. glass bowl; beat at high speed
with an electric mixer until blended. Place glass bowl over
simmering water, and beat at high speed 5 to 7 minutes or
until soft peaks form; remove from heat. Beat to spreading
consistency (about 2 to 3 minutes). Use immediately.

Candied Oranges

Makes about 19 pieces
Hands-on Time: 10 min. **Total Time:** 1 hr., 30 min.

  2   large navel oranges, thinly sliced
Parchment paper
  2   cups sugar
  ½   vanilla bean, split

1. Bring 4 cups water to a boil in a 3- to 3½-qt. saucepan
over medium-high heat. Add oranges. Return to a boil; cook
5 minutes. Transfer oranges to a parchment paper–lined
jelly-roll pan, using a slotted spoon; discard water.
2. Combine sugar and 2 cups water in saucepan. Scrape
seeds from vanilla bean into water; add vanilla bean to
water. Bring to a boil over medium-high heat, stirring
occasionally, until sugar is dissolved. Add orange slices.
Return to a boil; cover, reduce heat to medium, and simmer
10 minutes. Uncover and cook, stirring occasionally, 35 to
45 minutes or until rinds are softened and translucent.
3. Remove oranges, using tongs; arrange on parchment
paper–lined jelly-roll pan, folding oranges as desired. Blot
with paper towels.
4. Pour syrup through a fine wire-mesh strainer into a
bowl, reserving syrup and vanilla bean for another use.
Discard solids. Let oranges stand 15 minutes.

Spice Cake with Citrus Filling

Makes 12 servings
Hands-on Time: 25 min. **Total Time:** 2 hr., 23 min., including filling and icing

  1   cup chopped pecans
  1   cup butter, softened
  2   cups sugar
  3   large eggs
  3¼   cups all-purpose flour
  1   tsp. baking soda
  ½   tsp. salt
  1½   cups buttermilk
  1   tsp. vanilla extract
  ½   tsp. ground cinnamon
  ½   tsp. ground allspice
  ¼   tsp. ground cloves
       Citrus Filling
       White Icing

1. Preheat oven to 350°. Bake pecans in a single layer in a shallow pan 5 to 7 minutes or until lightly toasted and fragrant, stirring halfway through. Let cool.
2. Meanwhile, beat butter at medium speed with a heavy-duty electric stand mixer until creamy. Gradually add sugar, beating until light and fluffy. Add eggs, 1 at a time, beating just until blended after each addition.
3. Stir together flour, baking soda, and salt; add to butter mixture alternately with buttermilk, beginning and ending with flour mixture. Beat at low speed just until blended after each addition. Stir in vanilla.
4. Divide batter into 2 equal portions (about 3½ cups each); stir cinnamon, allspice, cloves, and pecans into 1 portion. Pour plain batter into 2 greased and floured 9-inch round cake pans (about 1¾ cups batter per pan). Pour spiced batter into 2 greased and floured 9-inch round cake pans (about 2 cups batter per pan).
5. Bake at 350° for 18 to 20 minutes or until a wooden pick inserted in center comes out clean. Cool in pans on wire racks 10 minutes; remove from pans to wire racks, and cool completely (about 1 hour).
6. Place 1 plain cake layer on a serving plate or cake stand; spread top of cake with ⅔ cup Citrus Filling, leaving a ¼-inch border around edges. Top with a spice cake layer, and spread top with filling as directed above. Repeat procedure with remaining plain cake layer and filling. Top with remaining spice cake layer. Prepare White Icing; spread icing over top and sides of cake.

Citrus Filling

Makes about 2 cups
Hands-on Time: 5 min. **Total Time:** 5 min.

  2   (10-oz.) jars lemon curd
  1½   cups sweetened flaked coconut
  1   Tbsp. orange zest
  1   Tbsp. fresh orange juice

1. Stir together lemon curd, coconut, and next 2 ingredients in a medium bowl until blended.

White Icing

Makes about 4 cups
Hands-on Time: 15 min. **Total Time:** 15 min.

  2   egg whites
  1¼   cups sugar
  1   Tbsp. corn syrup
  1   tsp. vanilla extract

1. Pour water to depth of 1½ inches into a 3½-qt. saucepan; bring water to a boil over medium-high heat. Reduce heat to medium, and simmer.
2. Combine egg whites, sugar, next 2 ingredients, and ¼ cup water in a 2½-qt. glass bowl; beat mixture at high speed with an electric mixer until blended. Place bowl over simmering water, and beat at high speed 5 to 7 minutes or until soft peaks form; remove from heat. Beat icing to spreading consistency (about 2 to 3 minutes). Use immediately.

Spice Cake with
Citrus Filling

editor's favorite

Caramel Italian Cream Cake

Brown sugar is the shortcut to quick caramel flavor in both the cake layers and the frosting. (Pictured on page 102)

Makes 12 servings
Hands-on Time: 25 min. **Total Time:** 2 hr., 33 min., including frostings

- 3 cups shaved coconut
- 1 cup finely chopped pecans
- ½ cup butter, softened
- ½ cup shortening
- 1½ cups granulated sugar
- ½ cup firmly packed dark brown sugar
- 5 large eggs, separated
- 1 Tbsp. vanilla extract
- 2 cups all-purpose flour
- 1 tsp. baking soda
- 1 cup buttermilk
- 1 cup sweetened flaked coconut
   Quick Caramel Frosting
   Cream Cheese Frosting

1. Preheat oven to 350°. Place shaved coconut in a single layer in a shallow pan. Place pecans in a second shallow pan. Bake coconut and pecans at the same time 5 to 7 minutes or until coconut is toasted and pecans are lightly toasted and fragrant, stirring halfway through.
2. Beat butter and shortening at medium speed with an electric mixer until fluffy; gradually add granulated and brown sugars, beating well. Add egg yolks, 1 at a time, beating until blended after each addition. Add vanilla extract, beating until blended.
3. Combine flour and baking soda; add to butter mixture alternately with buttermilk, beginning and ending with flour mixture. Beat at low speed just until blended after each addition. Stir in pecans and 1 cup sweetened flaked coconut.
4. Beat egg whites at high speed until stiff peaks form, and fold into batter. Pour cake batter into 3 greased and floured 9-inch round cake pans.
5. Bake at 350° for 23 to 25 minutes or until a wooden pick inserted in center comes out clean. Cool in pans on wire racks 10 minutes; remove from pans to wire racks, and cool completely (about 1 hour).
6. Prepare Quick Caramel Frosting. Immediately spread frosting between layers and on top of cake. Spread Cream Cheese Frosting over sides of cake; press 3 cups toasted shaved coconut onto sides of cake.

Quick Caramel Frosting

Like the classic caramel frosting, this one hardens quickly, so cool the cake layers before you start to make it.

Makes 5 cups
Hands-on Time: 20 min. **Total Time:** 20 min.

- 1 cup butter
- 1 cup firmly packed light brown sugar
- 1 cup firmly packed dark brown sugar
- ½ cup heavy cream
- 4 cups powdered sugar, sifted
- 2 tsp. vanilla extract

1. Bring first 3 ingredients to a rolling boil in a 3½-qt. saucepan over medium heat, whisking constantly (about 7 minutes).
2. Stir in cream, and bring to a boil; remove from heat. Pour into bowl of a heavy-duty electric stand mixer. Gradually beat in powdered sugar and vanilla at medium speed, using whisk attachment; beat 8 to 12 minutes or until thickened. Use immediately.

> ### test-kitchen secret
> Don't panic if you over-beat the frosting. Thin to a spreadable consistency by adding 1 to 2 tsp. hot water.

Cream Cheese Frosting

Makes about 1¾ cups
Hands-on Time: 10 min. **Total Time:** 10 min.

- ¼ cup butter, softened
- ½ (8-oz.) package cream cheese, softened
- 2 cups powdered sugar
- 1 tsp. vanilla extract

1. Beat butter and cream cheese at medium speed with an electric mixer until creamy. Gradually add powdered sugar, beating at low speed until blended; stir in vanilla.

Eggnog Pound Cake

Just when you thought pound cake couldn't get any better, try toasting the slices and spreading them with your favorite jam or preserves.

Makes 12 servings
Hands-on Time: 15 min. **Total Time:** 2 hr., 25 min.

- 1 (16-oz.) package pound cake mix
- 1¼ cups eggnog
- 2 large eggs
- ½ tsp. freshly grated nutmeg
- ½ tsp. vanilla extract

1. Preheat oven to 350°. Beat all ingredients together at low speed with an electric mixer until blended. Increase speed to medium, and beat 2 minutes. Pour into a lightly greased 9- x 5-inch loaf pan.

2. Bake at 350° for 1 hour to 1 hour and 5 minutes or until a long wooden pick inserted in center comes out clean. Cool in pan on a wire rack 10 minutes. Remove from pan to wire rack, and cool completely (about 1 hour).

Eggnog Pound Cake

Upside-Down Caramelized Apple Cake

To get a true reading of doneness, insert the wooden pick only halfway through the cake when testing.

Makes 8 to 10 servings
Hands-on Time: 38 min. **Total Time:** 1 hr., 38 min.

- ½ cup chopped pecans
- 2 large Granny Smith apples, peeled and cut into ½-inch-thick slices
- 1 Tbsp. lemon juice
- 2 tsp. vanilla extract, divided
- ¾ tsp. ground cinnamon, divided
- ½ cup butter, softened and divided
- 2 tsp. brandy
- 1 cup firmly packed light brown sugar
- ¾ cup granulated sugar, divided
- 2 large eggs, separated
- ¾ cup milk
- ½ cup sour cream
- 2 cups all-purpose baking mix
- ⅛ tsp. ground nutmeg

1. Preheat oven to 350°. Bake pecans in a single layer in a shallow pan 8 to 10 minutes or until toasted and fragrant, stirring after 5 minutes. Increase oven temperature to 375°.

2. Toss apple slices with lemon juice, 1 tsp. vanilla extract, and ½ tsp. cinnamon.

3. Melt ¼ cup butter in a 10-inch cast-iron skillet over low heat. Remove from heat; stir in brandy. Sprinkle with brown sugar. Sprinkle pecans over brown sugar mixture. Arrange apples in 2 concentric circles over pecans.

4. Beat ½ cup granulated sugar and remaining ¼ cup butter at medium speed with an electric mixer until blended. Add egg yolks, 1 at a time, beating just until blended after each addition. Add milk, sour cream, and remaining 1 tsp. vanilla, beating just until blended.

5. Whisk together baking mix, nutmeg, and remaining ¼ tsp. cinnamon in a medium bowl. Add nutmeg mixture to butter mixture, beating just until blended.

6. Beat egg whites in a large bowl at high speed until soft peaks form. Gradually beat in remaining ¼ cup granulated sugar until stiff peaks form. Fold into batter. Spread batter over apples in skillet.

7. Bake at 375° for 50 to 54 minutes or until a wooden pick inserted halfway into center of cake comes out clean.

8. Cool in skillet on a wire rack 10 minutes. Carefully run a knife around edge of cake to loosen. Invert cake onto a serving plate, replacing any topping on cake that sticks to skillet.

Upside-Down Caramelized
Apple Cake

**Pineapple Upside-Down
Carrot Cake**

Pineapple Upside-Down
Carrot Cake

Makes 8 servings
Hands-on Time: 20 min. **Total Time:** 1 hr., 15 min.

- ¼   cup butter
- ⅔   cup firmly packed brown sugar
- 1   (20-oz.) can pineapple slices in juice, drained
- 7   maraschino cherries (without stems)
- 1   cup granulated sugar
- ½   cup vegetable oil
- 2   large eggs
- 1   cup all-purpose flour
- 1   tsp. baking powder
- 1   tsp. ground cinnamon
- ¾   tsp. baking soda
- ½   tsp. salt
- 1½   cups grated carrots
- ½   cup finely chopped pecans

1. Preheat oven to 350°. Melt butter in a lightly greased 10-inch cast-iron skillet or a 9-inch round cake pan (with sides that are at least 2 inches high) over low heat. Remove from heat. Sprinkle with brown sugar. Arrange 7 pineapple slices in a single layer over brown sugar, reserving remaining pineapple slices for another use. Place 1 cherry in center of each pineapple slice.

2. Beat granulated sugar, oil, and eggs at medium speed with an electric mixer until blended. Combine flour and next 4 ingredients; gradually add to sugar mixture, beating at low speed just until blended. Stir in carrots and pecans. Spoon batter over pineapple slices.

3. Bake at 350° for 45 to 50 minutes or until a wooden pick inserted in center comes out clean. Cool in skillet on a wire rack 10 minutes. Carefully run a knife around edge of cake to loosen. Invert cake onto a serving plate, spooning any topping left in skillet over cake.

Mocha Java Cakes

Even the cook will have a hard time believing these take less than 45 minutes to assemble and bake.

Makes 6 servings
Hands-on Time: 15 min. **Total Time:** 41 min.

1	Tbsp. butter
1	cup butter
8	oz. bittersweet chocolate morsels
4	egg yolks
4	large eggs
2	cups powdered sugar
¾	cup all-purpose flour
1	tsp. instant espresso or instant coffee granules

Pinch of salt
Garnish: powdered sugar

1. Preheat oven to 425°. Grease 6 (6-oz.) ramekins or individual soufflé dishes with 1 Tbsp. butter.
2. Microwave 1 cup butter and bittersweet chocolate morsels in a microwave-safe bowl at HIGH 2 minutes or until chocolate is melted and mixture is smooth, whisking at 1-minute intervals.
3. Beat egg yolks and eggs at medium speed with an electric mixer 1 minute. Gradually add chocolate mixture, beating at low speed until well blended.
4. Sift together sugar and next 3 ingredients. Gradually whisk sugar mixture into chocolate mixture until well blended. Divide batter among prepared ramekins. Place ramekins in a 15- x 10-inch jelly-roll pan.

5. Bake at 425° for 16 minutes or until a thermometer inserted into cakes registers 165°. Remove from oven, and let stand 10 minutes. Run a knife around outer edge of each cake to loosen. Carefully invert cakes onto dessert plates. Garnish, if desired.

Note: We tested with Ghirardelli 60% Cacao Bittersweet Chocolate Chips.

Coffee Liqueur Java Cakes: Omit instant espresso. Prepare recipe as directed through Step 3. Sift together sugar, flour, and salt. Gradually whisk sugar mixture into chocolate mixture until well blended. Whisk in ⅓ cup coffee liqueur. Proceed with recipe as directed, baking cakes 14 to 16 minutes or until a thermometer inserted into cakes registers 165°.
Note: We tested with Kahlúa for coffee liqueur.

Orange Java Cakes: Prepare recipe as directed through Step 3. Sift together sugar and next 3 ingredients. Gradually whisk sugar mixture into chocolate mixture until well blended. Whisk in ¼ cup orange liqueur and 1 tsp. orange zest. Proceed with recipe as directed, baking cakes 14 to 16 minutes or until a thermometer inserted into cakes registers 165°.
Note: We tested with Grand Marnier orange liqueur.

Minty Mocha Java Cakes: Prepare recipe as directed through Step 4. Chop 12 thin crème de menthe chocolate mints. Sprinkle center of batter in ramekins with chopped mints. Press mints into batter gently just until submerged. Proceed with recipe as directed.
Note: We tested with Andes Crème de Menthe Thins.

Mocha Java Cakes

Red Velvet Loaf Cakes

Makes 16 servings
Hands-on Time: 25 min. **Total Time:** 2 hr., 15 min.

1	(18.25-oz.) package red velvet cake mix
1¼	cups buttermilk
¼	cup butter, melted
2	large eggs
1	tsp. vanilla extract
1½	(16-oz.) containers cream cheese frosting

Garnishes: white sparkling sugar, fresh mint sprigs

1. Preheat oven to 350°. Grease and flour 2 (8½- x 4½-inch) loaf pans.
2. Beat first 5 ingredients at low speed with an electric mixer just until dry ingredients are moistened. Increase speed to medium, and beat 1 minute or until batter is smooth, stopping to scrape down sides of bowl as needed. Pour batter into prepared pans.
3. Bake at 350° for 40 to 45 minutes or until a wooden pick inserted in center comes out clean. Cool in pans on wire racks 10 minutes; remove from pans to wire racks, and cool completely (about 1 hour).
4. Place loaves on a serving plate or cake pedestal. Spread frosting over tops and sides of cakes. Garnish, if desired.

Uptown Banana Pudding Cheesecake

Makes 10 to 12 servings
Hands-on Time: 15 min. **Total Time:** 9 hr., 20 min., including Meringue

1½	cups finely crushed vanilla wafers
¼	cup chopped walnuts, toasted
¼	cup butter, melted
2	large ripe bananas, diced
1	Tbsp. lemon juice
2	Tbsp. light brown sugar
3	(8-oz.) packages cream cheese, softened
1	cup granulated sugar
3	large eggs
1	Tbsp. coffee liqueur
2	tsp. vanilla extract

Meringue

1. Combine first 3 ingredients in a small bowl. Press evenly into bottom of a lightly greased 9-inch springform pan.
2. Bake at 350° for 10 minutes. Cool on a wire rack.
3. Combine diced bananas and 1 tablespoon lemon juice in a small saucepan. Stir in 2 tablespoons brown sugar. Place over medium-high heat, and cook, stirring constantly, about 1 minute or just until sugar has melted. Set aside.
4. Beat cream cheese at medium speed with an electric mixer 3 minutes or until smooth. Gradually add 1 cup granulated sugar, beating until blended. Add eggs, 1 at a time, beating until blended after each addition. Beat in coffee liqueur and vanilla. Pour into prepared vanilla wafer crust. Spoon tablespoonfuls of banana mixture evenly over top, and swirl gently into cream cheese mixture.
5. Bake at 350° for 35 to 40 minutes or until center is almost set.
6. Drop spoonfuls of Meringue gently and evenly over hot banana filling.
7. Bake at 400° for 10 minutes or until Meringue is golden brown. Remove from oven, and gently run a knife around edge of cheesecake in springform pan to loosen. Cool cheesecake completely on a wire rack. Cover loosely, and chill 8 hours. Release and remove sides of pan.

Meringue

Makes about 2 cups
Hands-on Time: 5 min. **Total Time:** 5 min.

3	egg whites
¼	tsp. salt
6	Tbsp. sugar

1. Beat egg whites and salt at high speed with an electric mixer until foamy. Add sugar, 1 tablespoon at a time, beating until soft peaks form and sugar dissolves (about 1 to 2 minutes).

make ahead

Red Velvet Soufflés with Whipped Sour Cream

Frozen soufflés bake for the same amount of time as those baked immediately after mixing.

Makes 6 servings
Hands-on Time: 20 min. **Total Time:** 45 min., including Whipped Sour Cream

1	Tbsp. butter
3	Tbsp. granulated sugar
1	(4-oz.) bittersweet chocolate baking bar, chopped
5	large eggs, separated
⅓	cup granulated sugar
3	Tbsp. milk
1	Tbsp. red liquid food coloring
1	tsp. vanilla extract

Pinch of salt
2 Tbsp. granulated sugar
Powdered sugar
Whipped Sour Cream

Red Velvet Soufflés with Whipped Sour Cream

1. Preheat oven to 350°. Grease bottom and sides of 6 (8-oz.) ramekins with butter. Lightly coat with 3 Tbsp. sugar, shaking out excess. Place on a baking sheet.
2. Microwave chocolate in a large microwave-safe bowl at HIGH 1 minute to 1 minute and 15 seconds or until melted, stirring at 30-second intervals. Stir in 4 egg yolks, ⅓ cup sugar, and next 3 ingredients. (Discard remaining egg yolk.)
3. Beat 5 egg whites and salt at high speed with a heavy-duty electric stand mixer until foamy. Gradually add 2 Tbsp. sugar, beating until stiff peaks form. Fold egg white mixture into chocolate mixture, one-third at a time. Spoon into prepared ramekins. Run tip of thumb around edges of ramekins, wiping clean and creating a shallow indentation around edges of mixture. (This will help the souffles rise.)
4. Bake at 350° for 20 to 24 minutes or until soufflés rise and are set. (A long wooden pick inserted in centers will have a few moist crumbs.) Dust with powdered sugar; serve immediately with Whipped Sour Cream.

Note: We tested with Ghirardelli 60% Cacao Bittersweet Chocolate Baking Bar. Soufflés can be assembled through Step 3 and frozen up to 1 week. Bake frozen soufflés as directed in Step 4.

Whipped Sour Cream

Makes about 2 cups
Hands-on Time: 5 min. **Total Time:** 5 min.

¾	cup whipping cream
½	cup sour cream
2	Tbsp. sugar

1. Beat together all ingredients at medium-high speed with a heavy-duty electric stand mixer 45 seconds or just until lightly whipped and pourable. Serve immediately.

So Easy Chocolate Soufflés

Before cooking, run your thumb around edges of ramekins or measuring cups (see Step 3) to help the chocolate soufflés rise higher.

Makes 4 servings
Hands-on Time: 10 min. **Total Time:** 28 min.

 2   tsp. butter
 2   Tbsp. sugar
 1   (4-oz.) semisweet chocolate baking bar
 ⅓   cup seedless strawberry jam
 1½   tsp. vanilla extract
 4   egg whites

1. Grease bottom and all sides of 4 (6-oz.) ramekins or 4 (1-cup) stainless steel dry measuring cups evenly with butter. Lightly coat bottom and sides with sugar, shaking out excess. Place cups on a baking sheet; set aside.
2. Microwave chocolate and jam in a small microwave-safe bowl at MEDIUM (50% power) 1 ½ minutes, stirring at 30-second intervals until melted. Stir in vanilla.
3. Beat egg whites at high speed with an electric mixer until soft peaks form. Stir about one-third of egg whites into chocolate mixture. Fold chocolate mixture into remaining egg whites. Spoon evenly into ramekins. Run tip of thumb around edges of each ramekin, wiping clean and creating a shallow indentation around edge of chocolate mixture.
4. Bake at 350° for 18 to 20 minutes or until soufflés rise and begin to brown on top.

White Chocolate–Cranberry Crème Brûlée

Makes 6 servings
Hands-On Time: 22 min. **Total Time:** 9 hr., 40 min.

 2   cups whipping cream
 4   oz. white chocolate
 1   tsp. vanilla extract
 5   egg yolks
 ½   cup sugar, divided
 ½   (15-oz.) can whole-berry cranberry sauce
 Garnish: Sugared Cranberries and Mint (see box at right)

1. Preheat oven to 300°. Cook ½ cup whipping cream and white chocolate in a heavy saucepan over low heat, stirring constantly, 2 to 3 minutes or until chocolate is melted.

Remove from heat; stir in vanilla extract and remaining 1½ cups cream.
2. Whisk together egg yolks and ¼ cup sugar until sugar is dissolved and mixture is thick and pale yellow. Add cream mixture, whisking until well blended. Pour mixture through a fine wire-mesh strainer into a large bowl.
3. Spoon 1½ Tbsp. cranberry sauce into each of 6 (4-oz.) ramekins. Pour cream-and-egg mixture into ramekins; place filled ramekins in a large roasting pan. Add water to pan to depth of ½ inch.
4. Bake at 300° for 45 to 55 minutes or until edges are set. Cool custards in pan on a wire rack 25 minutes. Remove ramekins from water bath; cover and chill 8 hours.
5. Preheat broiler with oven rack 5 inches from heat. Sprinkle 1½ to 2 tsp. remaining sugar over each ramekin. Fill a large roasting pan or 15- x 10- x 1-inch jelly-roll pan with ice; arrange ramekins in pan.
6. Broil 3 to 5 minutes or until sugar is melted and caramelized. Let stand 5 minutes. Garnish, if desired.

White Chocolate–Banana Crème Brûlée:
Omit cranberry sauce. Prepare recipe through Step 2. Slice 2 bananas; toss with ⅓ cup sugar. Melt 2 Tbsp. butter in a large nonstick skillet over medium-high heat. Add bananas, and cook 1 to 2 minutes on each side or until lightly browned. Place bananas in 6 (4-oz.) ramekins. Pour cream mixture into ramekins; place ramekins in a large roasting pan. Add water to pan to depth of ½ inch. Proceed as directed.

test-kitchen secret

How To Make Sugared Cranberries and Mint

Using a clean paintbrush, gently brush ¼ cup corn syrup onto the top side of ¼ cup dried cranberries and 1 bunch fresh mint sprigs. Sprinkle half of ¼ cup sugar over cranberries and mint. Let stand 5 minutes; sprinkle remaining sugar over cranberries and mint, gently shaking off excess. Hands-on Time: 15 min.; Total Time: 20 min.

White Chocolate–Cranberry
Crème Brûlée

Spiced Caramel-Apple Bread Pudding

Spiced Caramel-Apple Bread Pudding

Makes 8 servings
Hands-on Time: 22 min. **Total Time:** 2 hr., 41 min., including caramel sauce

- 1 Granny Smith apple, peeled and chopped
- ½ tsp. ground cinnamon, divided
- ½ (16-oz.) Italian bread loaf, cut into bite-size pieces
- Vegetable cooking spray
- 3 large eggs
- 1½ cups 2% reduced-fat milk
- 1 cup apple cider
- ¼ cup firmly packed brown sugar
- 1 tsp. vanilla extract
- ¼ tsp. ground nutmeg
- Toasted Pecan–Caramel Sauce

1. Sauté apple and ¼ tsp. cinnamon in a lightly greased skillet over medium-high heat 2 minutes or until tender. Stir together bread and apple in an 11- x 7-inch baking dish coated with cooking spray.
2. Whisk together eggs, milk, cider, brown sugar, vanilla, nutmeg, and remaining ¼ tsp. cinnamon; pour over bread mixture in baking dish. Cover and chill 1 hour.
3. Preheat oven to 350°. Bake bread 45 to 50 minutes or until top is crisp and golden brown. Serve warm with Toasted Pecan–Caramel Sauce.

Toasted Pecan–Caramel Sauce

Makes about ¾ cup
Hands-on Time: 24 min. **Total Time:** 34 min.

- ¼ cup chopped pecans
- ¾ cup sugar
- 1 tsp. light corn syrup
- ½ cup evaporated milk
- 1½ tsp. butter

1. Preheat oven to 350°. Bake pecans in a single layer in a shallow pan 8 to 10 minutes or until toasted and fragrant.
2. Sprinkle sugar in an even layer in a small saucepan. Stir together syrup and ⅓ cup water, and pour over sugar in saucepan. Cook, without stirring, over medium-high heat 12 to 14 minutes or until sugar is dissolved and syrup mixture is golden.
3. Remove from heat. Gradually whisk in evaporated milk. (Mixture will bubble.) Stir in butter and toasted pecans.

test kitchen secret

Use this versatile, scrumptious sauce as a topper for ice cream—or even for pancakes or waffles.

Caramel–Cream Cheese Flan

The custard of choice in Spain, flan is similar to créme caramel; it bakes in a caramel-lined mold and is turned out before serving. Flan, though, is richer than créme caramel because the custard is made with more eggs and yolks, as well as half-and-half, evaporated milk, or sweetened condensed milk.

Makes 8 servings
Hands-on Time: 15 min. **Total Time:** 7 hr., 10 min.

1½   cups sugar, divided
7   egg yolks
1   (14-oz.) can sweetened condensed milk
1   (12-oz.) can evaporated milk
¾   cup milk
1½   tsp. vanilla extract
⅛   tsp. salt
4   egg whites
1   (8-oz.) package cream cheese, softened

1. Cook 1 cup sugar in a 9-inch round cake pan over medium heat, stirring occasionally, 5 minutes or until sugar melts and turns golden brown. Remove pan from heat, and let stand 5 minutes. (Sugar will harden.)
2. Meanwhile, whisk together egg yolks, milks, vanilla, and salt in a large bowl.
3. Process egg whites, cream cheese, and remaining ½ cup sugar in a blender until smooth. Add 2 cups egg yolk mixture, and process until smooth. Stir egg white mixture into remaining egg yolk mixture until blended. Pour custard over caramelized sugar in pan.
4. Place cake pan in a large shallow pan. Add hot water one-third up sides of cake pan.
5. Bake at 350° for 50 to 60 minutes or until a knife inserted into center of flan comes out clean. Remove pan from water; cool completely on a wire rack (about 2 hours). Cover and chill 4 hours to 2 days.
6. Run a knife around edge of flan to loosen; invert onto a serving plate. (Once inverted, the flan will take about 30 seconds to slip from the pan. Be sure to use a serving plate with a lip to catch the extra caramel sauce.)

Caramel–Cream Cheese Flan

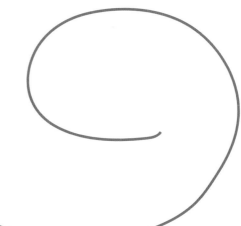

test-kitchen secret

The flan will continue to set as it cools in the pan and will set completely when it's chilled.

step-by-step

Tipsy Spiced Fruit Tart with Buttermilk Whipped Cream

1. Go with the flow: Don't worry if juices from the fruit run toward the edges of the crust. Just start folding, and tuck all that goodness inside.

2. Wrap it up: Fold the edges of the crust up and over the fruit mixture, loosely shaping pleats and turning the parchment paper as you go.

3. Make it sparkle: Brush the crust with beaten egg, and sprinkle with large golden crystals of Demerara sugar or coarse sparkling sugar.

Tipsy Spiced Fruit Tart with Buttermilk Whipped Cream

The bourbon-soaked fruits and bold flavors in this rustic pie make it an adults-only dessert. Splurge for a premium brandy or bourbon—it's worth it.

Makes 8 servings
Hands-on Time: 35 min. **Total Time:** 2 hr., including whipped cream, plus 24 hr. for chilling

- ⅔ cup bourbon or brandy
- ¾ tsp. ground cinnamon
- ¼ tsp. ground allspice
- ¾ cup granulated sugar, divided
- 1 cup halved dried Mission figlets
- 1 (7-oz.) package dried apricots, coarsely chopped
- 1 cup jumbo raisins
- 3 ripe Bartlett pears, peeled and chopped
- 2 Tbsp. all-purpose flour
- 2 tsp. finely grated fresh ginger
- 1 (14.1-oz.) package refrigerated piecrusts
- Parchment paper
- 1 large egg, beaten
- 2 tsp. Demerara sugar*
- Buttermilk Whipped Cream

1. Cook bourbon, next 2 ingredients, and ½ cup granulated sugar in a medium saucepan over medium-low heat, stirring often, 3 minutes or until sugar is dissolved and mixture is hot. Remove from heat, and stir in figlets, apricots, and raisins. Pour mixture into a large zip-top plastic freezer bag. Seal bag, removing as much air as possible; chill 24 hours.
2. Preheat oven to 350°. Transfer fruit mixture to a large bowl; stir in pears, flour, ginger, and remaining ¼ cup sugar.
3. Unroll and stack piecrusts on parchment paper. Roll into a 12-inch circle. Mound fruit mixture in center of piecrust (mixture will be slightly runny), leaving a 2- to 2½-inch border. Fold piecrust border up and over fruit, pleating as you go, leaving an opening about 5 inches wide in center. Brush piecrust with egg, and sprinkle with 2 tsp. Demerara sugar. Slide parchment paper onto a baking sheet.
4. Bake at 350° for 50 minutes or until filling is bubbly and crust is golden brown. Cool on baking sheet on a wire rack 30 minutes. Serve warm or at room temperature with Buttermilk Whipped Cream.

*Granulated sugar may be substituted.

Buttermilk Whipped Cream

Freeze the bowl and beaters, and use cream and buttermilk right out of the fridge for perfect results.

Makes 3 cups
Hands-on Time: 5 min. **Total Time:** 5 min.

- 1 cup heavy cream
- ½ cup buttermilk
- 2 Tbsp. sugar

1. Beat first 2 ingredients at high speed with an electric mixer until foamy; gradually add sugar, beating until soft peaks form. Serve immediately, or cover and chill up to 2 hours.

Rustic Spiced Apple Tart

Makes 8 servings
Hands-on Time: 35 min. **Total Time:** 2 hr., 30 min., including whipped cream

- 1½ lb. Honeycrisp or Braeburn apples, peeled and sliced
- ½ cup sugar
- ⅓ cup pear preserves
- 1 tsp. vanilla extract
- ¼ tsp. ground allspice
- 1 Tbsp. all-purpose flour
- 1 (14.1-oz.) package refrigerated piecrusts
- Parchment paper
- 1 large egg, lightly beaten
- 1 Tbsp. sugar
- Buttermilk Whipped Cream

1. Preheat oven to 350°. Stir together first 5 ingredients in a large bowl. Let stand 30 minutes, stirring occasionally. Stir in flour.
2. Unroll and stack piecrusts on parchment paper. Roll into a 12-inch circle. Mound apple mixture in center of piecrust using a slotted spoon (mixture will be slightly runny), leaving a 2- to 2½-inch border. Fold piecrust border up and over fruit, pleating as you go, leaving an opening 5 inches wide in center. Drizzle apples with any remaining juice in bowl. Brush piecrust with egg, and sprinkle with 1 Tbsp. sugar. Slide parchment paper onto a baking sheet.
3. Bake at 350° for 50 to 55 minutes or until filling is bubbly and crust is golden brown. Cool on a baking sheet on a wire rack 30 minutes. Serve warm with Buttermilk Whipped Cream.

Tiny Caramel Tarts

Add a festive touch. Just before serving, sprinkle tarts with finely chopped chocolate, crystallized ginger, toffee, or Buttered Pecans.

Makes 6 dozen
Hands-on Time: 30 min. **Total Time:** 4 hr., 35 min., including pastry shells

- 2   cups sugar, divided
- ½   cup cold butter, sliced
- 6   Tbsp. all-purpose flour
- 4   egg yolks
- 2   cups milk
- Cream Cheese Pastry Shells
- Sweetened whipped cream

1. Cook 1 cup sugar in a medium-size heavy skillet over medium heat, stirring constantly, 6 to 8 minutes or until sugar melts and turns golden brown. Stir in butter until melted.
2. Whisk together flour, egg yolks, milk, and remaining 1 cup sugar in a 3-qt. heavy saucepan; bring mixture just to a simmer over low heat, whisking constantly. Add sugar mixture to flour mixture, and cook, whisking constantly, 1 to 2 minutes or until thickened. Cover and chill 4 hours.
3. Meanwhile, prepare Cream Cheese Pastry Shells. Spoon caramel mixture into pastry shells, and top with sweetened whipped cream.

Cream Cheese Pastry Shells

Makes 6 dozen
Hands-on Time: 35 min. **Total time:** 2 hr., 20 min.

- 1   cup butter, softened
- 1   (8-oz.) package cream cheese, softened
- 3½   cups all-purpose flour

1. Beat butter and cream cheese at medium speed with a heavy-duty electric stand mixer until creamy. Gradually add flour to butter mixture, beating at low speed just until blended. Shape dough into 72 (¾-inch) balls, and place on a baking sheet; cover and chill 1 hour.
2. Place dough balls in cups of lightly greased miniature muffin pans; press dough to top of cups, forming shells.
3. Bake at 400° for 10 to 12 minutes. Remove from pans to wire racks, and cool completely (about 15 minutes).

Buttered Pecans

Makes 2 cups
Hands-on Time: 10 min. **Total Time:** 22 min.

- 2   cups coarsely chopped pecans
- ¼   cup butter, melted

1. Preheat oven to 350°. Stir together pecans and melted butter. Spread in a single layer in a 13- x 9-inch pan. Bake 12 to 15 minutes or until toasted and fragrant, stirring halfway through. Remove from oven, and let cool in pan.

Orange–Sweet Potato Pie with Rosemary-Cornmeal Crust

Makes 8 servings
Hands-on Time: 35 min. **Total Time:** 4 hr., 35 min.

Rosemary-Cornmeal Crust:
- ¾   cup all-purpose flour
- ½   cup plain white cornmeal
- ¼   cup powdered sugar
- 2   tsp. chopped fresh rosemary
- ¼   tsp. salt
- ½   cup cold butter, cut into pieces
- ¼   cup very cold water

Orange–Sweet Potato Filling:
- 1½   lb. sweet potatoes
- 3   large eggs
- ¾   cup granulated sugar
- 1   cup evaporated milk
- 3   Tbsp. butter, melted
- 2   tsp. orange zest
- 1   Tbsp. fresh orange juice
- ½   tsp. ground cinnamon
- ¼   tsp. ground nutmeg
- 1½   tsp. vanilla extract

1. Prepare crust: Whisk together first 5 ingredients in a medium bowl until well blended. Cut butter into flour mixture with a pastry blender or fork until mixture resembles small peas and is crumbly.
2. Sprinkle cold water, 1 Tbsp. at a time, over surface of mixture in bowl; stir with a fork until dry ingredients are moistened. Place dough on a plastic wrap–lined flat surface, and shape into a disc. Wrap dough in plastic wrap, and chill 30 minutes.

3. Unwrap dough, and roll between 2 new sheets of lightly floured plastic wrap into a 12-inch circle. Fit into a 9-inch pie plate. Fold edges under, and crimp. Chill 30 minutes. Preheat oven to 400°. Bake crust 20 minutes, shielding edges with aluminum foil to prevent excessive browning. Cool completely on a wire rack (about 1 hour).

4. Meanwhile, prepare filling: Bake sweet potatoes at 400° on a baking sheet 50 to 55 minutes or until tender. Let stand 5 minutes. Cut potatoes in half lengthwise; scoop out pulp into a bowl. Mash pulp. Discard skins.

5. Whisk together eggs and granulated sugar until well blended. Add milk, next 6 ingredients, and sweet potato pulp, stirring until blended. Pour mixture into Rosemary-Cornmeal Crust.

6. Bake at 400° for 20 minutes. Reduce heat to 325°, and bake 20 to 25 more minutes or until center is set. Let cool completely on a wire rack (about 1 hour).

test-kitchen secret

Substitute ½ (15-oz.) package refrigerated piecrusts for cornmeal crust ingredients. Unroll on a lightly floured surface. Sprinkle with 1 Tbsp. plain white cornmeal and 2 tsp. chopped fresh rosemary. Lightly roll cornmeal and rosemary into crust. Fit into a 9-inch pie plate according to package directions. Fold edges under; crimp. Proceed as directed, beginning with Step 5.

Orange–Sweet Potato Pie with Rosemary-Cornmeal Crust

Sweet Potato Pie with Marshmallow Meringue

Be sure to lightly pack the mashed sweet potatoes in your measuring cup for a fluffy filling.

Makes 8 to 10 servings
Hands-on Time: 20 min. **Total Time:** 2 hr., 31 min.

Crust:
- ½ (14.1-oz.) package refrigerated piecrusts
- Parchment paper
- 1 egg yolk, lightly beaten
- 1 Tbsp. whipping cream

Filling:
- ¼ cup butter, melted
- 1 cup sugar
- ¼ tsp. salt
- 3 large eggs
- 3 cups lightly packed, cooked, mashed sweet potatoes (about 2½ lb. sweet potatoes)
- 1 cup half-and-half
- 1 Tbsp. lemon zest
- 3 Tbsp. lemon juice
- ¼ tsp. ground nutmeg

Marshmallow Meringue:
- 3 egg whites
- ½ tsp. vanilla extract
- ⅛ tsp. salt
- ¼ cup sugar
- 1 (7-oz.) jar marshmallow crème

1. Prepare crust: Preheat oven to 425°. Roll piecrust into a 13-inch circle on a lightly floured surface. Fit into a 9-inch pie plate; fold edges under, and crimp. Prick bottom and sides with a fork. Line piecrust with parchment paper; fill with pie weights or dried beans. Bake 9 minutes. Remove weights and parchment paper.

2. Whisk together egg yolk and cream; brush bottom and sides of crust with yolk mixture. Bake 6 to 8 more minutes or until crust is golden. Transfer to a wire rack, and cool. Reduce oven temperature to 350°.

3. Prepare filling: Stir together melted butter, sugar, and next 2 ingredients in a large bowl until mixture is well blended. Add sweet potatoes and next 4 ingredients; stir until mixture is well blended. Pour sweet potato mixture into prepared piecrust. (Pie will be very full.)

4. Bake at 350° for 50 to 55 minutes or until a knife inserted in center comes out clean, shielding top with aluminum foil to prevent excessive browning. Transfer pie to wire rack, and cool completely (about 1 hour).

5. Prepare meringue: Beat egg whites, vanilla extract, and salt at high speed with a heavy-duty electric stand mixer until foamy. Gradually add sugar, 1 Tbsp. at a time, beating until stiff peaks form.

6. Beat one-fourth of marshmallow crème into egg white mixture; repeat 3 times with remaining marshmallow crème, beating until smooth (about 1 minute). Spread over pie.

7. Bake at 400° for 6 to 7 minutes or until meringue is lightly browned.

Note: Pie can be made up to a day ahead. Prepare recipe as directed through Step 4; cover and chill up to 24 hours. Proceed as directed in Steps 5 through 7.

Pumpkin Pie
Spectacular

Pumpkin Pie Spectacular

Makes 8 servings
Hands-on Time: 20 min. **Total Time:** 3 hr., 25 min., including streusel and topping

½ (14.1-oz.) package refrigerated piecrusts
2 cups crushed gingersnaps (about 40 gingersnaps)
1 cup pecans, finely chopped
½ cup powdered sugar
¼ cup butter, melted
1 (15-oz.) can pumpkin
1 (14-oz.) can sweetened condensed milk
2 large eggs, beaten
½ cup sour cream
1 tsp. ground cinnamon
½ tsp. vanilla extract
¼ tsp. ground ginger
Pecan Streusel
7 thin ginger cookies, halved
Garnish: Ginger-Spice Topping, ground cinnamon

1. Preheat oven to 350°. Fit piecrust into a 9-inch deep-dish pie plate according to package directions; fold edges under, and crimp.
2. Stir together crushed gingersnaps and next 3 ingredients. Press mixture on bottom and ½ inch up sides of piecrust.
3. Bake at 350° for 10 minutes. Let cool completely on a wire rack (about 30 minutes).
4. Stir together pumpkin and next 6 ingredients until well blended. Pour into prepared crust. Place pie on an aluminum foil–lined baking sheet.

5. Bake at 350° for 30 minutes. Sprinkle Pecan Streusel around edge of crust. Bake 40 to 45 more minutes or until set, shielding edges with aluminum foil during last 25 to 30 minutes of baking, if necessary. Insert ginger cookies around edge of crust. Let cool completely on a wire rack (about 1 hour). Dollop with Ginger-Spice Topping; dust with cinnamon.

Pecan Streusel

Makes about 1 cup
Hands-on Time: 10 min. **Total Time:** 10 min.

¼ cup all-purpose flour
¼ cup firmly packed dark brown sugar
2 Tbsp. melted butter
¾ cup pecans, coarsely chopped

1. Stir together all ingredients.

Ginger-Spice Topping

Makes 3 cups
Hands-on Time: 5 min. **Total Time:** 5 min.

1. Stir together 1 (8-oz.) container frozen whipped topping, thawed; ¼ tsp. ground cinnamon; and ¼ tsp. ground ginger.

Scrumptious Apple Pie

Scrumptious Apple Pie

Makes 8 servings
Hands-on Time: 30 min. **Total Time:** 1 hr., 55 min.

7   cups peeled and sliced Granny Smith apples (about 5 medium)
½   cup granulated sugar
2   tsp. lemon juice
¾   cup all-purpose flour, divided
½   tsp. salt, divided
¾   cup butter
1   cup firmly packed brown sugar
½   cup uncooked quick-cooking oats
½   (14.1-oz.) package refrigerated piecrusts
½   cup chopped pecans
Jarred caramel topping, vanilla ice cream

1. Preheat oven to 375°. Stir together first 3 ingredients, ¼ cup flour, and ¼ tsp. salt until well blended.
2. Cut butter into remaining ½ cup flour with a pastry blender or fork until mixture resembles small peas. Stir in brown sugar, oats, and remaining ¼ tsp. salt.
3. Fit piecrust into a 9-inch pie plate according to package directions; fold edges under, and crimp. Place apple mixture in piecrust, and top with brown sugar mixture, pressing gently to adhere. Shield edges of crust with aluminum foil. Place pie on a foil-lined baking sheet.
4. Bake at 375° for 25 minutes. Remove foil from crust, and bake 25 more minutes or until golden brown. Sprinkle with pecans, and bake 5 to 7 minutes or until pecans are toasted. Let pie stand 30 minutes to 2 hours before serving. Serve with caramel topping and ice cream.

Upside-Down Apple-Pecan-Raisin Pie

Sprinkling 1 to 2 tsp. lemon juice over cut apples will help prevent browning.

Makes 8 servings
Hands-on Time: 28 min. **Total Time:** 2 hr., 31 min.

1   cup pecan halves
4   Tbsp. butter, melted
½   cup firmly packed light brown sugar
1   (14.1-oz.) package refrigerated piecrusts
½   cup granulated sugar
2   Tbsp. all-purpose flour
½   tsp. ground cinnamon
¼   tsp. freshly grated nutmeg
1½   lb. peeled and sliced Granny Smith or Rome apples (about 3 medium)
1   cup golden raisins
2   Tbsp. butter, cut into pieces

1. Preheat oven to 350°. Bake pecans in a single layer in a shallow pan 8 to 10 minutes or until toasted and fragrant, stirring after 5 minutes. Let cool 30 minutes. Increase oven temperature to 375°.
2. Stir together melted butter and brown sugar. Stir in pecans, and spread mixture on bottom of a lightly greased 9-inch pie plate. Unroll 1 pie crust, and fit into pie plate over top of pecan mixture.
3. Combine granulated sugar and next 3 ingredients in a large bowl. Add apples and raisins, and toss to coat.
4. Spoon apple mixture into prepared crust. Dot butter pieces over apple mixture.
5. Unroll remaining piecrust; place over filling. Fold edges under, and crimp; cut slits in top for steam to escape. Place pie on a baking sheet.
6. Bake at 375° for 50 to 55 minutes, shielding edges with foil during last 30 minutes, if necessary. Cool on a wire rack 5 minutes. Invert pie onto a plate, and let cool 1 hour.

Pecan-Cheesecake Pie

Makes 8 servings
Hands-on Time: 15 min. **Total Time:** 2 hr., 10 min.

½ (14.1-oz.) package refrigerated piecrusts
1   (8-oz.) package cream cheese, softened
4   large eggs, divided
¾ cup sugar, divided
2   tsp. vanilla extract, divided
¼ tsp. salt
1¼ cups chopped pecans
1   cup light corn syrup

1. Fit piecrust into a 9-inch pie plate according to package directions. Fold edges under, and crimp.
2. Beat cream cheese, 1 egg, ½ cup sugar, 1 tsp. vanilla, and salt at medium speed with an electric mixer until smooth. Pour cream cheese mixture into piecrust; sprinkle evenly with chopped pecans.
3. Whisk together corn syrup and remaining 3 eggs, ¼ cup sugar, and 1 tsp. vanilla; pour mixture over pecans. Place pie on a baking sheet.
4. Bake at 350° on lowest oven rack 50 to 55 minutes or until pie is set. Cool on a wire rack 1 hour or until completely cool. Serve immediately, or cover and chill up to 2 days.

Raspberry–Ice Cream Pie

Makes 10 servings
Hands-on Time: 30 min. **Total Time:** 4 hr., 25 min.

- ½ (18-oz.) package cream-filled chocolate sandwich cookies (about 22 cookies)
- 2 Tbsp. butter, melted
- 1 (1.5-qt.) container vanilla ice cream
- ¾ cup seedless raspberry jam
- 1½ Tbsp. orange juice
- 1 (4-oz.) semisweet chocolate baking bar, finely chopped

Garnish: fresh raspberries

1. Preheat oven to 350°. Process first 2 ingredients in a food processor until cookies are finely crushed. Firmly press mixture on bottom and up sides of a lightly greased 9-inch springform pan.
2. Bake at 350° for 10 minutes. Cool completely in pan on a wire rack (about 30 minutes).
3. Meanwhile, let vanilla ice cream stand at room temperature 20 minutes or until slightly softened. Stir together raspberry jam and orange juice until smooth.
4. Place ice cream in a large bowl; cut into 3-inch pieces. Gently fold chocolate and ½ cup raspberry mixture into ice cream until just blended. Spoon mixture into prepared crust. Drizzle top of ice cream mixture with remaining raspberry mixture, and gently swirl with a long wooden skewer or knife. Freeze 3 hours or until firm. Let stand at room temperature 15 minutes before serving. Garnish, if desired.

Triple Chocolate–Cookie Trifle Pie

Makes 10 to 12 servings
Hands-on Time: 25 min. **Total Time:** 8 hr., 45 min., including glaze

- 3¼ cups heavy cream, divided
- 1½ (4-oz.) bittersweet chocolate baking bars, chopped
- 1 (4-oz.) white chocolate baking bar, chopped
- 1 tsp. vanilla extract, divided
- 1 (12.5-oz.) package assorted cookies
- 2 Tbsp. mocha liqueur (optional)
- 2 (6-oz.) containers fresh raspberries

Raspberry Glaze

1. Microwave ½ cup heavy cream at HIGH 30 seconds to 1 minute or until hot (do not boil). Place bittersweet chocolate in a large bowl. Pour hot cream over chocolate, and stir until smooth. Repeat procedure with ¼ cup cream and white chocolate. (If chocolate does not melt completely after stirring, microwave at HIGH for 10-second intervals just until chocolate is melted and mixture is smooth.) Stir ½ tsp. vanilla into each chocolate mixture until well blended. Cool 20 minutes.
2. Meanwhile, let 2½ cups cream stand at room temperature 20 minutes. Beat 1½ cups cream at medium-high speed with an electric mixer until medium peaks form. Gently fold one-fourth of whipped cream into cool bittersweet chocolate mixture. Fold in remaining whipped cream.
3. Beat remaining 1 cup cream at medium-high speed until medium peaks form. Gently fold one-fourth of whipped cream into cool white chocolate mixture. Fold in remaining whipped cream.
4. Crush 6 to 7 cookies to equal ½ cup crumbs. Sprinkle on bottom of a lightly greased 9-inch springform pan. Spread half of bittersweet chocolate mixture over crushed cookies in pan. Arrange assorted cookies around sides of pan (about 19 cookies). Spread white chocolate mixture over bittersweet chocolate mixture.
5. Crush remaining cookies, and sprinkle pieces over white chocolate mixture in springform pan. Drizzle with liqueur, if desired. Spread remaining bittersweet chocolate mixture over crushed cookies. Cover and chill 8 to 24 hours.
6. Remove sides from pan. Mound raspberries in center of trifle; brush with Raspberry Glaze. Serve immediately.

Note: We tested with Ghirardelli 60% Cacao Bittersweet Baking Bars, Ghirardelli White Chocolate Baking Bar, Pepperidge Farm Distinctive Entertaining Cookie Collection, and Godiva Mocha Liqueur.

Raspberry Glaze

Makes ¼ cup
Hands-on Time: 5 min. **Total Time:** 5 min.

1. Combine 3 Tbsp. seedless raspberry jam and 2 tsp. water in a small glass bowl. Microwave at HIGH 10 to 15 seconds or until smooth.

Triple Chocolate–Cookie Trifle Pie

Sweet-Hot Honey Mustard;
Italian-Parmesan Herb Mix

ITALIAN
PARMESAN
HERB MIX

SWEET HOT
HONEY
MUSTARD

GIFTS *from the kitchen*

make ahead

Sweet-Hot Honey Mustard

This is a delicious complement to holiday ham and turkey. Spread it on a grilled chicken sandwich or over the crust of a quiche before adding the filling. Straight from the jar, it makes a bold and spicy dip for egg rolls.

Makes 4 cups
Hands-on Time: 15 min. **Total Time:** 15 min.

- 2   cups sugar
- 1½ cups dry mustard
- 2   cups white vinegar
- 3   large eggs, lightly beaten
- ½   cup honey

1. Whisk together sugar and mustard in a heavy 3-qt. saucepan; gradually whisk in vinegar and eggs until blended. Cook mustard mixture over medium heat, whisking constantly, 10 to 12 minutes or until smooth and thickened. Remove from heat, and whisk in honey. Let cool, and store in airtight containers in the refrigerator up to 1 month.

Cranberry-Pecan Chicken Salad: Stir together 8 cups chopped cooked chicken; 3 celery ribs, diced; 5 green onions, thinly sliced; 1½ cups chopped toasted pecans; 1 (6-oz.) package sweetened dried cranberries; 1 cup mayonnaise; and ½ cup Sweet-Hot Honey Mustard. Hands-on Time: 20 min.; Total Time: 20 min.

Note: Made with Sweet-Hot Honey Mustard, Cranberry-Pecan Chicken Salad is great to keep on hand for casual get-togethers. Serve as a festive luncheon entrée with sliced avocado and fresh fruit, or tuck tiny scoops into miniature tart shells for a quick appetizer. It also makes a terrific tea sandwich. For holiday gift-giving, pack into pretty jars, and deliver to family and friends along with a fresh loaf of bakery bread.

make ahead

Italian-Parmesan Herb Mix

Italian-Parmesan Herb Mix is one of our most versatile seasoning blends. Toss with hot cooked pasta, steamed veggies, or a bag of popped microwave popcorn. Sprinkle it over French bread and croutons; or dip frozen rolls and biscuits into melted butter, and dredge with the mixture before baking. Combined with an equal amount of soft, fresh breadcrumbs, it makes an irresistibly crisp coating for pan-fried chicken cutlets and pork chops or a flavorful binder for homemade meatballs and meatloaf.

Makes about 2 cups
Hands-on Time: 5 min. **Total Time:** 5 min.

- 1   (8-oz.) container grated Parmesan cheese
- 3   Tbsp. dried Italian seasoning
- 3   Tbsp. dried parsley flakes
- 1   Tbsp. granulated garlic
- ½   tsp. ground red pepper

1. Stir together all ingredients. Store mixture in airtight containers in refrigerator up to 6 weeks.

Holiday Herb Butter: Stir together 1 cup softened butter and ¼ cup Italian-Parmesan Herb Mix. Makes 1 cup. Hands-on Time: 5 min.; Total Time: 5 min.

Note: Pack this flavorful butter into colorful pottery crocks, or mold into festive shapes using holiday cookie cutters. Inexpensive sheets of plastic candy molds, sold at crafts stores, are perfect for shaping individual portions of butter. To make the Christmas tree-shaped butter, place a tree-shaped cookie cutter on a plate lined with wax paper; fill with butter, and garnish with pink peppercorns. Freeze 4 hours or until firm enough to remove from mold. Place in a zip-top plastic freezer bag, and freeze up to 1 month.

Carrot Pickles with Shallots and Dill

Makes 2 pt.
Hands-on Time: 15 min. **Total Time:** 2 hr., 50 min.

- 1½ lb. carrots
- 2 large shallots, thinly sliced
- 6 fresh dill sprigs
- 4 garlic cloves, peeled and crushed
- 2 tsp. black peppercorns
- ½ tsp. celery seeds
- 2 cups white wine vinegar
- 2 tsp. kosher salt
- 2 tsp. sugar

1. Cut carrots diagonally into ⅛-inch-thick slices. Combine carrots, shallot, and next 4 ingredients in 2 (1-pt.) canning jars with lids.
2. Bring vinegar and remaining ingredients to a simmer in a medium saucepan. Remove from heat, and pour hot vinegar mixture over carrot mixture. Cover loosely, and let cool to room temperature (about 30 minutes). Seal and chill 2 hours before serving mixture. Store in refrigerator up to 2 weeks.

Fig-and-Bourbon Compote

Makes 1 pt.
Hands-on Time: 15 min. **Total Time:** 44 min.

- 1 cup apple cider
- ⅔ cup bourbon
- 1 Tbsp. dark brown sugar
- 10 oz. dried Mission figlets (about 2 cups), halved
- ½ cup whipping cream
- 1½ Tbsp. powdered sugar

1. Combine cider, bourbon, and brown sugar in a small saucepan. Stir in figlets, and let stand 10 minutes.
2. Bring figlet mixture to a simmer; cook 10 minutes or until figlets are soft. Transfer figlets to a medium bowl using a slotted spoon. Simmer liquid until thickened and reduced by half (about 4 minutes). Pour liquid over figlets. Serve warm, or store in refrigerator up to 1 week.
3. Beat cream at medium speed with an electric mixer until soft peaks form. Add powdered sugar, beating until stiff peaks form. Serve over compote.

Cheese Relish

Serve this tangy cousin to pimiento cheese on crackers or in grilled sandwiches. Make sure the cheese is well chilled before grating.

Makes 2 cups
Hands-on Time: 15 min. **Total Time:** 2 hr., 25 min.

- 2 Tbsp. capers, drained
- 10 oz. Swiss cheese, finely grated (about 3½ cups)
- 1 (12-oz.) jar sliced mild banana peppers, drained and minced
- 2 Tbsp. minced fresh chives
- 3 Tbsp. sour cream
- ¼ tsp. pepper
- ¼ tsp. dried crushed red pepper
- ¼ tsp. kosher salt

1. Soak capers in water to cover 10 minutes; drain.
2. Stir together capers and remaining ingredients. Cover and chill 2 hours before serving. Store in refrigerator up to 2 days.

Smoky Pecan Relish

Makes about 1½ cups
Hands-on Time: 15 min. **Total Time:** 2 hr., 53 min.

- ½ cup pecan halves
- 1 (12-oz.) jar roasted red bell peppers, drained and rinsed
- 3 Tbsp. extra virgin olive oil
- 1 Tbsp. red wine vinegar
- 1 garlic clove, minced
- 1½ tsp. smoked paprika*
- ½ tsp. salt
- ¼ tsp. ground red pepper

1. Preheat oven to 350°. Bake pecans in a single layer in a shallow pan 8 to 10 minutes or until toasted and fragrant. Let cool 15 minutes.
2. Pat peppers dry with paper towels. Combine peppers, pecans, oil, and remaining ingredients in a food processor. Pulse 8 to 10 times or until finely chopped (but not smooth). Cover and chill 2 hours before serving. Store in refrigerator up to 1 week. Let stand at room temperature 30 minutes before serving.

*1 tsp. regular paprika with ½ tsp. ground cumin may be substituted for smoked paprika.

Pickled Okra

Makes 7 (1-pt.) jars
Hands-on Time: 30 min. **Total Time:** 12 hr., 45 min., including cooling

1	(9-piece) canning kit, including canner, jar lifter, and canning rack
7	(1-pt.) canning jars
2½	lb. small fresh okra
7	small fresh green chile peppers
7	garlic cloves
2	Tbsp. plus 1 tsp. dill seeds
4	cups white vinegar (5% acidity)
½	cup salt
¼	cup sugar

1. Bring canner half-full with water to a boil; simmer. Meanwhile, place jars in a large stockpot with water to cover; bring to a boil, and simmer. Place bands and lids in a large saucepan with water to cover; bring to a boil, and simmer. Remove hot jars 1 at a time using jar lifter.

2. Pack okra into hot jars, filling to ½ inch from top. Place 1 pepper, 1 garlic clove, and 1 tsp. dill seeds in each jar. Bring vinegar, salt, sugar, and 4 cups water to a boil over medium-high heat. Pour over okra, filling to ½ inch from top.

3. Wipe jar rims; cover at once with metal lids, and screw on bands (snug but not too tight). Place jars in canning rack, and place in simmering water in canner. Add additional boiling water as needed to cover by 1 to 2 inches.

4. Bring water to a rolling boil; boil 10 minutes. Remove from heat. Cool jars in canner 5 minutes. Transfer jars to a cutting board; cool 12 to 24 hours. Test seals of jars by pressing center of each lid. If lids do not pop, jars are properly sealed. Store in a cool, dry place at room temperature up to 1 year.

step-by-step

Step 1

Step 2

Step 3

Step 4

Pickled Grapes with Rosemary and Chiles

1. Pack grapes into 4 (1-pt.) canning jars with lids. Add 1 rosemary sprig to each jar.
2. Bring vinegar, next 4 ingredients, 1 cup water, and remaining 2 rosemary sprigs to a simmer in a medium saucepan. Remove from heat, and discard rosemary sprigs. Pour hot vinegar mixture over grapes. Cover loosely, and let cool to room temperature (about 30 minutes). Seal and chill 1 hour before serving. Store in refrigerator up to 1 week.

Pecan Pesto

Package this tasty treat in a glass jar tied with a festive bow. Add a gift tag with serving suggestions, which could include pasta, meats, salads, and chicken.

Makes 2 cups
Hands-on Time: 15 min. **Total Time:** 15 min.

    4   cups loosely packed fresh basil leaves
    1   cup (4 oz.) freshly shredded Parmesan cheese
    1   cup toasted pecans
    1   cup olive oil
    4   garlic cloves
    2   Tbsp. lemon juice
    ½   tsp. salt
    ½   tsp. pepper

1. Process all ingredients in a food processor until smooth.

make ahead

Pickled Grapes with Rosemary and Chiles

We love these unusual "pickles" with everything from chicken salad to antipasto. They're also delicious straight off a fork.

Makes 4 pt.
Hands-on Time: 10 min. **Total Time:** 1 hr., 45 min.

    3   cups seedless green grapes (about 1 lb.)
    3   cups seedless red grapes (about 1 lb.)
    6   (4-inch-long) fresh rosemary sprigs, divided
    2   cups white wine vinegar
    3   garlic cloves, thinly sliced
    2   Tbsp. kosher salt
    2   tsp. sugar
    ½   tsp. dried crushed red pepper

Pecan Pesto

make ahead • freezer friendly

Pecan-Honey Butter

Makes 1 cup
Hands-on Time: 5 min. **Total Time:** 5 min.

- ½ cup butter, softened
- ½ cup finely chopped toasted pecans
- 2 Tbsp. honey

1. Stir together butter, pecans, and honey. Store in refrigerator up to 1 week, or freeze up to 1 month.

Note: Be sure to cool pecans completely after toasting.

Chili-Lime Pecans

Makes 3 cups
Hands-on Time: 10 min. **Total Time:** 22 min.

- 2 Tbsp. lime juice
- 1 Tbsp. olive oil
- 1 tsp. paprika
- 1 tsp. salt
- 1 tsp. chili powder
- ½ tsp. ground red pepper
- 3 cups pecans

1. Preheat oven to 350°. Stir together lime juice, olive oil, paprika, salt, chili powder, and ground red pepper. Add 3 cups pecans; toss. Spread in a lightly greased aluminum foil–lined jelly-roll pan. Bake at 350° for 12 to 14 minutes or until pecans are toasted and dry, stirring occasionally. Cool completely.

test-kitchen secret

Toasting pecans brings out even more flavor. Use your sense of smell to judge when they're toasted; the smaller the pieces, the quicker they toast, so don't turn your back! Preheat oven to 350°. Bake pecans in a single layer in a shallow pan until lightly toasted and fragrant, stirring occasionally. (This should take about 8 to 10 minutes.)

Pecan-Honey Butter

Chili-Lime Pecans

Santa Snack Mix

make ahead

Santa Snack Mix

Makes 8 cups
Hands-on Time: 15 min. **Total Time:** 1 hr., 35 min.

4	cups toasted oat bran cereal
1	cup multigrain cluster cereal
1	cup chopped pecans
1	tsp. ground allspice
¼	tsp. salt
¾	cup honey
½	cup butter
1	cup jumbo red raisins

Wax paper

1. Preheat oven to 250°. Combine first 5 ingredients in a large bowl.
2. Cook honey and butter together in a small saucepan over low heat, stirring occasionally, until butter is melted and mixture is blended and smooth (about 5 minutes).
3. Pour honey mixture over cereal mixture, stirring to coat. Spread in a single layer on a lightly greased aluminum foil–lined 15- x 10-inch jelly-roll pan.
4. Bake at 250° for 55 minutes, stirring mixture once every 10 to 15 minutes. Stir in raisins, and bake 5 more minutes. Spread immediately on wax paper; cool 20 minutes. Store in an airtight container up to 1 week.

Note: We tested with Quaker Oat Bran for toasted oat bran cereal and Kashi GOLEAN Crunch for multigrain cluster cereal.

make ahead

Holiday Power Mix

We used a dried fruit–mix blend of blueberries, cherries, cranberries, and plums.

Makes about 7½ cups
Hands-on Time: 5 min. **Total Time:** 5 min.

2	(5-oz.) packages dried fruit blend
2½	cups pretzel twists
1½	cups candy-coated dark chocolate pieces
1	cup roasted, salted almonds
⅓	cup coarsely chopped crystallized ginger

1. Toss all ingredients together in a large bowl. Store in a zip-top plastic freezer bag up to 1 week.

Note: We tested with M&Ms Dark Chocolate Candies for the Holidays.

Microwave Snack Mix

Use a glass bowl when you zap this in the microwave. (Don't use a plastic bowl; we tried it, and the mixture got too hot and could possibly burn.) Package these tasty treats in plastic gift sacks tied with festive ribbon.

Makes 13 cups
Hands-on Time: 15 min. **Total Time:** 45 min.

2	(1-oz.) envelopes Ranch dressing mix
½	cup vegetable oil
3	cups crisp oatmeal cereal squares
3	cups corn-and-rice cereal
3	cups crisp wheat cereal squares
2	cups pretzel sticks

Wax paper

1	cup dried cherries
1	cup candy-coated chocolate pieces

1. Whisk together Ranch dressing mix and vegetable oil in a large microwave-safe glass bowl. Stir in oatmeal cereal squares and next 3 ingredients.
2. Microwave cereal mixture at HIGH 2 minutes, and stir well. Microwave at HIGH 2 more minutes, and stir well. Spread mixture in a single layer on wax paper, and let cool 30 minutes. Add cherries and candy pieces. Store in an airtight container up to 5 days.

Note: We tested with Quaker Essentials Oatmeal Squares for crisp oatmeal cereal squares, Crispix for corn-and-rice cereal, and Wheat Chex for wheat cereal squares.

Santa Fe Snack Seeds

Divide this hip food gift evenly among small airtight storage jars available from import or home stores. Use a funnel to fill the jars with the seed mix.

Makes 4 cups
Hands-on Time: 18 min. **Total Time:** 18 min.

- ¼ cup olive oil
- 1 tsp. ground cumin
- 1 tsp. chili powder
- ¼ cup sugar
- 2 Tbsp. honey
- 2 cups pumpkin seeds
- 2 cups sunflower seeds

1. Heat oil in a large nonstick skillet until hot; add cumin and chili powder. Cook over medium-high heat 30 seconds, stirring constantly. Add sugar and honey, and stir until sugar dissolves.
2. Stir in pumpkin and sunflower seeds; cook seeds, stirring constantly, 8 minutes or until seeds are toasted and mixture smells good.
3. Carefully spoon seed mixture onto a big piece of lightly greased aluminum foil. Cool completely. Store seeds in an airtight container up to 2 weeks.

Cheese Straws

If you like cheese straws less spicy, use the smaller amount of red pepper.

Makes about 2 dozen
Hands-on Time: 30 min. **Total Time:** 1 hr., 54 min.

- 1½ cups (6 oz.) shredded extra-sharp Cheddar cheese
- ¾ cup all-purpose flour
- ¼ cup unsalted butter, cut into 4 pieces and softened
- ½ tsp. kosher salt
- ¼ to ½ tsp. dried crushed red pepper
- 1 Tbsp. half-and-half

1. Combine first 5 ingredients in a food processor; pulse in 5-second intervals until mixture resembles coarse crumbs. Add half-and-half, and process 10 seconds or until dough forms a ball.

2. Turn dough out onto a well-floured surface, and roll into an 8- x 10-inch rectangle (about ⅛ inch thick). Cut dough with a sharp knife into ¼- to ½-inch-wide strips, dipping knife in flour after each cut to ensure clean cuts. Place on ungreased baking sheets.
3. Bake at 350° for 12 minutes or until ends are slightly browned. Cool on baking sheets on a wire rack 30 minutes. Break into desired lengths.

Note: To make cheese rounds, roll dough to ⅛-inch thickness; cut with a 1½-inch round cutter. Place on ungreased baking sheets. Bake and cool as directed. Freeze baked cheese straws or rounds in a zip-top plastic freezer bag up to 3 months. Thaw at room temperature 30 minutes before serving.

Cheddar Cheese Straws

Makes about 9 dozen
Hands-on Time: 30 min. **Total Time:** 1 hr., 40 min.

- 1½ cups butter, softened
- 1 (1-lb.) block sharp Cheddar cheese, shredded
- 1½ tsp. salt
- 1 to 2 tsp. ground red pepper
- ½ tsp. paprika
- 4 cups all-purpose flour
- Parchment paper

1. Preheat oven to 350°. Beat first 5 ingredients at medium speed with a heavy-duty electric stand mixer until blended. Gradually add flour, beating just until combined. Use a cookie press fitted with a star-shaped disk to shape dough mixture into 12-inch-long strips on parchment paper–lined baking sheets, following manufacturer's instructions. Cut each strip into 3 (4-inch) straws.
2. Bake at 350°, in batches, 12 minutes or until lightly browned. Remove to wire racks, and let cool completely (about 10 minutes).

Cheese Wafers: Prepare recipe as directed in Step 1; cover and chill dough 2 hours. Shape dough into 4 (8-inch-long) logs; wrap each in plastic wrap, and chill 8 hours. Cut each log into ¼-inch-thick slices; place on parchment paper–lined baking sheets. Bake at 350° for 13 to 15 minutes or until lightly browned. Remove to wire racks, and let cool completely (about 10 minutes). Store in an airtight container 1 week. Makes about 10 dozen. Hands-on Time: 30 min.; Total Time: 11 hr., 40 min, including chilling

Santa Fe Snack Seeds

Cheese Straws

Cheddar Cheese Straws

Whole Grain Marshmallow Crispy Bars

Makes 24 squares
Hands-on Time: 20 min. **Total Time:** 30 min.

- 3 Tbsp. butter
- 1 (10.5-oz.) bag miniature marshmallows
- 1 (15-oz.) box multigrain cluster cereal
- 1¼ cups dried cranberries, divided
- Vegetable cooking spray

1. Melt butter in a large saucepan over low heat. Add marshmallows, and cook, stirring constantly, 4 to 5 minutes or until melted and smooth. Remove from heat.
2. Stir in cereal and 1 cup cranberries until well coated.
3. Press cereal mixture into a 13- x 9-inch baking dish coated with cooking spray. Chop remaining ¼ cup cranberries, and sprinkle on top. Let stand 10 to 15 minutes or until firm. Cut into 24 bars.

Note: We tested with Kashi GOLEAN Crunch! cereal.

Cinnamon-Pecan Crispy Bars: Place ⅓ cup pecan halves, chopped, in a single layer on a shallow pan. Bake at 350° for 8 to 9 minutes or until toasted, stirring once after 5 minutes. Prepare Whole Grain Marshmallow Crispy Bars as directed through Step 2. Press mixture as directed into baking dish coated with cooking spray. Sprinkle with toasted chopped pecans and 1 tsp. ground cinnamon. Proceed with recipe as directed.

Benne Brittle

make ahead

Benne Brittle

Makes about 1 lb.
Hands-on Time: 23 min. **Total Time:** 43 min.

- 1¼ cups benne (sesame) seeds
- 2 cups sugar
- 1 tsp. vanilla extract

1. Cook benne seeds in a large heavy skillet over medium heat, stirring often, 8 minutes or until seeds begin to turn brown. Remove from skillet.
2. Cook sugar and 2 Tbsp. water in skillet over low heat, stirring constantly, 10 minutes or until sugar is melted. Quickly stir in benne seeds and vanilla. Pour onto a well-buttered baking sheet. Quickly spread to ⅛-inch thickness, using a metal spatula. Cool completely (20 minutes). Break into pieces. Store in an airtight container.

Whole Grain Marshmallow
Crispy Bars

Almond Brittle

When making almond brittle candy, start with a heavy nonaluminum saucepan to encourage even cooking and to prevent the mixture from over-browning. This tasty snack makes a great gift for teachers

Makes about 1 lb.
Hands-on Time: 30 min. **Total Time:** 1 hr.

   Butter
  3   Tbsp. butter
1¼   cups whole almonds
  1   cup sugar
  ½   tsp. baking soda

1. Line a baking sheet or 15- x 10-inch jelly-roll pan with aluminum foil; grease foil with butter. Set pan aside.
2. Melt 3 tablespoons butter in a small skillet over medium heat. Add almonds, and cook, stirring constantly, 2 minutes. Remove from heat.
3. Cook sugar and ¼ cup water in a small heavy saucepan over medium-high heat, stirring constantly, until mixture starts to boil. (Use a small brush dipped in cold water to brush down sugar crystals that cling to sides of pan.). Boil without stirring about 10 minutes or until a candy thermometer reaches 310° (hard-crack stage). (Mixture should be golden.) Remove from heat, and stir in almond mixture and baking soda.
4. Pour mixture immediately onto prepared baking sheet, spreading mixture quickly into an even layer with a metal spatula. Allow to stand 30 minutes or until hardened. Break into pieces.

test-kitchen secret

Choose a sunny, dry day to make this candy. It's sensitive to humidity. Store it in an airtight container to keep the candy crisp, crunchy, and not sticky to the touch.

Praline Pecans

freezer friendly • make ahead

Praline Pecans

Make pralines when the weather is dry—humidity tends to make them grainy. Use a heavy saucepan, and work quickly when spooning the pecan mixture onto the wax paper.

Makes about 8 cups
Hands-on Time: 20 min. **Total Time:** 40 min.

1½   cups granulated sugar
 ¾   cup firmly packed brown sugar
 ½   cup butter
 ½   cup milk
 2   tablespoons corn syrup
 5   cups toasted pecan halves
Wax paper

1. Stir together first 5 ingredients in a heavy 3-qt. saucepan. Bring to a boil over medium heat, stirring constantly. Boil, stirring constantly, 7 to 8 minutes or until a candy thermometer registers 234°.
2. Remove from heat, and vigorously stir in pecans. Spoon pecan mixture onto wax paper, spreading in an even layer. Let stand 20 minutes or until firm. Break praline-coated pecans apart into pieces. Store in an airtight container at room temperature up to 1 week. Freeze in an airtight container or zip-top plastic freezer bag up to 1 month.

Crunchy–Pecan Pie Bites

Velvety Pecan Candy

Crunchy–Pecan Pie Bites

Makes about 6 dozen
Hands-on Time: 15 minutes **Total Time:** 1 hr., 17 min.

- 3   cups chopped pecans
- ¾   cup sugar
- ¾   cup dark corn syrup
- 3   large eggs, lightly beaten
- 2   Tbsp. melted butter
- 1   tsp. vanilla extract
- ⅛   tsp. salt
- 5   (2.1-oz.) packages frozen mini-phyllo pastry shells

1. Preheat oven to 350°. Bake pecans in a single layer in a shallow pan 8 to 10 minutes or until toasted and fragrant.
2. Stir together sugar and corn syrup in a medium bowl. Stir in pecans, eggs, and next 3 ingredients.
3. Spoon about 1 heaping teaspoonful pecan mixture into each pastry shell, and place on 2 large baking sheets.
4. Bake at 350° for 20 to 22 minutes or until set. Remove to wire racks, and let cool completely (about 30 minutes). Store in an airtight container for up to 3 days.

Mini Pecan Pies: Substitute 1½ (8-oz.) packages frozen tart shells for frozen mini-phyllo pastry shells. Prepare recipe as directed through Step 2. Spoon about ¼ cup pecan mixture into each tart shell. Place tart shells on a large baking sheet. Proceed with recipe as directed in Step 4, increasing bake time to 25 to 30 minutes or until set. Garnish with currants, if desired. Makes 1 dozen.

Velvety Pecan Candy

Makes about 3 dozen (about 3 lb.)
Hands-on Time: 10 min. **Total Time:** 2 hr., 20 min.

- 3   cups coarsely chopped pecans
  Wax paper
- 1½   lb. vanilla or chocolate candy coating, coarsely chopped
- 1   (14-oz.) can sweetened condensed milk
- ¼   tsp. salt
- 1   tsp. vanilla extract

1. Preheat oven to 350°. Bake pecans in a single layer in a shallow pan 8 to 10 minutes or until toasted and fragrant.

2. Line a 15- x 10-inch jelly-roll pan with wax paper. Lightly grease wax paper.
3. Microwave chopped candy coating, sweetened condensed milk, and salt in a 2-qt. microwave-safe bowl at HIGH 3 to 5 minutes, stirring at 1-minute intervals. Stir until smooth. Stir in vanilla and pecans. Spread in an even layer in prepared pan. Cover and chill 2 hours or until set.
4. Turn candy out onto cutting board, and cut into squares. Store, covered, at room temperature.

Mildred's Toffee

Makes about 1½ lb.
Hand-on Time: 30 min. **Total Time:** 1 hr., 30 min.

1½ cups chopped toasted pecans, divided
1 cup sugar
1 cup butter
1 Tbsp. light corn syrup
1 cup semisweet chocolate morsels

1. Spread 1 cup pecans into a 9-inch circle on a lightly greased baking sheet.
2. Bring sugar, next 2 ingredients, and ¼ cup water to a boil in a heavy saucepan over medium heat, stirring constantly. Cook until mixture is golden brown and a candy thermometer registers 290° to 310° (about 15 minutes). Pour sugar mixture over pecans on baking sheet.
3. Sprinkle with chocolate morsels; let stand 30 seconds. Spread melted chocolate morsels evenly over top; sprinkle with remaining ½ cup chopped pecans. Chill 1 hour. Break into bite-size pieces. Store in an airtight container.

Bourbon-Pecan Toffee: Substitute ¼ cup bourbon for ¼ cup water. Proceed as directed.

Almond Toffee: Substitute 1 cup chopped toasted slivered almonds for 1 cup chopped pecans to sprinkle on baking sheet. Substitute ½ cup toasted sliced almonds for ½ cup chopped pecans to sprinkle over chocolate. Proceed with recipe as directed.

Hawaiian Toffee

Makes about 1½ lb.
Hand-on Time: 30 min. **Total Time:** 1 hr., 30 min.

1 cup chopped toasted macadamia nuts
1 cup sugar
1 cup butter
1 Tbsp. light corn syrup
1 cup semisweet chocolate morsels
½ cup toasted sweetened flaked coconut

1. Spread macadamia nuts into a 9-inch circle on a lightly greased baking sheet.
2. Bring 1 cup sugar, next 2 ingredients, and ¼ cup water to a boil in a heavy saucepan over medium heat, stirring constantly. Cook until mixture is golden brown and a candy thermometer registers 290° to 310° (about 15 minutes). Pour sugar mixture over pecans on baking sheet.
3. Sprinkle with chocolate morsels; let stand 30 seconds. Spread melted morsels evenly over top; sprinkle with coconut. Chill 1 hour. Break into bite-size pieces. Store in an airtight container.

test-kitchen secrets

Toffee Tips

- Simmer sugar mixture over medium heat until sugar and butter melt.
- Cook until sugar mixture reaches 290° to 310° on a candy thermometer. The color will change to a deep golden brown, and the mixture will get slightly thicker.
- Carefully pour sugar mixture over nuts that have already been spread into a 9-inch circle on a baking sheet lightly greased with cooking spray.
- Sprinkle morsels evenly on top, and let stand for 30 seconds or until they are totally melted. Spread melted morsels over surface.
- Sprinkle chopped toasted nuts over chocolate, and chill until firm
- Break toffee into small pieces before storing in an airtight container.

**Bacon-Peanut
Truffles**

make ahead

Bacon-Peanut Truffles

Makes about 2 dozen
Hands-on Time: 30 min. **Total Time:** 4 hr.

2   Tbsp. dark brown sugar
¼   tsp. salt
¾   cup honey-roasted peanuts
8   thick bacon slices, cooked and divided
⅓   cup creamy peanut butter
6   oz. bittersweet chocolate, chopped
Parchment paper

1. Process first 3 ingredients and 6 bacon slices in a food processor 20 to 30 seconds or until finely ground. Stir together bacon mixture and peanut butter in a small bowl until smooth. Cover and chill 2 hours.
2. Shape rounded teaspoonfuls of bacon mixture into ¾-inch balls. Place on a parchment paper–lined baking sheet; chill 1 hour.
3. Chop remaining 2 bacon slices. Microwave chocolate in a microwave-safe bowl at HIGH 1 to 1½ minutes or until melted and smooth, stirring at 30-second intervals. Dip chilled bacon balls into chocolate. Place on a parchment paper–lined baking sheet. Immediately sprinkle tops with chopped bacon. Chill 30 minutes before serving. Store in an airtight container in refrigerator up to 2 weeks.

make ahead

Peanut Butter Truffles

If you over-beat the chocolate mixture in Step 2, beat in 2 to 3 Tbsp. more whipping cream to return mixture to a smooth consistency.

Makes about 2 dozen
Hands-on Time: 20 min. **Total Time:** 3 hr., 30 min.

- 1 (12-oz.) package semisweet chocolate morsels
- ½ cup whipping cream
- 3 Tbsp. creamy peanut butter
- ¾ cup finely chopped, lightly salted roasted peanuts
- Wax paper

1. Microwave morsels, cream, and peanut butter in a medium-size microwave-safe bowl at HIGH 1 to 1½ minutes or until melted and smooth, stirring at 30-second intervals. Let cool 10 minutes.
2. Beat chocolate mixture at medium speed with an electric mixer 1 to 2 minutes or until whipped and smooth. Cover and chill 2 hours or until firm.
3. Shape chocolate mixture into 1-inch balls, using a small ice-cream scoop. Roll in chopped peanuts. (If chocolate mixture becomes too soft to shape, refrigerate until firm.) Place on wax paper–lined baking sheets. Chill 1 hour before serving. Store truffles in an airtight container in refrigerator up to 5 days.

Hazelnut-Chocolate Truffles

Makes 20 truffles
Hands-on Time: 20 min. **Total Time:** 2 hr., 30 min.

- ¾ cup whipping cream
- 1 cup finely chopped bittersweet chocolate
- 1 Tbsp. unsalted butter
- 2 Tbsp. hazelnut liqueur
- ¾ cup hazelnuts
- 1 (3-oz.) dark chocolate bar, chopped*

1. Bring cream to a boil in a medium saucepan over medium-high heat; whisk in bittersweet chocolate, butter, and hazelnut liqueur until well combined. Chill at least 2 hours.
2. Place hazelnuts on a baking sheet. Bake at 350° for 10 minutes or until hazelnuts are toasted. Place warm nuts in a dish towel, and rub vigorously to remove skins.

Peanut Butter Truffles

3. Process toasted hazelnuts in a food processor until ground. Place in a shallow dish. Shape chocolate mixture into 1-inch balls. Melt chopped dark chocolate bar in a small saucepan over low heat. Roll each ball in 1 tsp. of melted dark chocolate, and immediately roll in toasted, ground hazelnuts.
4. Cover and chill truffles until ready to serve.

Note: We tested with Ghirardelli Dark Chocolate for dark chocolate bar.

*½ cup semisweet morsels may be substituted for dark chocolate bar.

test-kitchen secret
Make sure the truffles are well chilled before you dip them in the melted chocolate.

1. Preheat oven to 350°. Cook ¾ cup chocolate morsels and oil in a small saucepan over low heat, stirring constantly, 2 minutes or until chocolate melts. Pour chocolate mixture into a large bowl, and cool 5 minutes.

2. Stir together flour, powdered sugar, and next 3 ingredients.

3. Stir brown sugar, next 3 ingredients, and 2 Tbsp. water into chocolate mixture; stir in flour mixture and remaining chocolate morsels. (Dough will be stiff.)

4. Drop dough by level tablespoonfuls 2 inches apart onto lightly greased baking sheets.

5. Bake at 350° for 8 minutes. Cool on baking sheets 2 minutes; transfer to wire racks, and cool completely (about 20 minutes).

test-kitchen secret

The dough for these cookies with the ooey-gooey centers freezes well. Shape into 3 logs, wrap in parchment paper, and freeze. Bake for last-minute guests, or give dough logs as gifts. Thaw dough at room temperature 15 minutes, and spoon from log by level tablespoonfuls. Bake as directed. Store in an airtight container for 1 week.

Double-Chocolate Chews

Double-Chocolate Chews

Makes 3 dozen
Hands-on Time: 27 min. **Total Time:** 1 hr., 29 min.

1	cup semisweet chocolate morsels, divided
3	Tbsp. vegetable oil
1¾	cups all-purpose flour
⅔	cup sifted powdered sugar
⅓	cup unsweetened cocoa
2¼	tsp. baking powder
⅛	tsp. salt
1	cup firmly packed light brown sugar
3	Tbsp. light corn syrup
2½	tsp. vanilla extract
1	large egg

Pistachio-and-Cherry Cookies

Makes about 5 dozen
Hands-on Time: 30 min. **Total Time:** 1 hr., 20 min.

¾	cup butter, softened
¾	cup sugar
¾	cup firmly packed light brown sugar
2	large eggs
1	tsp. almond extract
2¼	cups all-purpose flour
1	tsp. baking soda
¾	tsp. salt
1	(6-oz.) package dried cherries, coarsely chopped
1	(4-oz.) bittersweet chocolate baking bar, chopped
1	(4-oz.) white chocolate baking bar, chopped
1	cup chopped pistachios
Parchment paper	

1. Preheat oven to 350°. Beat butter and sugars at medium speed with a heavy-duty electric stand mixer until creamy. Add eggs and almond extract, beating until blended.

2. Combine flour, baking soda, and salt in a small bowl; gradually add to butter mixture, beating just until blended. Stir in cherries and next 3 ingredients just until combined. Drop dough by tablespoonfuls onto parchment paper–lined baking sheets.

3. Bake at 350° for 10 to 14 minutes or to desired degree of doneness. Remove from baking sheets to wire racks, and cool completely (about 15 minutes).

Paradise Pecan Cookies

Makes 1 dozen
Hands-on Time: 15 min. **Total Time:** 1 hr., 2 min.

  1 cup chopped pecans
Parchment paper
  3 egg whites
  1 cup sugar
20 saltine crackers, crushed

1. Preheat oven to 350°. Bake pecans in a single layer in a shallow pan 8 to 10 minutes or until toasted and fragrant.

2. Line a baking sheet with parchment paper; lightly grease parchment paper.

3. Beat egg whites at high speed with an electric mixer until soft peaks form. Gradually add sugar, and beat until stiff peaks form. Fold pecans and crackers into egg whites. Drop by rounded tablespoonfuls onto prepared baking sheet.

4. Bake at 350° for 17 minutes or until lightly browned. Cool on baking sheet 1 minute. Remove cookies to wire racks, and cool completely (about 20 minutes).

Pecan Sandies

Makes about 7 dozen
Hands-on Time: 20 min. **Total Time:** 3 hr.

  ⅓ cup finely chopped pecans
  1 cup butter, softened
  ½ cup sugar
2½ cups all-purpose flour
  1 tsp. vanilla extract
Parchment paper

1. Preheat oven to 350°. Bake pecans in a single layer in a shallow pan 6 to 8 minutes or until toasted and fragrant, stirring halfway through.

2. Beat butter and sugar at medium speed with an electric mixer until fluffy. Gradually add flour, beating just until blended. Stir in pecans and vanilla.

3. Divide dough in half, and shape each portion into 2 (1¼-inch-thick) logs (about 12 inches long). Wrap in parchment paper, and cover and chill 1 hour or until firm.

4. Preheat oven to 325°. Cut logs into ¼-inch-thick rounds, and place rounds ½ inch apart on parchment paper–lined baking sheets.

5. Bake at 325° for 18 to 20 minutes or until lightly golden. Let cool on baking sheets 5 minutes. Transfer to wire racks, and let cool completely (about 20 minutes).

Candy Bar–Peanut Butter Cookies

Makes 3 dozen
Hands-on Time: 20 min. **Total Time:** 1 hr., 50 min.

  1 cup butter, softened
  1 cup granulated sugar
  1 cup firmly packed brown sugar
  1 cup creamy peanut butter
  2 large eggs
  1 tsp. vanilla extract
  2 cups all-purpose flour
  1 tsp. baking soda
  ½ tsp. salt
36 bite-size chocolate-covered caramel-peanut nougat bars
Parchment paper

1. Beat first 4 ingredients at medium speed with an electric mixer until smooth. Add eggs and vanilla, and beat mixture until blended.

2. Stir together flour and next 2 ingredients in a small bowl. Add to butter mixture, beating until blended. Cover and chill 30 minutes.

3. Preheat oven to 350°. Shape about 2 Tbsp. dough around each nougat bar, using lightly floured hands, and roll into balls. Place 3 inches apart on ungreased or parchment paper–lined baking sheets.

4. Bake at 350° for 13 to 14 minutes or until lightly browned. Cool on baking sheets 5 minutes. Transfer to wire racks.

Sour Cream–Coffee Cake Muffins

Makes 24 muffins
Hands-on Time: 20 min. **Total Time:** 52 min.

- 1 cup butter, softened
- 2 cups sugar
- 2 large eggs
- 1 cup sour cream
- ½ tsp. vanilla extract
- 2 cups all-purpose flour
- 1 tsp. baking powder
- ¼ tsp. salt
- ⅛ tsp. baking soda
- 24 paper baking cups
- 1 cup pecan halves, finely chopped
- ¼ cup sugar
- 1½ tsp. ground cinnamon

1. Preheat oven to 350°. Beat butter at medium speed with an electric mixer 2 minutes or until creamy. Gradually add 2 cups sugar, beating 2 to 3 minutes. Add eggs, 1 at a time, beating until blended after each addition. Add sour cream and vanilla, beating until blended.
2. Whisk together flour and next 3 ingredients; gradually stir into butter mixture. (Batter will be thick.)
3. Place baking cups in muffin pans. Spoon batter into cups, filling two-thirds full.
4. Stir together pecans, ¼ cup sugar, and cinnamon. Sprinkle pecan mixture over batter.
5. Bake at 350° for 20 to 25 minutes or until a wooden pick inserted in center comes out clean. Remove muffins from pans, and cool completely on wire racks (about 12 to 15 minutes).

Peanut Streusel–Mango Muffins

Remove muffins from pan after baking using a knife or metal spatula instead of inverting and losing streusel.

Makes 1 dozen
Hands-on Time: 15 min. **Total Time:** 1 hr., 7 min.

- ½ cup coarsely chopped dry roasted, salted peanuts
- ¼ cup light roast peanut flour made with peanuts
- 2 cups all-purpose flour, divided
- ½ cup firmly packed light brown sugar, divided
- 5½ Tbsp. butter, melted and divided
- 1 tsp. baking soda
- ½ tsp. baking powder
- ½ tsp. ground cinnamon
- ¼ tsp. salt
- 2 medium mangoes (about 2 lb.), peeled and chopped*
- ½ cup granulated sugar
- ½ cup low-fat buttermilk
- 1 large egg
- 12 aluminum foil baking cups

1. Preheat oven to 375°. Stir together chopped peanuts, peanut flour, ½ cup all-purpose flour, ¼ cup light brown sugar, and 3½ tablespoons melted butter until mixture is crumbly.
2. Stir together baking soda, baking powder, cinnamon, salt, and remaining 1½ cups all-purpose flour in a bowl.
3. Process chopped mango in a blender or food processor 15 to 20 seconds or until pureed. Pour puree into a measuring cup to equal 1 cup. (Reserve any remaining mango puree for another use.)

Sour Cream–Coffee Cake Muffins

4. Whisk together 1 cup mango puree, granulated sugar, buttermilk, egg, and remaining ¼ cup brown sugar and 2 tablespoons melted butter in a medium bowl until well blended. Gradually whisk in flour mixture just until combined.

5. Place baking cups in a muffin pan. Spoon batter into cups, filling two-thirds full. Sprinkle peanut streusel mixture over batter.

6. Bake at 375° for 22 to 24 minutes or until a wooden pick inserted in center comes out clean. Cool in pan on a wire rack 10 minutes. Gently transfer muffins from pan to a wire rack using a knife or metal spatula, and cool completely (about 20 minutes).

*2 cups frozen cubed mango, thawed, may be substituted.

make-ahead tip

Freeze baked, cooled muffins in a zip-top plastic freezer bag up to 1 month. To reheat, remove muffins from baking cups, wrap in a paper towel, and microwave at HIGH 20 seconds or until thoroughly heated. We tested with 12% fat light roast peanut flour.

Gingerbread

Makes 9 servings
Hands-on Time: 20 min. **Total Time:** 1 hr.

- ½ cup butter, softened
- ½ cup granulated sugar
- ½ cup firmly packed dark brown sugar
- 1 large egg
- ⅔ cup molasses
- 2½ cups all-purpose flour
- 2 tsp. ground cinnamon
- 1 tsp. baking soda
- 1 tsp. ground ginger
- ½ tsp. salt
- ½ tsp. ground allspice
- ½ tsp. ground nutmeg
- ¼ tsp. ground cloves
- ⅛ tsp. baking powder
- 1 cup buttermilk
  Whipped cream (optional)
  Rum Glaze (optional)

1. Preheat oven to 350°. Beat butter at medium speed with an electric mixer until creamy; gradually add sugars, beating well. Add egg, beating until blended. Add ⅔ cup molasses, beating until smooth.

2. Whisk together flour and next 8 ingredients in a large bowl. Add to butter mixture alternately with buttermilk, beginning and ending with flour mixture. Beat at low speed just until blended after each addition. Pour into 9 lightly greased (6-oz.) ramekins.

3. Bake at 350° for 24 to 28 minutes or until a wooden pick inserted in center comes out clean. Let cool on a wire rack 15 minutes. Serve warm with whipped cream, or drizzle with Rum Glaze, if desired.

Note: Gingerbread may be baked in a greased and floured 9-inch square pan. Increase bake time to 50 to 55 minutes.

Rum Glaze

We also love this rich glaze drizzled over pound cake slices and ice cream.

Makes about ½ cup
Hands-on Time: 10 min. **Total Time:** 10 min.

- ½ cup firmly packed dark brown sugar
- ¼ cup rum
- 2 Tbsp. butter
- 1 tsp. molasses

1. Stir together all ingredients in a small saucepan.

2. Bring to a boil over medium-high heat, stirring constantly. Reduce heat to low, and simmer, stirring occasionally, 3 to 4 minutes or until brown sugar is dissolved and mixture is thickened and bubbly. Transfer to a serving dish. Serve immediately.

Note: If glaze becomes too thick to pour, return saucepan to stovetop, and whisk in 1 to 2 Tbsp. water. Cook over low heat, whisking mixture until Rum Glaze thins and becomes a pourable consistency.

Peanut Butter Cakes

No time to make frosting? This cake has a baked-on topping.

Makes 7 loaves
Hands-on Time: 20 min. **Total Time:** 1 hr., 45 min., including topping

    1   cup creamy peanut butter
    ½   cup butter, softened
    2   cups sugar
    4   large eggs
    1   cup milk
    1½ Tbsp. vanilla extract
    2   cups all-purpose flour
    1½ tsp. baking powder
    ½   tsp. salt
        Peanutty Topping

1. Preheat oven to 350°. Beat peanut butter and butter at medium speed with an electric mixer until creamy; gradually add sugar, beating well. Add eggs, 1 at a time, beating until blended after each addition. Stir in milk and vanilla extract.
2. Sift together flour, baking powder, and salt; stir into peanut butter mixture. Pour batter into 7 greased and floured 5- x 3-inch disposable aluminum foil loaf pans, filling each pan half-full. Place pans on a baking sheet; sprinkle with Peanutty Topping.
3. Bake at 350° for 55 to 60 minutes or until a long wooden pick inserted in center comes out clean. Cool completely in pans on wire racks (about 20 minutes).

Chocolate Chip–Peanut Butter Cakes: Stir 2 cups semisweet chocolate morsels into batter.

Peanutty Topping

Makes about 2 cups
Hands-on Time: 10 min. **Total Time:** 10 min.

    1   cup powdered sugar
    1   cup creamy peanut butter
    ½   cup all-purpose flour
    ½   cup uncooked regular or quick-cooking oats
    ¼   cup peanuts, chopped
    ½   tsp. salt

1. Stir together all ingredients in a medium bowl until thoroughly blended.

Two-Step
Pound Cake

Two-Step Pound Cake

You'll need a heavy-duty stand mixer with a 4-qt. bowl and paddle attachment for this recipe.

Makes 10 to 12 servings
Hands-on Time: 15 min. **Total Time:** 2 hr., 55 min.

    4   cups all-purpose flour
    3   cups sugar
    2   cups butter, softened
    ¾   cup milk
    6   large eggs
    2   tsp. vanilla extract

1. Preheat oven to 325°. Place flour, sugar, butter, milk, eggs, and vanilla (in that order) in 4-qt. bowl of a heavy-duty electric stand mixer. Beat at low speed 1 minute, stopping to scrape down sides. Beat at medium speed 2 minutes.
2. Pour into a greased and floured 10-inch (16-cup) tube pan, and smooth. Bake at 325° for 1 hour and 30 minutes or until a long wooden pick inserted in center comes out clean. Cool in pan on a wire rack 10 minutes. Remove from pan to wire rack, and cool completely (about 1 hour).

test-kitchen secret

"It's simple to soften butter to that just-right stage," says Angela Sellers, Test Kitchen Professional. "Remove butter from the refrigerator 2 hours before using, and let it stand in a cool, shaded spot. Test softness by gently pressing the top of the stick with your index finger. If an indentation remains and the stick of butter still holds its shape, it's ready to use."

Chocolate-Marble Sheet Cake

Makes 12 servings
Hands-on Time: 20 min. **Total Time:** 1 hr., 53 min., including frosting

- 1 cup butter, softened
- 1¾ cups sugar, divided
- 2 large eggs
- 2 tsp. vanilla extract
- 2½ cups all-purpose flour
- 1 Tbsp. baking powder
- ½ tsp. salt
- 1 cup half-and-half
- ¼ cup unsweetened cocoa
- 3 Tbsp. hot water
- Mocha Frosting

1. Preheat oven to 325°. Beat butter and 1½ cups sugar at medium speed with a heavy-duty electric stand mixer 4 to 5 minutes or until creamy. Add eggs, 1 at a time, beating just until blended after each addition. Beat in vanilla extract.
2. Sift together flour, baking powder, and salt. Add to butter mixture alternately with half-and-half, beginning and ending with flour mixture. Beat at low speed just until blended after each addition, stopping to scrape bowl as needed.
3. Spoon 1¼ cups batter into a 2-qt. bowl, and stir in cocoa, hot water, and remaining ¼ cup sugar until well blended.
4. Spread remaining vanilla cake batter into a greased and floured 15- x 10-inch jelly-roll pan. Spoon chocolate cake batter onto vanilla batter in pan; gently swirl with a knife or small spatula.

5. Bake at 325° for 23 to 28 minutes or until a wooden pick inserted in center comes out clean. Cool completely in pan on a wire rack (about 1 hour). Spread top of cake with Mocha Frosting.

Mocha Frosting

Makes 2⅓ cups
Hands-on Time: 10 min. **Total Time:** 10 min.

- 3 cups powdered sugar
- ⅔ cup unsweetened cocoa
- 3 Tbsp. hot brewed coffee
- 2 tsp. vanilla extract
- ½ cup butter, softened
- 3 to 4 Tbsp. half-and-half

1. Whisk together sugar and cocoa in a medium bowl. Combine coffee and vanilla.
2. Beat butter at medium speed with a heavy-duty electric stand mixer until creamy; gradually add sugar mixture alternately with coffee mixture, beating at low speed until blended. Beat in half-and-half, 1 Tbsp. at a time, until batter is smooth and mixture has reached desired consistency.

Mocha-Almond Frosting: Decrease vanilla extract to 1 tsp. Proceed with recipe as directed, adding ½ tsp. almond extract to coffee mixture in Step 1.

Hot Chocolate Mix

This makes a great gift for the kids in the neighborhood.

Makes 14 servings
Hands-on Time: 5 min. **Total Time:** 5 min.

 1 (9.6-oz.) package nonfat dry milk
 4 cups miniature marshmallows
 1½ cups powdered sugar
 1 cup unsweetened cocoa

1. Stir together all ingredients in a large bowl. Store chocolate mixture in an airtight container at room temperature until ready to serve.

Hot Chocolate: Stir ½ cup Hot Chocolate Mix into 1 cup hot milk. Makes 1 serving.

Minted–Hot Chocolate Mix

Makes about 16 servings
Hands-on Time: 10 min. **Total Time:** 10 min.

 3 (4½-inch) soft peppermint candy sticks
 1 cup sugar
 ¾ cup instant nonfat dry milk
 ¾ cup powdered nondairy coffee creamer
 ½ cup unsweetened cocoa

1. Place peppermint sticks in a zip-top plastic freezer bag; seal bag, and crush candy with a mallet.
2. Combine crushed candy and remaining ingredients in an airtight container, and store at room temperature up to 1 month.

Minted Hot Chocolate: Stir about 2½ to 3 Tbsp. Minted Hot Chocolate Mix into 1 cup hot milk, stirring until dissolved. Top with marshmallows, if desired. Makes 1 serving.

Hot Fudge Sauce

Makes 3¼ cups
Hands-on Time: 10 min. **Total Time:** 10 min.

 1 (8-oz.) package unsweetened chocolate baking squares
 ½ cup butter
 2 cups sugar
 1 cup milk
 1 tsp. vanilla extract
 ⅛ tsp. salt

1. Melt baking squares and butter in a large, heavy saucepan over low heat, stirring constantly. Add sugar, and cook, stirring constantly, 30 seconds or until blended. Add milk, and cook, stirring constantly, 3 minutes or until thoroughly heated and sugar is dissolved. (Do not boil.) Remove from heat. Stir in vanilla and salt. Cover and chill fudge sauce up to 2 weeks.

Note: To reheat, microwave sauce in a microwave-safe bowl, stirring occasionally, at HIGH for 15- to 30-second intervals or until warm.

Espresso–Hot Fudge Sauce: Add 2 Tbsp. instant espresso with sugar.

Whiskey–Hot Fudge Sauce: Stir in 3 Tbsp. Southern Comfort with vanilla and salt.

Brown Sugar–Cinnamon–Hot Fudge Sauce: Substitute 1 cup firmly packed brown sugar for 1 cup granulated sugar. Stir in ½ tsp. ground cinnamon with vanilla and salt.

Peanut Butter Sauce

Makes 2½ cups
Hands-on Time: 10 min. **Total Time:** 10 min.

 1⅓ cups miniature marshmallows
 1 (14-oz.) can sweetened condensed milk
 1 cup chunky peanut butter
 ⅓ cup light corn syrup

1. Melt marshmallows and sweetened condensed milk in a small saucepan over medium heat, stirring constantly. Add peanut butter and corn syrup, stirring until blended. Store Peanut Butter Sauce in the refrigerator up to 1 month, and reheat before serving.

Hot Fudge Sauce

year-round all-occasion MENUS

This at-a-glance planner offers menus based on recipes in the book.

Company Brunch
Serves 6

- Ham-and-Cheese Croissant Casserole, **page 107**
- Fresh fruit
- Morning Glory Muffins, **page 206**

Easter Dinner
Serves 8

- Lela's Baked Ham, **page 137**
- Spinach-Apple Salad with Maple-Cider Vinaigrette, **page 193**
- Tee's Corn Pudding, **page 178**
- Jordan Rolls, **page 205**
- Caramel Italian Cream Cake, **page 235**

Special Birthday Dinner
Serves 6

- Perfect Prime Rib, **page 147**
- Golden Potato and Leek Gratin, **page 186**
- Basic Green Bean Casserole, **page 180**
- Triple Chocolate–Cookie Trifle Pie, **page 254**

One-Dish Dinner
Serves 6

- Tomato 'n Beef Casserole with Polenta Crust, **page 165**
- Mixed salad greens
- French bread

New Orleans Supper
Serves 4

- Muffuletta Calzones, **page 160**
- Potato chips
- Dill pickles
- Spiced Caramel-Apple Bread Pudding, **page 244**

Italian Night
Serves 8

- Vanessa's Make-Ahead Beefy Lasagna, **page 166**
- Green Salad with Orange Vinaigrette, **page 193**
- Garlic bread
- Caramel–Cream Cheese Flan, **page 245**

Ladies' Lunch
Serves 4

- Spicy Pork-and-Orange Chopped Salad, **page 163**
- Refrigerator Yeast Rolls, **page 203**
- Salted Caramel-Pecan Bars, **page 225**

Supper Club
Serves 6

- Roast Pork Loin with Crumb Crust, **page 143**
- Perfect Mashed Potatoes, **page 185**
- Balsamic Root Vegetables, **page 190**
- Red Velvet Soufflés with Whipped Sour Cream, **page 241**

Create a Snowflake Garnish

Place tissue or wax paper over the template, and trace. Place a sheet of parchment paper over snowflake stencil on a jelly-roll pan. Microwave 1 (4-oz.) white chocolate baking bar, chopped, in a 2-qt. microwave-safe glass bowl at HIGH 1 minute or until chocolate is glossy. Let stand 5 minutes; stir just until melted and smooth. (Be careful not to overstir or chocolate will lose its gloss and firm up.) Spoon chocolate into a zip-top plastic freezer bag. Snip 1 corner of bag to make a small hole. Pipe chocolate onto parchment paper, using stencil as a guide. Freeze 10 minutes or until chocolate hardens. Carefully lift snowflake from parchment paper using a spatula, and place on cheesecake.

Snowflake
Template

metric EQUIVALENTS

The recipes that appear in this cookbook use the standard U.S. method for measuring liquid and dry or solid ingredients (teaspoons, tablespoons, and cups). The information on this chart is provided to help cooks outside the United States successfully use these recipes. All equivalents are approximate.

Metric Equivalents for Different Types of Ingredients

A standard cup measure of a dry or solid ingredient will vary in weight depending on the type of ingredient. A standard cup of liquid is the same volume for any type of liquid. Use the following chart when converting standard cup measures to grams (weight) or milliliters (volume).

Standard Cup	Fine Powder (ex. flour)	Grain (ex. rice)	Granular (ex. sugar)	Liquid Solids (ex. butter)	Liquid (ex. milk)
1	140 g	150 g	190 g	200 g	240 ml
¾	105 g	113 g	143 g	150 g	180 ml
⅔	93 g	100 g	125 g	133 g	160 ml
½	70 g	75 g	95 g	100 g	120 ml
⅓	47 g	50 g	63 g	67 g	80 ml
¼	35 g	38 g	48 g	50 g	60 ml
⅛	18 g	19 g	24 g	25 g	30 ml

Useful Equivalents for Liquid Ingredients by Volume

¼ tsp	=						1 ml
½ tsp	=						2 ml
1 tsp	=						5 ml
3 tsp	=	1 Tbsp	=		½ fl oz	=	15 ml
	=	2 Tbsp	=	⅛ cup	1 fl oz	=	30 ml
	=	4 Tbsp	=	¼ cup	2 fl oz	=	60 ml
	=	5⅓ Tbsp	=	⅓ cup	3 fl oz	=	80 ml
	=	8 Tbsp	=	½ cup	4 fl oz	=	120 ml
	=	10⅔ Tbsp	=	⅔ cup	5 fl oz	=	160 ml
	=	12 Tbsp	=	¾ cup	6 fl oz	=	180 ml
	=	16 Tbsp	=	1 cup	8 fl oz	=	240 ml
	=	1 pt	=	2 cups	16 fl oz	=	480 ml
	=	1 qt	=	4 cups	32 fl oz	=	960 ml
					33 fl oz	=	1000 ml = 1 l

Useful Equivalents for Dry Ingredients by Weight

(To convert ounces to grams, multiply the number of ounces by 30.)

1 oz	=	1⁄16 lb	=	30 g
4 oz	=	¼ lb	=	120 g
8 oz	=	½ lb	=	240 g
12 oz	=	¾ lb	=	360 g
16 oz	=	1 lb	=	480 g

Useful Equivalents for Length

(To convert inches to centimeters, multiply the number of inches by 2.5.)

1 in				=	2.5 cm		
6 in	=	½ ft		=	15 cm		
12 in	=	1 ft		=	30 cm		
36 in	=	3 ft	1 yd	=	90 cm		
40 in				=	100 cm	=	1 m

Useful Equivalents for Cooking/Oven Temperatures

	Fahrenheit	Celsius	Gas Mark
Freeze Water	32° F	0° C	
Room Temperature	68° F	20° C	
Boil Water	212° F	100° C	
Bake	325° F	160° C	3
	350° F	180° C	4
	375° F	190° C	5
	400° F	200° C	6
	425° F	220° C	7
	450° F	230° C	8
Broil			Grill

INDEX